CANADA AND THE UNITED STATES

The Politics of Partnership

TWAYNE'S INTERNATIONAL HISTORY SERIES

Akira Iriye, editor
Harvard University

CANADA AND THE UNITED STATES

The Politics of Partnership

Robert Bothwell
University of Toronto

TWAYNE PUBLISHERS • NEW YORK
MAXWELL MACMILLAN INTERNATIONAL • NEW YORK OXFORD SINGAPORE SYDNEY

Twayne Publishers
Macmillan Publishing Company
866 Third Avenue
New York, New York 10022

Macmillan Publishing Company is part of the Maxwell Communications Group of Companies.

Twayne's International History Series, No. 10

The paper used in this publication meets the minimum requirements of American National
Standard for Information Sciences—Permanence of Paper for Printed Library Materials,
ANSI Z39.48-1984. ⊚™
Printed and bound in the United States of America.

Library of Congress Cataloging-in-Publication Data

Bothwell, Robert.
    Canada and the United State / Robert Bothwell.
      p.   cm.—(Twayne's international history series ; no. 10)
    Includes bibliographical references and index.
    ISBN 0-8057-7914-0
      1. United States—Foreign relations—Canada. 2. Canada—Foreign
relations—United States. I. Title. II. Series.
    E183.8C2B68   1992
    327.73071—dc20
                                                          91-41404
                                                              CIP

ISBN 0-8057-7914-0 (alk. paper). 10 9 8 7 6 5 4 3 2 1
ISBN 0-8057-9213-9 (pbk.: alk. paper) 10 9 8 7 6 5 4 3 2 1
First printing, 1992

For Willis and Louise Armstrong

CONTENTS

ILLUSTRATIONS

FOREWORD

Twayne's International History Series seeks to publish reliable and readable accounts of post-World War II international affairs. Today, nearly fifty years after the end of the war, the time seems opportune for a critical assessment of world affairs in the second half of the twentieth century. What themes and trends have characterized international relations since 1945? How have they evolved and changed? What connections have developed between international and domestic affairs? How have states and peoples defined and pursued their objectives, and what have they contributed to the world at large? How have conceptions of warfare and visions of peace changed?

These questions must be addressed if one is to arrive at an understanding of the contemporary world that is international—with an awareness of the linkages among different parts of the world—and historical—with a keen sense of what the immediate past has brought to human civilization. Hence Twayne's *International History* Series. It is hoped that the volumes in this series will help the reader to explore important events and decisions since 1945 and to develop the global awareness and historical sensitivity required for confronting today's problems.

The first volumes in the series examine the United States' relations with other countries, groups of countries, or regions. The focus on the United States is justified in part because of the nation's predominant position in postwar international relations, and also because far more extensive documentation is available on American foreign affairs than is the case with other countries. The series addresses not only those interested in international relations, but also those studying America's and other countries' histories, who will find here useful guides and fresh insights into the recent past. Now more than ever, it is imperative to understand the linkages between national and international history.

In this volume, Professor Bothwell, a distinguished historian of Canadian foreign affairs, exemplifies this principle, providing in-depth analysis both for the United States and for Canada as they have dealt with one another since the end of the Second World War. Of course, there has been something asymmetrical about this relationship:

for the United States, Canada has been just one part of an overall global strategy, whereas for the latter the neighbor to the south has been the dominant reality in its external affairs. But the picture is complicated, the book shows, because Canadian domestic politics and public opinion are just as volatile as in the United States, and often internal circumstances dictate contradictory foreign policy decisions. Economically and culturally, too, there have been areas of obvious interdependence as well as self-conscious opposition between the two countries. Only a balanced historical account such as is presented here will enable one to understand the full story. At a time when the two nations prepare for further economic integration and ponder the future political and cultural definition of the bilateral relationship, the book will provide valuable insights as North America prepares for the twenty-first century.

Akira Iriye

chapter 1:

DISTANT NEIGHBORS, 1763–1945

In March 1945, not long after the Yalta conference, President
Franklin D. Roosevelt received Prime Minister Mackenzie King of Canada.
King was in Washington to discuss Canadian-American relations and the
progress of the war, but he had something else in mind as well. While he was
in Washington, King wanted to hold a press conference.[1]

The news was not well received among the White House press corps.
"William Lyon Mackenzie King," they chanted, "Never tells us a goddamn
thing." He would not have to: Roosevelt dominated the press conference, as
he usually did, uttering a few complimentary phrases designed to help King's
chances in Canada's approaching general election. They would have been
even less happy had they known that the president and the prime minister
were whiling away their time imagining how to produce a real newspaper, four
pages long, reprinted all across America via radio photography, featuring
what King described as "the main news truthfully."[2]

It was a typical Roosevelt-King get-together. Over time and through many
meetings (Roosevelt had been continuously in office since 1933, and King
since 1935), these two liberal politicians—Harvard men both—wandered
amiably over subjects as diverse as the future of French Canada to a proposed
universal peace conference to be held in the Canary Islands in 1937 or 1938.
They dealt with more pressing matters when required: Canadian-American
trade, munitions purchases, and this time, the design of the United Nations
and Roosevelt's proposed trip to Europe in June, when victory assuredly would
have been won.

King never saw Roosevelt again. The Canadian prime minister, eight years

1

older than the president, was shaken at the deterioration of his friend's health and disquieted by the president's tales of how he and Churchill and Stalin were reshaping world order. "The point is," King wrote in his diary, "no human mortal was ever meant to possess the kind of power that these three men have come to have today."[3] That power, King sensed, fixed a gulf between himself and Roosevelt, and between Canada and the United States.

Roosevelt did not enjoy his power for long. In April he was dead; King attended the burial at Roosevelt's estate at Hyde Park, New York. He naturally reflected on what had bound him to Roosevelt: It was not the war he remembered, but the fight for social justice against "the bitterest kind of enmity and hatreds."[4] King not only liked and admired Roosevelt; he empathized with the president and associated his domestic policies and political style with Canada's own. On such issues, power and nationality did not count so much—what mattered was the convergence of Canadian and American attitudes and habits.

EARLY CONVERGENCES

No Canadian was absolutely unfamiliar with the United States. Nova Scotia had been largely settled from prerevolutionary Massachusetts. Colonial American soldiers served in the British campaigns that conquered Canada during the Seven Years War (aptly known in the United States as the French and Indian War). The French and the Indians were the great losers in that war, which determined that English would be the predominant language in North America; New France, renamed Quebec, became a subordinate unit in an English-speaking universe, far from mother France and very far from French armies and ships.

The Peace of Paris of 1763 that gave New France to Great Britain also removed a proximate menace from the British colonies to the south. A revolution in the thirteen colonies saw the defeat of Great Britain and the liberation of the Atlantic seaboard from European domination. (Ironically enough, a French army assisted the colonies but never came close to challenging Britain's hold on French-speaking America.) The revolution that created the republic also created Canada, still a monarchy and a colony. The colonies of Nova Scotia and Quebec did not join the revolution; there, the British maintained a predominance of force sufficient to overawe local would-be revolutionaries and drive out invaders from the thirteen rebellious colonies. That was fortunate for the thousands of Americans who did not support the revolution, many of whom chose exile over citizenship in the new republic. There was still a "British North America," much smaller after the peace with the United States in 1783 than it had been before. Among its inhabitants were 40,000 refugees from the United States, the Loyalists. The new international boundary sheltered them, although it took some sixty years for the frontier to assume its final shape.

The Loyalist presence, the persistence of monarchy, the existence of a French-speaking culture in the valley of the St. Lawrence clustered around eighteenth-century Quebec City, not to mention Canada's previous colonial history, gave observers the impression that the northern country was somehow *older* than the United States. Ideologically, that may have been so; physically, it was not. Very little of Canada outside the St. Lawrence valley was long-settled. The people were newer, with shallower roots—a phenomenon that continued to be true as settlement advanced across the continent. Moreover, there was less land on which to settle, though there was plenty of rock and muskeg to accommodate wildlife. It followed that there was less opportunity to accumulate wealth and therefore, at any particular historical point, a more compressed and constrained society north of the border. Some have seen in this blending of ideology and circumstance the roots of a Canadian toryism, a conservative and collective pattern of life that distinguishes Canadians from Americans.

For years, soldiers made sure the difference, whatever it was, persisted. Mackenzie King's paternal grandfather, Sergeant John King of the Royal Artillery, was one of them. There was only one war between the British colonies and the United States, 1812–1815, a minor, bloody, and bitter episode in the larger Napoleonic Wars. The war left the border where it was, but it also consolidated the British identity of the colonies north of the line.

King's other grandfather, William Lyon Mackenzie, challenged that identity in 1837, in loose association with a group of French-Canadian rebels in the St. Lawrence Valley. Mackenzie failed and fled for his life. His cause, a Canadian republic—a northern version of Texas that probably would have joined the United States—collapsed with him.

The United States government remained studiously neutral during Mackenzie's rebellion, as it did whenever the question of annexing Canada came up. Though individual Americans trumpeted the "Manifest Destiny" of the United States to absorb all of North America, the American government as such never did. Before the Civil War, the absorption of Canada would have upset the balance between slave states and free. During the Civil War, when uncivil Confederates used British territory and ports to raid American towns and prey on shipping, war was avoided. That was just as well for the thousands of Canadians who had enlisted in the Union Army and who were spared the choice of fighting against their native land. In the enthusiasm of northern victory, Secretary of State William Seward boasted "that Nature designs that this whole continent . . . shall be, sooner or later, within the magic circle of the American Union."[5] Nevertheless, Seward did little or nothing to bring that prospect about.

When Canadians or Americans crossed the border in the eighteenth and nineteenth centuries, they necessarily adapted their politics, but they did not have to do much to alter other aspects of their culture. And passage over the frontier was simple—simpler for people (for there was free emigration and immigration) than for commerce, encumbered by tariffs. In the early nineteenth century, American settlers flowed through Canada from upstate New York to get to Michigan, and many stayed. Others crossed the frontier from Vermont into what is now Quebec and implanted their characteristic architecture. They brought with them their nonconformist tastes in religion and found that the laws and institutions of the provinces of British North America were remarkably and even increasingly similar to those of the states to the south.

New Englanders had an affinity to the three Maritime Provinces (New Brunswick, Prince Edward Island, and Nova Scotia after the 1780s), and to the Eastern Townships adjacent to Vermont and New Hampshire. Language and accents became closely aligned; those of the Maritime Provinces with the flat tones and slang of New England, those of Ontario with the tones of Michigan and points west. (There are a few points on which Canadian speech can be distinguished, such as the diphthong *ou*, as in *around* and *about*.) Loyalist and postloyalist immigrants to Upper Canada brought with them Georgian and federal styles of architecture.[6]

The French language, the Catholic Church, and particular institutions (such as civil law) distinguished Lower Canada (modern Quebec) from all its English-speaking and mostly Protestant neighbors. Yet it is unwise to set too much store on the differences wrought by language and its attendant cultural baggage. Language was distinguishing and separating, but not to the point of negating economic pressures. French Canadians moved off their overcrowded farms south into New England in search of work; by 1900, they numbered 573,000 and formed the majority in certain areas.[7] French Canadians preferred New England to farming in the Canadian west, even though moving to New England meant occupying the lower rungs of an urban labor force.

It may have seemed at first that the French-Canadian immigration into New England might make a permanent impact. "They seemed very much out of place in what was still an old New England community," according to one witness. "They segregated themselves in the mill towns and had very little to do with their neighbors." But, Franklin D. Roosevelt concluded, that was a mirage. "Today, forty or fifty years later," he told Mackenzie King in 1942, "the French Canadian elements in Maine, New Hampshire, Massachusetts and Rhode Island are at last becoming a part of the American melting pot. . . . They are inter-marrying with the original Anglo-Saxon stock; they are good, peaceful citizens and most of them are speaking English at home." There was, admittedly, more to be done. Roosevelt suggested "planning," even unofficially, to "hasten the objective of assimilating the New England French Canadians and Canada's French Canadians into our respective bodies politic."[8] Mackenzie King did not respond, but the episode all the same speaks volumes as to Roosevelt's view of Canada.

Not all the migration went south. When the Canadian prairies were opened to effective settlement after 1896, Americans were eager homesteaders. Across the forty-ninth parallel, migrants ebbed and flowed, as opportunity dictated (two and a half million Canadians to the United States, 375,000 Americans to Canada, by 1921).[9] The flow was assisted by the fact that aspects of basic life were essentially the same on either side of the border. But the transfers of population did not alter one basic fact: The ratio of population between Canada and the United States remained below ten to one—where, indeed, it remained until comparatively recently. The population statistics confirm what the boundary treaties had defined: that Canada occupied the less fertile, more inhospitable part of North America, and that its dreams of rivaling the United States in wealth and population were mere fantasy. The disparity between American income and Canadian gave rise to one of the staple jokes of the Canadian-American relationship.

"What is the difference between a Canadian and an American?"

"Twenty-five percent."

Certainly differences in life-style were insufficient to either explain or justify the border. Yet even in the legislative sphere the resemblances were striking. In British North America, as in the United States of America, there were elections and assemblies, parties and partisanship. Often the issues were the same: schools, disestablishment, political patronage. The two countries enjoyed a similar legal structure. Except for the two civil law exceptions of Quebec and Louisiana, common law in the United States and Canada derived from England. Methods of interpretation were familiar, the jury system was the same, and the principles were nearly identical. Canadians from the maritime provinces had no difficulty in traveling to the United States for their legal education. Indeed, if they wanted education as opposed to apprenticeship, they had to go south at least until the 1880s.[11]

Law is modified by experience, and Canadian legislators were delighted to take advantage of American spadework. So, in one example, laws governing railroad development and property in the northern tier of the United States swiftly found their way onto Canadian statute books.[12]

Freedom of trade was closely related to freedom of movement—or to the propensity to take advantage of an open frontier. Both Canadians and Americans imbibed theories of tariff protection in the mid-nineteenth century, although there was a brief interval from 1854 to 1866 when a different philosophy prevailed. A partial free-trade zone resulted, but it was free trade by commodity—what would later be called sectoral free trade. The Canadians profited by it, but the Americans grew increasingly disgruntled as Canadi-

Table 1:   Comparative Population

(in millions of people; Canadian censuses are taken one year after U.S. censuses)

	1860–61	1890–91	1920–21	1950–51	1987 (est.)
United States	31.4	62.9	105.7	150.7	243.9
Canada	3.2	4.8	8.8	14.0	26.9

Table 2:   Comparative Per Capita Annual Income

	1870s	1890	1900	1910	1920	1930
United States	170*	208	246	382	860	734
Canada	126*	168	199	319	576	561

*U.S. figure is an average, 1869–78; the Canadian figure is an estimate.[10]
All figures in US dollars.

ans levied tariffs on items not covered by the agreement. In the indignation against Britain and Canada that accompanied Confederate depredations during the Civil War, the Reciprocity Agreement was abrogated by the United States. Its disappearance was a factor in the subsequent union of the British North American colonies to form the self-governing, but still colonial, Dominion of Canada in 1867.

The memory of reciprocity lingered in Canada. In the haze of recollection, the 1850s and 1860s seemed an era of prosperity and abundance: to later generations of Canadians, reciprocity with the United States was a prescription for affluence. Best of all, economic reciprocity guaranteed contentment with the government at home, at least on the economic front. Paradoxically, free trade with the United States could be used to shore up Canada's British identity. Canada's first governments were mainly Conservative, stressing, among other things, tradition and loyalty to the British Empire. In their view, loyalty to the empire and a transatlantic connection did not preclude a quest for economic advantage in relations with the United States. That was no more than a recognition that the United States was Canada's best, or second-best, trading partner in the late nineteenth century.[13]

The Canadian desire for reciprocity was a case of unrequited love. In the United States, the Republican administrations of the late nineteenth century were engaged elsewhere, and Congress was interested principally in raising the tariff. Negotiations between Canada and the United States in the 1870s and 1880s failed, complicated as they were by disputes over Atlantic fisheries and Pacific seals. Canadian interest in reciprocity abated, a process aided by special interest groups that had become attached to the Canadian government's high tariff policy. That policy was almost a mirror image of the American tariff, and the resemblances did not end there. As in the United States, government subsidized transcontinental railroads, three of them by 1914, for a population totaling 8 million. The effect of these policies was to counteract geography by emphasizing internal, east-west, connections rather than north-south linkages.

Canadians began to be less pessimistic about their prospects. The "Confederation" of 1867 created a Canadian federal state with a powerful central government located in Ottawa. There were four provinces (later ten), which were analogous to states. The central government refocused political activity; for some it was an alternative to the imperial government in London, although Canadian nationalism and British Empire patriotism were far from incompatible. In the Canadian general election of 1891 the Conservative prime minister, Sir John A. Macdonald, proclaimed, "A British subject I was born, a British subject I will die." (He did, in fact, expire some months after the election, but he died happy, having defeated the Liberal opposition.)

The Canadian structure of government before and after 1867 evolved differently from the American. Unlike the United States, but like nineteenth-century Britain, the head of government and his cabinet sat in the legislature. "Governors" became ceremonial and were succeeded in power by prime ministers (federal) and premiers (provincial). Although the American and Canadian party systems closely resembled one another until about 1900, further reforms in the United States in the twentieth century loosened party bonds and diluted the link between executive and legislature. As a result, Canadians tended to regard the American political system as more responsive—and less responsible. A typical comment came from a Canadian diplomat in Washington, Lester B. Pearson, who wrote in 1943 that the U.S. Congress was "probably the most irresponsible legislative body in the world." The comment betrays the frustrations of the moment, but it also reveals a gap in political culture that should not be underestimated.[14] Occasionally Americans reciprocated with their own unflattering assessments of their northern neighbor.[15] The fact that Canadian-American relations frequently spilled over into domestic housekeeping did make for confusion, controversy, and a certain amount of chest-pounding on behalf of whichever system seemed for the moment to be functioning better. It is a characteristic that is still present.

American politicians, responding to domestic political imperatives, hiked the tariff in 1891, and again in 1897. Each rise in rates was followed by a decline in Canadian exports to the United States. While almost 50 percent of Canada's exports were consigned to the United States in 1888, a mere 27 percent went south a decade later. Canadian trade with Great Britain meanwhile grew, proportionately and absolutely. Reversing the 1850s, it was not difficult to associate economic connections with political loyalty; as a result Canada and the United States were in some respects further apart, economically and politically, in 1900 than they had been in 1865. Even American investment in Canada did not operate to assist economic rapprochement. American companies located branch plants in Canada to get around the Canadian tariff. By 1900, such American firms as Singer Sewing Machine, Edison Electric, Gillette, Swift's, Parke Davis, and Coca Cola had branches in Canada. Canadian towns and cities begged for more and dreaded the disappearance of the tariff.[16] If the tariff were abolished, would the departure of these plants and the employment and technology they brought be far behind? American investment brought cultural convergence, a homogenization of technology and management styles, and a familiarization of the Canadian consumer to American-style (if Canadian-made) products. Investment stimulated cultural imitation, but not political absorption.

Canada's British connection was, on the contrary, reinforced. British immigration, British investment, particularly in railroads, and British political ideas were powerful factors in shaping late-nineteenth-century Canada. The development of Canada's wheatlands in the west also furnished a powerful link across the Atlantic, where Canadian and American grains competed. The wheat farmers, to be sure, did not favor the tariff, which forced them to buy high-cost Canadian manufactures from short production runs; but they themselves were a powerful link in a transatlantic economy centered on Great Britain.

As the balance of power tilted away from Britain in the 1870s and 1880s, British statesmen discovered unsuspected advantages in their empire that, it was held, could contribute substantially to the salvation of the mother country in time of need. The British also discovered unsuspected advantages in friendly relations with the United States. As opinion in the mother country warmed toward the Americans, so in the colonies: "Canada has a mission to perform," one pundit wrote in 1872, "and that mission is to act as an intermediate between the two great Anglo-Saxon nations."[17] The mission—to be a linchpin between the two larger countries—was reinforced as British power declined, although that was sometimes difficult for Canadian politicians to grasp. Britain, Colonial Secretary Joseph Chamberlain explained in 1897, had become "a weary titan, laboring under the too vast orb of its destiny."

British interest in Canada met a mixed response. Canadian prime minister Sir Wilfrid Laurier wanted something concrete, such as British support in Canada's occasional disputes with the United States. He was disappointed. The British, craving American friendship more than Canadian affection, made the inevitable choice to please a power ten times the size of Canada and with more than ten times the wealth. In view of Britain's relative diplomatic isolation, it was a wise choice; and in the end the adverse consequences for Canada were not too serious.[18]

The increasing volume of transboundary affairs caused the British to press the Canadians to relieve the British embassy in Washington by establishing a Canadian foreign office that would take responsibility for Canada's external affairs. This was done, after a fashion, in 1909. The British retained their ultimate authority in the area, but henceforth minor matters would be transacted between Washington and Ottawa, using the British embassy as a post office. The same year Canada (via Britain) and the United States signed a Boundary Waters Treaty establishing an International Joint Commission to investigate and if possible arbitrate disputes arising from the many shared waterways and water systems along the border. The commission (called the IJC by the relatively few people who know of it) was eventually established and undertook as one of its first tasks the pressing problem of pollution in the Great Lakes.

Over the years (it is still in existence), the IJC resolved a fair number of transboundary annoyances, but it fell short of the hopes of Elihu Root, the

American secretary of state and one of the signatories of the 1909 treaty. Root had hoped "to dispense with the Hague Tribunal as far as possible . . . and set an example to the world by the creation of a judicial Board as distinguished from a diplomatic and partisan one to deal with all these matters."[19] Root was not the last to sound this particular note, nor was the IJC the last such board to be created. On the other hand, Canada and the United States continue to use the Hague Tribunal to settle important disputes.

Laurier finally achieved a reciprocity agreement with Roosevelt's successor, William Howard Taft, in 1911. He held an epic election on the issue and lost, in a campaign notable for its vehement British chauvinism. The American consul general in Ottawa observed, "I have rarely known such manifestations of extreme feeling [among Canadians]. They claim that reciprocity would destroy the home because divorces would immediately become prevalent, that the present judicial system would be replaced by an elected judiciary, and that every conceivable kind of ill would be let loose."[20] Thereafter, "1911" symbolized the negative side of Canadian-American relations.

The American consul general concluded that beneath the placid waters of the Canadian character there lurked a demon of easily aroused Canadian nationalism. Later historians and novelists have extrapolated a deep Canadian unease in the face of American vigor and self-assertion; some have gone on to speculate that Canadians transferred their sense of their own defects to their image of their southern twin.[21] At the time, with the election over and the Liberals out of office, the demon returned to its subconscious lair. The Conservatives, who took office under their leader, Sir Robert Borden, prime minister from 1911 to 1920, were not all anti-American. No Canadian government wanted to get along badly with the Americans, and Borden, who had once lived in the United States and liked Americans, was happy to praise Anglo-Saxon harmony. He dreamt of a role for himself as mediator between the United States and Great Britain.

Perhaps if the world had continued to be peaceful, Borden's ambition would have had a run for its money. But when war broke out between Britain and Germany in August 1914, Canada's interest turned eastward, not southward. Canada followed the rest of the British Empire in sending troops and supplies to the western front: more than 600,000 troops, out of a total population of just over 8 million. The strain was great, particularly because French Canadians took a more distant view of the war than did their English-speaking fellow citizens and refused to enlist in any great numbers. In 1917, when the United States joined the war and enacted a military draft, Canada followed suit, with the assurance that conscripts could no longer escape over the border. French Canadians, concentrated in Quebec, were not happy, and the memory of 1917 became a long-lasting grievance inside Canada.

The burden of war caused the British government to concede a role for its self-governing colonies in directing the war. Borden took the occasion to argue a special and privileged place for Canada where the empire's American policy was concerned. His views received a polite hearing, but in practice Borden was ignored. Anglo-American relations, especially after the United States entered the war, were too important and too complicated to allow for Canadian interference.

That was especially the case once it became clear that the British treasury was running dry. One of the first consequences was to throw Canada onto its own resources and those of the New York capital market. Later in the war, the Canadians worked out a special arrangement with the Wilson administration that allowed for American procurement of war supplies in Canada. The Americans got scarce munitions, and the Canadians got scarce U.S. dollars; both sides were satisfied.

Political relations with the United States remained tangential during the war. Canadian troops in Europe served with the British Army, and in North America contacts between the two armies were not particularly extensive. The focus of Canadian attention, official and popular, was still London, and the war's effect was naturally to increase nationalistic fervor with some anti-American side effects. Because Canada remained officially a colony, the American government treated it as such at the Paris Peace Conference of 1919. Eventually and rather grudgingly, American representatives conceded that Canada and the other self-governing British dominions could sign the Versailles treaty and become members of the League of Nations. President Wilson's adviser, Colonel House, explained in his diary that it was merely a stage in "the eventual breakup of the British Empire."[22]

The League of Nations proved to be a sideshow as far as Canada was concerned. Because the United States did not become a member, Canadian-American relations were not enhanced by President Wilson's creation, and some Canadian politicians speculated nervously whether league commitments might not lead them into a clash with the American government. That was a situation to be avoided at almost all costs.

A crisis almost occurred in 1921, when the British government proposed, over Canadian objections, to renew its alliance with Japan. Canada's Conservative prime minister, Arthur Meighen, threatened to withdraw his support of British policy because of the disastrous impact renewal would have on American opinion. The British government was not deterred, but it abandoned the struggle once it became clear that Meighen's assessment of American views was all too correct. The British Foreign Office nevertheless concluded from the experience that running a foreign policy that included Canada was too great a strain. By the mid-1920s a common imperial foreign policy was a thing of the past, and Canada (not to mention the other British dominions) was on its own if it wanted to be.

A change of governments in Canada brought William Lyon Mackenzie King and the Liberal party to power in 1921. King was an oddity as a political leader. Dull and verbose, he left many people cold. Self-preoccupied and psychologically eccentric, he married himself to his party and was rewarded

Mackenzie King: "dull and verbose." Cartoon by Robert LaPalme from *Le Cercle du Livre de France. Courtesy Robert LaPalme.*

by keeping it—and himself—in power most of the time from 1921 to 1948. Internationalist by his training and friendships, King was resolutely preoccupied with Canadian domestic politics. Yet like most of his electors, King remained British in his view of the world.

King's British-centered politics contrasted with American-directed cultural and economic trends. American investment in Canada surpassed British investment in value in 1922 or 1923; by 1926, the United States accounted for over half of all nonresident-owned capital in Canada. Minerals, pulp and paper, and the automobile industry attracted investment to the point of overcapacity. Culturally, the two countries marched to the beat of the same drum. Prohibition in the United States was mirrored by prohibition laws in most of Canada; paradoxically, it remained legal to produce liquor *for export.* Some Canadian distilleries were located right on the Detroit River, and it became a cottage industry in adjacent American states to seek out Canadian supplies. The manufacture of "beverage spirits" soared from 3.8 million gallons in 1920 to 15.7 million in 1929—a decade when most Canadians found it difficult to get a legal drink. Relations between the Canadian and American government cooled somewhat as a result.

American control of certain sectors of the Canadian economy rose during the 1920s. In mining and smelting, for example, American control increased from 32 percent in 1926 to 42 percent in 1930. That figure records only the viable investment; Canadian mining stocks were notoriously risky in the 1920s, and the Toronto Stock Exchange was widely viewed as a den of thieves specializing in fleecing the unwary and gullible American investor.[23]

Automobile factories were as easy for Americans to establish in Windsor, Ontario, as in Detroit across the river. With the new factories came mass production, admittedly for the smaller Canadian market but with no limitation on exports. Needless to say, Canadian farm boys flocked to the auto plants. According to John Kenneth Galbraith, who witnessed the phenomenon, the new autoworkers "liked their work, were fascinated by their surroundings, debated ardently the merits of Fisher Body and Briggs . . . and were profound admirers of Henry Ford."[24]

If American capital could be exported, so could labor unions. Canadian branches of American unions dated back to the nineteenth century. "International" unions, overwhelmingly American, dominated the Canadian labor scene; even the Trades and Labour Congress, the largest union central in the country, was run to all intents and purposes by the American Federation of Labor. It was not an entirely happy marriage, and a rival, Canadian-dominated organization was established as a counterweight.

American influence in Canada was not confined to the economy. American magazines, books, and music found a ready market, and the twentieth century brought movies (with the odd Canadian star, like Mary Pickford, thrown in). In the 1920s they were joined by a new medium, radio. Every night Canadians gathered around their radios to listen to their favorite shows. Because of a lag in Canadian investment in radio, Canadians listened mostly to American stations. Even remote Royal Canadian Mounted Police detachments got their news bulletins from Pittsburgh.

Not everyone approved. Canadian nationalists took umbrage and pressured the government to do something. Jamming American transmissions was unthinkable, and private-enterprise competition in Canada was likely to do little more than rebroadcast American programs. So in the 1930s, the Canadian government established its own radio network, the Canadian Broadcasting Corporation or CBC, with the specific mandate to promote a Canadian identity.

In some areas that identity had already been lost. Canadian sports fans cheered, every summer, for American baseball. Hockey was admittedly more Canadian, but it was hard to resist the lure of American money. In 1924 the (Canadian) National Hockey League granted its first American franchise to a Boston grocery magnate. His team, the Boston Bruins, sported his store colors when they battled their rivals. Boston was followed by New York, Detroit, and Chicago; by the 1940s only two Canadian teams, those of Toronto and Montreal, survived.[25] (A belated expansion of the National Hockey League in the 1970s added teams in western Canada.)

Under the circumstances it was hard to disagree with McGill University professor P. E. Corbett when he wrote in 1931 that more and more Canadians found the difference between Canadians and Americans "imperceptible." In certain areas of culture, he was assuredly right.[26] It would have been hard to distinguish English Canadians from Americans by dress, accent, or taste in entertainment. Increasingly, it was hard to distinguish Canadians by employer (General Motors, Ford, or General Electric) or by labor union. French Canadians *were* different, to be sure, but even in Quebec, American radio reached into the home, while French-Canadian youths dreamed of careers as hockey players in far-off Chicago or New York.

Many Canadians did more than dream. Between 1921 and 1927, 630,016 moved to the republic. A survey of the living graduates of eight Canadian universities in 1927 showed that 13 percent had gone south; in engineering and medicine the proportions were much higher. According to a Canadian doctor in Detroit, "In five years' time I am making more than the eminent practitioners in Toronto, men who have been there twenty-five years or more." Fully 77 percent of those answering a questionnaire cited economic or educational advantage as their reason for moving away; in terms of opportunity, they argued, Canada was a "headless pyramid."[27] Professor Corbett needed to look no further for his "differences."

For those who remained, politics loomed larger than economics. Canada's political culture continued to be dominated by British symbols. When the country celebrated its sixtieth anniversary in 1927, Prime Minister King chose the phrase "the Britain of the West" to signify the occasion. Canadian magazines published effusive homages to "their most excellent majesties," George V and his consort. Despite the dreary king, London, as much as New York, was the fashionable metropolis that drew young Canadians.

Nor was Canadian acceptance of American culture unmixed. To some, the United States was progressive and prosperous; to others, it was "fast," immoral, if not actually decadent. Surveys of Canadian opinion conducted for the Carnegie Foundation in the 1930s indicated that Canadians were not sure that American life was to be imitated. Canadians were happy to pay money to gawk at the gangster films of Edward G. Robinson or Jimmy Cagney on Saturday evenings, or to swoon over the fashionable life-styles of Cary Grant or Katharine Hepburn. These life-styles fell into the category of forbidden pleasures: they were titillating but to be avoided.

American politics failed to make much of an impression. The dour Republican politicians of the 1920s were not popular in Canada, and their propensity to raise the American tariff against Canadian exports did not contribute much to fellow-feeling. Canada and the United States did finally exchange diplomatic missions (at the level of legations) in 1927. Intergovernmental communication improved somewhat, especially on technical bilateral issues: there was a tremendous "volume of business" to be transacted, according to a Canadian diplomat, but "95 percent of it I can do while thinking of something else and the rest is just dull—like international double taxation and similar monstrosities."[28]

American isolationism naturally differentiated American views of foreign policy from Canadian, but only on an official level, and only some of the time. American isolationism was not directed against Canada, and the isolationist impulse fed on a common perception that a new world had developed that was different in nature from the old, and in conflict with Europe.[29] "North American" enthusiasts in Canada drew closer to the United States between the wars, stressing continental values and linkages—connections that they hoped would save Canada from another war.

North American sentiment did not spill over into economic policy. On the more important or fundamental questions, there was little meeting of minds. The American tariff of 1922 crippled Canadian agricultural exports to the United States; throughout the 1920s they never recovered to the level of 1921. When the U.S. Congress enacted the Smoot-Hawley Tariff of 1930 and President Hoover signed it into law, the Canadian government grumbled, lamented, and retaliated, but it made little difference. Canadian trade with the United States plummeted, but by the time the figures were in, it was difficult to know how much of the decline was owing to the tariff, and how much to the onset of the Great Depression. One consequence was obvious: American and Canadian government policies continued to hobble north-south trade and thereby maintained unchallenged Canada's internal political economy on an east-west and transatlantic axis.

The Depression devastated both North American economies. The American net national product declined by 53 percent between 1929 and 1933; Canada's dropped by 49 percent.[30] Neither country was much help to the other during the crisis. The Canadian government, reacting to sky-high American tariffs, raised its own and concluded, at the Ottawa conference of 1932, preferential tariff agreements with the other parts of the British Empire, principally Great Britain. Cordell Hull, the American secretary of state from 1933 to 1944, termed the Ottawa Agreements "the greatest injury, in a commercial sense, that has been inflicted on this country since I have been in public life."[31] They remained a bone of contention until changed attitudes and circumstances brought about the General Agreement on Tariffs and Trade in 1947.

In social life the impact of the Depression north and south of the border was not greatly different, nor was there much difference in its political effects. Sitting politicians were tossed out, and the mood of the two countries was radicalized. Mackenzie King was the first casualty, in 1930. He was lucky— his Conservative successor had to take the blame for even worse times. Then the Republican Hoover administration was beaten, just when economic indicators reached their lowest point, in 1932. The American vote and its aftermath made a profound impression north of the border.

The election of Franklin Delano Roosevelt as U.S. president puzzled Canadians. Roosevelt had been an unimpressive governor of adjacent New York. Unimpressive or not, he was a Democrat and presumably favored lower tariffs. In Canada, a Democratic president was assured of an initially sympathetic hearing. Roosevelt's administration was not merely heard, but felt. The "Hundred Days" of 1933 and the New Deal, the appearance of purpose and compassion, all greatly impressed. Canada's minister in Washington, William Herridge (who was also the Conservative prime minister's brother-in-law), sought out the New Dealers and made his home one of their principal watering holes.

It would be an exaggeration to say that Canadian-American relations flourished as a result, but there was advantage. Dean Acheson, a frequent guest at the Canadian legation, admired Herridge's ability to elicit "helpful suggestions" from his guests on thorny Canadian-American issues.[32] It helped that the administration (and particularly Secretary of State Hull) badly wanted to get tariffs down. They proposed tariff reductions, which were implemented via the Reciprocal Trade Agreements Act, passed in 1934. The act had a twist. The U.S. government could negotiate 50 percent reductions in its very high tariffs, but only with the "principal supplier" of a given commodity. Concessions negotiated in bilateral talks could be extended to all countries with "most favored nation" status—or not, according to circumstance. The act, and the trend it represented, would eventually help considerably, or so Roosevelt and Hull believed. Meanwhile the Canadians had to be content with changes in the atmosphere and the promise of sunnier days to come. Negotiations on a trade pact, the first since 1911, were opened.

The improved atmosphere went far beyond mere bilateral questions. The influence of the United States on Canada and on Canada's political agenda was never greater. The New Deal impressed Canadians. They sensed that radical measures were called for, and they saw New Deal labor legislation as a possible model. The new Congress of Industrial Organizations (CIO) moved into Canada, and with it came a revival of labor zealotry. Canadian businessmen and the managers of American branch plants opposed it; the Canadians said the CIO was copying "American" radicalism. The American model therefore had its limits in terms of its impact on the very conservative society of Canada. As late as 1942, an American observer commented that "Canadian industrialists . . . have preserved a strength and an arrogance surprising to an American."[33]

Canada was obviously a more conservative society than the United States, and even in the Depression Canadian governments considered that they had fewer resources and less public tolerance for social experiments. Unemployment projects that in the United States were run by social workers were in Canada run by the army. Canadian welfare agencies did not tolerate people's art or radical theater of the New Deal variety. But style was easier to mimic than substance. Roosevelt's radio chats were heard across the border and stimulated a Canadian imitation. Unfortunately, the apprentice—Conservative prime minister R. B. Bennett—had little of the master's credibility. His supporters believed he had gone mad, while his the electorate scorned a deathbed repentance. In October 1935, in a federal election, Bennett was out, and Mackenzie King and his Liberal Party were in.

Foreign policy also played a role in the Canadian election. Relations with the United States were not in question, despite the tariff; relations with the empire, Europe, and the League of Nations were. In October 1935, Italy, a league member, invaded Ethiopia, another league member. Canada's Conservative government, in its last days, authorized Canadian participation in economic sanctions against Italy. Its Liberal successor was not so sure.

Mackenzie King wanted to see Roosevelt, and in preparing for a trip to Washington, he uttered an uncharacteristically memorable phrase. He told the American minister in Ottawa that he proposed to take "the American road" in his foreign policy; he did not add—and the minister did not point out—that all he had to do was discover what that road might be.[34]

So King immediately conferred with Roosevelt. After deciding that they had met before, when King received an honorary degree at Harvard, Roosevelt announced that his visitor was "an old personal friend."[35] The two newfound friends did more. They sped up negotiations for a trade agreement, so much so that one of Roosevelt's critics complained of its "furtive character."[36] It was duly signed on 15 November. Roosevelt proclaimed an opening to trade with a country that "prior to 1929 bought from the United States more goods of all kinds than all of Latin America put together." Those days could come again, because Canadians were "a nation adjoining us—same general stock—same general conditions of life." Trade, he predicted, would double in two years. (American exports to Canada did double, in fact, in four years; Canadian exports to the United States did not fare so well.)

The public part of King's visit over, the president and the prime minister chatted about foreign policy, a subject on which Roosevelt's hands were tied by isolationist feelings at home. That this was so was often frustrating to some American officials, who like their Canadian counterparts professed a commitment to liberal international policies, a repugnance for the antidemocratic tides that were sweeping Europe and undermining peace, and a preference, seldom overtly expressed, for collective security. With their respective governments trammeled by cautious or hostile public opinion, these diplomats could only dream of better days. They consoled themselves that they might outlast their political overlords, dreaming that their generation would construct a very different kind of international order.[37]

Roosevelt and King met frequently in the years that followed. Foreign policy and the drift to war in Europe increasingly dominated their conversations, but paradoxically their discussions did not increase American influence over Canadian foreign policy in this period. The unreal nature of some of the discussions helps account for this; for example, early in 1937 the president and the prime minister dreamed together of summoning an international conference in the Canary Islands to examine and remove the economic causes that were at the root of international tension. These deliberations, which were privately reported as far away as London, had no practical sequel. (The British ambassador in Washington called the idea "western vapourings," and his superior in London, Sir Robert Vansittart, termed it "drivel, and dangerous drivel.")[38]

Canadian sentiment (or rather, English-Canadian sentiment) accepted that if Great Britain went to war against Hitler, Canada would join in. King explained as much to Hitler's ministers in the summer of 1937, and presumably Roosevelt knew of it as well. King's task was not to oppose the drift of opinion in Canada—the evidence suggests he sympathized with the trend—but to channel it in such a way as not to alienate French Canadians, with their well-known opposition to British imperial adventures and to forced drafts of Canadian soldiers to European wars.

Roosevelt understood what was likely to happen. Possibly he derived some vicarious satisfaction, since his own sentiments—pro-British and anti-Nazi—were not in doubt. He occasionally tapped Canadians in his own entourage—notably Lauchlin Currie, an economist—for their views on what was happening in Canada, but for the most part he seems to have relied on his own instincts, on Mackenzie King, and on larger considerations.[39] In a speech at Kingston, Ontario, in August 1938, Roosevelt told his audience that if Canada were invaded by "any other Empire" than the British, the United States would come to the rescue. Some weeks later, King made a reciprocal pledge.

Roosevelt hoped that his words would help to deter Hitler, but his hope was in vain. Even in North America, no special notice was taken of these entangling commitments, which had greater significance over the long term than in the short haul. Canadians appreciated Roosevelt's evident charm; that was assimilated to his already high reputation. As a result, one historian has remarked, "I have no doubt he was far more popular with Canadians than Mackenzie King ever was."[40] At the time that was unremarkable; and in September 1938 there were other events to preoccupy attention.

Within a month the Canadian government confronted the possibility of going to war. Hitler was threatening Czechoslovakia, and it seemed that the British government would be obliged to support the Czechs. Opinion in Canada was divided, with the English-language majority inclined to support the British and the French minority inclined to remain neutral. The King government did not publicize its deliberations: King had a well-founded dread of provoking foreign policy divisions before it was absolutely necessary. Canadian officers in civilian clothes were sent south to confer with their American counterparts on war plans and war production—the first contacts of this kind.

The Canadian government was resolved to go to war if war came. But when war did not come, it was content to leave heroics to others and rejoiced in the reprieve. The avoidance of war through the Munich conference enhanced the standing of the British government in Mackenzie King's eyes, for the British appeasement policy showed more clearly than ever before that the blame for war would incontrovertibly lie with the Germans. This was no small consideration for a government that was liberal as well as Liberal in complexion.

By the time war actually came, with the German invasion of Poland in September 1939, Mackenzie King had resolved most of Canada's internal political problems between English and French Canadians. There was therefore no politically significant opposition to Canadian entry into the war, which took effect on 10 September 1939.

WORLD WAR II

Canada entered World War II as an act of faith. There was no certainty that the country could afford the luxury of going to war. Finance was shaky, and foreign exchange reserves were insufficient for heavy expenditure. French and English Canadians regarded one another warily: the French expected that the English would seize the moment to conscript them all, the English believed that the French would again leave the sacrifice of the war to others.

Before Canada officially declared war, Roosevelt shipped all the war supplies he could north of the border, circumventing the provisions of the American Neutrality Act. The Canadian government knew that its American counterpart took an active and sympathetic interest in the war effort; for the time being there were few legal ways in which that interest could be expressed.

The German conquest of Western Europe in May and June 1940, and the prospect that Great Britain itself might be invaded and defeated, changed all that. Roosevelt feared that the British fleet would fall into German hands if the British surrendered. The president asked Mackenzie King to find out what might happen; this was one of the few examples of the "linchpin" theory, mentioned earlier. Roosevelt suggested it would be best that King present the American concern as his own.

To King, as he told his diary, "it seemed . . . that the United States was seeking to save itself at the expense of Britain." He had no desire to be the instrument of fate, and he had reason to doubt his capacity to fill the role Roosevelt was assigning him. King's relations with the new British prime minister, Winston Churchill, were cool; during the 1930s the Canadian prime minister had viewed Churchill as the most dangerous man in England and prayed that he might never return to power. Churchill, for his part, did not like King. Fortunately, after May 1940, when Churchill's stirring speeches came over the airwaves, King changed his mind. It was just as well, for Churchill needed King's help to stave off Britain's military and financial collapse.

Though King dutifully transmitted Roosevelt's interest in the fleet, he was careful to attribute the idea to its originator; and as he expected, it met a chilly response. Churchill wanted American ships sent east, not British ships sent west. In the "destroyers for bases" deal of 1940 he got what he wanted, even if he had to use the threat of an eventual pro-German administration in Great Britain to get it.[41]

The experience showed that it was more useful for the British and Americans not to rely on an interpreter or a linch pin. King, who did not want to be a go-between, must have breathed a sigh of considerable relief. That the great strategic decisions of World War II would be taken without his participation or even his knowledge bothered him very little. The responsibility of power on a grand scale was beyond his grasp, as well as Canada's capacity.

There were other problems to solve. The defense of North America against Germany was one; it was the subject of staff talks and a conference between King and Roosevelt at Ogdensburg, New York, on 17–18 August 1940. This conference spawned a Permanent Joint Board of Defense (PJBD) to study "mutual problems of defense" of the United States and Canada; the PJBD began to meet almost at once. A senior Canadian civil servant called it "certainly the best day's work done for many a year. It did not come by chance, but as the inevitable sequence of public policies and personal relationships, based upon the realization of the imperative necessity of close understanding between the English-speaking peoples."[42]

The creation of a joint defense board between a neutral United States and a belligerent Canada caused almost no objections, even from isolationist Americans. Only Churchill disapproved, seeing the PJBD as a wedge between the Canadians and the British, and a token of lack of faith in Britain's powers of survival.

The PJBD busied itself with plans, but at least on the American side its activities were not taken entirely seriously. As the war drew on and American entry became more probable, the fighting moved farther and farther away. Meanwhile the Canadians raised an overseas volunteer air force and an army and sent them to England, where they served for the balance of the war. A conscript army was also created, but it found a purpose only when the Japanese attacked Pearl Harbor. As a result, Canada's draftees were sent to the

Pacific coast where they sat out much of the war in rain-soaked camps in the British Columbia forest, with the occasional mutiny to pass the time. The war in any serious form never came to North America, and the PJBD never had to firm up its plans. It did nevertheless justify its name: it was indeed permanent.

The Canadian government early on decided to make a substantial economic contribution to war supply. After Dunkirk, the British were glad to accept the proposition. But the Canadian economy was small and incomplete. War production in Canada, which was aimed largely to meet British rather than Canadian demand, meant getting raw materials, such as coal and iron ore, machine tools, and aircraft engines from the United States. Because Canada's foreign exchange reserves were slender and its reserves of U.S. dollars slimmer still, this supply requirement soon brought on a crisis in the management of Canada's balance of payments with the United States. Canada's economic war effort was faced with bankruptcy.

Fortunately for the Canadian government, the Roosevelt administration needed Canadian war supplies, which were just beginning to come off production lines at the beginning of 1941. Some of King's officials and ministers were able to match things up with their American counterparts, and Roosevelt and King ratified the results in a meeting at Roosevelt's estate at Hyde Park, New York, in April 1941. The draft was King's; Roosevelt is reported to have made one small change.

The Hyde Park Declaration or agreement provided that "in mobilizing the resources of this continent each countrry should provide the other with the defense articles it is best able to produce." In other words, Canada was free to sell the United States anything it could manufacture, for the purpose of the war. Since the United States bought war supplies from Canada, Canada was able in return to buy war supplies from the United States, on a cash basis. Supplies that were to be incorporated in products destined for Britain could be purchased on the British lend-lease account. Alone of the wartime Allies, Canada did not have to rely directly on the generosity of American lend-lease.

The decision not to take lend-lease was conscious and political. Acceptance of lend-lease risked, in the eyes of some Canadian officials, becoming an American client. Canada was ten times smaller than the United States, its economy twelve times smaller. These disproportions were large enough without adding to them the burden of clientage. Well-informed Canadians knew that the United States had in any case supplanted the United Kingdom as their country's primary external connection; there was no reason to suppose the British would soon recover the ground lost during the war.

Canadian trade moved heavily into surplus after 1942: favorable balances reached well over a billion dollars (Canadian) in each of 1943, 1944, and 1945. Current account transactions were also in surplus, though American investment in Canada rose by only $400 million from 1939 to 1945. Because Canadian-American trade could take care of itself, there was no further need for special arrangements. This encouraged the American government to see Canada more as a partner (a much smaller partner) than as a client.

Other linkages were enhanced by the war. Canadian officials from various economic departments and government-owned companies ("crown companies") flocked to Washington during the war. It proved impossible, and not merely difficult, to keep track of the Canadian government's multifarious activities in the United States, especially when Ottawa was not much harder to get to than Chicago on the overnight train and was just as easy to reach on the long distance telephone. For American officers and officials, Ottawa was friendly and familiar, if dull; but it did have more meat in the last years of the war, and few official travelers returned from Canada without a few unrationed steaks.

Canadian economic priorities and controls resembled American ones. Because their respective expectations and commitments were so nearly identical during the war, it proved possible to short-circuit complicated formalities in shipping necessary supplies north or south of the border. Yet it was less the mechanisms that were important than a more basic consideration—an identical commitment to victory, without unduly exploiting the war for unfair advantage afterward.

The war also marked a high point in the prestige and effectiveness of the American way of doing things. Canada's most spectacularly successful war production programs utilized American-style assembly lines and American-style management; in some cases, when Canadian managers were not available, management teams were imported directly from the United States.[43] Full order books superseded, for the duration, competitive concerns. In one example, reported by the American minister in Ottawa in June 1941, American aluminum interests "were no longer opposing the plans of the Canadian aluminum Company [to expand] their development at Arvida."[44]

Links were especially close among the captains of industry recruited for the war effort. Their friendships and associations outlasted the war, creating connections that endured as long as the wartime generation and that matched, in a different sphere, the linkages that already existed among Canadian and American civil servants and diplomats. That matters could be handled on a personal, individual, and especially, a sectoral level probably maximized Canada's negotiating advantage: a few American officials suspected the Canadians were following a policy of dividing and ruling, but their suspicions had no great effect.[45]

Things were not different on the labor front. Both Canada and the United States managed a rapid expansion of the labor force during the war. That labor force, in turn, experienced a rapid rise in living standards even under wartime taxation. Average wages and total payrolls increased dramatically. According to one estimate, 16 percent of the population moved up into the middle-income range and thereby acquired middle-class interests, if not a middle-class identity.[46] Per capita GNP rose fastest of all, with the Canadian rate of increase surpassing the American. Canadian industry was enhanced, and its comparative relationship with the United States improved.[47]

It would be an exaggeration to say that bilateral relations were invariably fruitful or friendly. Yet considering the volume of contacts and the economic importance of transborder trade, it is surprising how few problems had to be resolved at the diplomatic or political level. The unobtrusiveness of U.S.-Canadian relations contributed in no small part to their smoothness; so did the infrequency of Prime Minister King's calls on President Roosevelt's diplomatic time or political capital.

There was always the danger that King's toothless diplomacy would omit some larger Canadian interest. "Canada certainly plays a very minor part down here now in American attention," a Canadian reporter wrote in October 1941. "We are looked on somewhat as poor cousins who can be depended on to do whatever Uncle Sam wants and perhaps that is so."[48] But on bilateral issues, the reciprocal was true: the Canadian minister in Washington informed his prime minister "that, during the war, they had given us pretty much all we had asked for; that they could make our position very difficult if they ceased to adopt a co-operative attitude."[49]

When Roosevelt and Churchill met in Quebec City in 1943 and 1944, King was there for the photographs and the ceremonies. Once the photos were taken, he left. He had little to add to the great powers' deliberations, and his reluctance to force even that little on them had doubtless been a sine qua non for the choice of Canada as the location for the highly publicized Allied meetings. As far as the people of Canada were concerned, a picture was worth a thousand words. That the photos of Mackenzie King hobnobbing with the great men of the Allied world were illusions was not something Canadians had to know about—at least, not until after the next election.

There was also the difficult consideration of British weakness. The Canadian government was financing much of British war supply in North America, and it was obvious that Britain's economic weakness would inhibit that country's ability to balance or offset American influence in Canada. King explained as much to Churchill when the British prime minister visited Ottawa in August 1943. It was important to avoid giving the impression that the British Empire (or Commonwealth, as it was by then being called) was "ganging up" on the Americans. King, needless to say, would have nothing to do with a policy designed to reduce American influence, or interest, in the rest of the world.[50] That, in his view and the view of his officials, was not going to be the problem.

Canadian diplomatic opinion considered enlightened American involvement in the international system a rather fragile flower, to be encouraged if possible. Lester B. Pearson, the legation counselor, reported throughout 1943 the wide-spread feeling in the United States that any participation in international affairs was to be considered as a benefit from, rather than a benefit for, the Americans. They seem to think, in Pearson's opinion, that they would be doing all the giving while others would be doing all the receiving.[51] Canadians sought to persuade Americans that this was not so, but with slight success.

The trouble was, Pearson wrote, that countries like Canada were "necessary but not necessary enough." It was an apt comment. Canada was obviously "necessary" to bilateral relations. Depending on the issue, it would be treated as an equal. But multilateral arrangements were another matter. On the great issues of strategy, Canada's views were not sought. Mackenzie King willingly acquiesced; indeed, Roosevelt could have been pardoned some surprise that the government of Canada had any views at all.

COMING TOGETHER AND GROWING APART

Roosevelt seems to have believed that the worldviews of Canadians and Americans were essentially the same. It was an easy conclusion for a boy from "the nineties," when notions of Anglo-American friendship and identity of interest were in vogue. Canadians, as British North Americans, were closer to Americans than the British themselves, and it might be, as Colonel House foresaw in 1919, that eventually Canadians would leave the shelter of the declining British Empire and throw their lot in with the United States.

The similarities between Canadian society and that of the United States seemed to bear this out. Canada was easily perceived as a calmer, slower, poorer version of the United States, and in the 1920s many thousands of Canadians testified to this view by moving south. The differences that existed between Canada and the United States appeared to be differences of degree rather than of real principle. On fundamental matters, such as the assimilation of immigrants toward an existing dominant culture, there was no particular distinction.[52]

Since there was no particular distinction between them, it could be anticipated that the 1940s and 1950s would see a resumption of the patterns of the 1920s—normalcy. An imbalance of economic opportunity would stimulate Canadian emigration to the United States, while Canada served as the resource frontier for North America—a role more essential than ever, given the depletion of American natural resources during World War II.

Yet that was not the relationship that emerged during the abnormal years of economic crisis and world war. Canada ended World War II more prosperous and stable than it entered it. During the war it had avoided direct economic clientage with the United States; the fact that Canada had paid its own way through the sale of useful products to the U.S. war effort encouraged the U.S. administration to look fondly on Canada as an exception to the general rule of mendicancy that obtained in the wartime alliance.

Mackenzie King exploited that exception in his relations with Roosevelt, and to it he added some advantageous cultural baggage. The concept of an Anglo-Saxon identity of interest, modified by North American geography and economics and combined in the melting pot, was never far away, as the two men saw the world. But was it a tactic or a strategic truth? That was the conundrum Mackenzie King had to contemplate after his last conversation with Roosevelt in 1945. It would remain a puzzle for his fellow citizens over the next fifty years.

chapter 2

POWER AND ATTRACTION, 1945–1950

Victory in Europe was celebrated on 8 May 1945. The celebrations fell amidst the San Francisco conference, where Allied diplomats, including Canadians and Americans, were struggling with the details of the United Nations charter.

"I have one very vivid impression," a member of the Canadian delegation recalled. "I went for a walk, and it was just as though it was an ordinary evening. There was no interest whatever, no crowds, no cheering, no nothing, and it was perfectly clear to me that night that the European war didn't mean anything in San Francisco. It was the war across the Pacific that did; and it wasn't over."[1]

The Pacific war would also be the principal concern of the new administration in Washington, under Roosevelt's former vice president, Harry Truman. Truman would have no time to spare for Canada or Canadian problems, but as on many subjects he had preconceived notions about the northern neighbor. "Canada is fine, it's all right," Truman later wrote. "Canada's government is along the same lines as our own"—which was just as well, since otherwise western Canada, which Truman believed was largely settled by Americans, would long since have sought admission to the American union. Canadian-American relations were a model of fairness and friendship. Canada had benefited greatly from its proximity to the United States and its "love of freedom," and that happy situation would continue if Truman had anything to do with it.[2] Truman had correctly identified the two countries' sense of community; but could he—would he—see beyond it?

There was neither time nor occasion to find out in the spring of 1945. The senior Canadians at San Francisco soon packed up and went home, leaving the diplomats to complete the particulars. The diplomats would have to worry about whether the Americans shared Canada's eastward orientation to the Atlantic and Europe, rather than a western orientation to Asia and the Pacific. In Canada, there was an election, and for any politician, first things had to come first.

Prime Minister King and his Liberal party won the election. They won narrowly, but they prevailed because enough citizens mistrusted change. By extension, people coveted the security of a known commodity—King and the Liberals. The Liberals were a fairly broadly based party, attracting at least some support from every part of the country and from every class. Admittedly they attracted less support from business and the well-heeled, but those groups were by definition a minority. They attracted more support from those groups that had done well out of the war—those who had gotten jobs or improved their wages—and their numbers and distribution were rather more useful to the Liberal party. In fact, many more people were better off in 1945 than in 1939, despite heavy taxation.[3] The similarity to the American experience was marked.

The Canadian election of 1945 was about prosperity and security, not about foreign policy or relations with the United States. Those topics belonged to the government; on such issues Canadians expected that nothing much would change in the generally satisfactory situation. In a broader sense, the 1945 election confirmed, or ratified, that Canada and the United States would travel convergent paths in lifestyle, in culture, and in economic activity and policy.

Canadians in 1945 wanted job security and an assured income—and something to spend it on. They already had war savings, and they wanted to spend them—on stoves, clothes, a house in the suburbs, a car in the garage, a refrigerator, and as many other creature comforts as they could imagine.[4] That ambition generated a paradox. Canadians craved security, to judge from their votes in the 1945 general election; but they were impatient with restrictions and irritated by high taxes. They wanted stable prices and higher take-home pay. The end of the war meant the end of overtime and a reduction in their pay packets. It was not surprising that one of the first fruits of victory after the war was a wave of strikes on both sides of the border in the most

Table 3: Per Capita Annual Income, 1940–1970

(in U.S. dollars)

	1940	1950	1960	1970
United States	754	1,877	2,788	4,808
Canada	535	1,248	2,232	3,725

All figures in U.S. dollars

integrated North American industry, the auto plants that straddled the Canadian-American border.[5]

Americans would not have seen anything strange in Canadians' aspirations or anything unfamiliar in the products they wanted to buy. Even the brand names were the same. So was the advertising. And because Canadians read *Look* and *Life* and *Better Homes and Gardens,* and because they listened to NBC and CBS in addition to their indigenous media, they more often than not absorbed American tastes and products in an undiluted form.

Not everything was available north of the border, and what was available usually cost more. (The author recalls having had an unsatisfied craving for Wheaties cereal and Crayola crayons.) The Canadian tariff accounted for some of the lack, as it also accounted for many American-owned branch plants. Shortage of supply in both the United States and Canada also counted; sometimes the U.S. government had to exert itself to keep short supplies flowing north, using the Hyde Park agreement and the argument of "sharing" as ammunition.

But scarcity apart, Canadian prices were higher, and the selection of goods was more limited. Automobile companies compensated for shorter production runs by limiting the models that were available for Canadian purchasers. The shorter production runs, of course, resulted in higher unit costs. The higher prices that resulted had to be paid by Canadians out of a per capita income that was more than 25 percent lower than that of Americans.

The effect is not surprising. Canadians did not live as well as Americans, and up to a point they knew it. As a result, there were some psychological blinders and, inevitably, some compensating mechanisms. Canadians "used to talk a lot about quality of life back 25 years ago," an American diplomat remembered, "but it wasn't that great."[6] Materially speaking, that was undoubtedly true, not only in private life but in public services such as highways and urban transport. In these, Canadians paid a price for their vast distances and sparse population—a price usually collected in higher taxes. In an era of exchange control, tariff across the border was, as far as the Canadian government could direct, one-way.[7] But what was possible was very limited: a long and porous border meant that Canadians would exercise their option to travel and buy in the United States whether their government wanted them to or not. Worse, from the government's point of view, Canadians simply expected that their dollar would be convertible with the American dollar. Non-convertibility could be accepted as a war sacrifice, but with the war over, the pressure to return to the normal prewar practice was overwhelming. In May 1945 exchange restrictions were relaxed in view of substantial Canadian reserves of gold and U.S. dollars.

In July 1946 the Canadian government inadvertently encouraged travel south of the border by raising the Canadian dollar to par with the American. The idea was to combat inflation at home; the effect was to make spending in the United States even more attractive to Canadian travelers and importers.

Circumstances in 1946 and 1947 aggravated the problem considerably. In the event, in November 1947, the government proclaimed a crisis, reimposed stringent controls on Canadian purchases in the United States, and told an alarmed citizenry that they must restrain their spending habits. The burden of these restrictions fell on Canadian-American trade, but the causes of the crisis lay far beyond Canadian-American relations as such.

TRADE, CONTINENTAL AND INTERCONTINENTAL

Political stability in Canada and the perpetuation of the Liberals in power depended on the Canadian economy operating at a high and stable level. That level, economists and politicians agreed, hinged on trade. The government accordingly gave trade intense attention and high priority. The size of Canada's trade was important, Ottawa collectively decided, but so was security of supply, and predictability of markets. Security could be multilateral, but the depleted state of Europe's—especially, Great Britain's—exchange accounts made this an arguable goal. Or security could be found bilaterally, and in Canada *bilateral* meant only one thing: the United States.

There was no substantial difference over the line. In the United States, however, trade policy was a matter of negotiation if not competition. What the bureaucrats and diplomats, both Canadian and American, preferred was not necessarily what the administration could secure from Congress; the outcome could, to the diplomats, resemble a caricature of an original grand design.

During the war the United States government had attempted to exploit lend-lease to secure a more congenial international trading system.[8] The Canadian government was now understandably nervous at the prospect that Britain would bargain away imperial preference (that is, its tariff concessions to Canada) to ensure the continuation of American aid. If the U.S. government devised and then followed a consistent policy that linked present aid and future trade and pressed it upon the British, then Canada's trade with Britain would suffer—especially because many American products were highly competitive with Canadian products. On the other hand, given the state of the British economy, preference with Britain might turn out to be privileged access to nothing at all. Lord Keynes, Great Britain's principal expert on trade policy at the end of the war, succinctly termed the prospect "Starvation Corner" in a seminar for Canadian officials in May 1945.[9]

The Canadians held similar exploratory discussions with officials from the U.S. State and Treasury departments in 1944 and 1945. A variety of options, bilateral and multilateral, were explored, but without much progress. The Canadians wanted broad multilateral trade concessions, only to be told that Congress would not go along. Instead, Congress had just renewed the Reciprocal Trade Agreements Act, effectively confining future trade negotiators to the straitjacket of the principal supplier rule of the previous 1937 Act, and eliminating the possibility of across-the-board tariff cuts.[10]

Canadian anxiety for the future was not allayed by the terms of an American loan to Great Britain in the fall of 1945. The United States lent the British $3.75 billion, but with interest and with onerous requirements for the convertibility of the British pound. The American embassy in Ottawa reported the Canadian reaction: "we struck a hard bargain with a man who was down."[11]

The Canadians topped up the American loan with a $1.25 billion of their own—on the same terms as the American loan. The loan was justified to a skeptical Liberal caucus (with a heavy admixture of anti-British French Canadians) in terms of Canada's desperate need for markets. There were other reasons too. In his diary, Mackenzie King wrote of "the great menace" posed by the USSR. Obviously, shoring up the British was a strategic act, politically justifiable in terms other than Canada's traditional affection for the mother country.[12]

The loans, American and Canadian, did not work. They gave the British a bridge through 1946 and into 1947, but they did nothing to restore the basic imbalance of British trade. They did not convert Great Britain from a "soft currency" country requiring exchange control into a powerful "hard currency" partner. This was a particular disappointment from the Canadian point of view because the Canadians had hoped that a trade surplus with the British could be used to offset a trade deficit with the Americans. Instead, the British loan complicated Canada's dwindling reserves of gold and U.S. dollars and helped bring on an exchange crisis in the summer of 1947. Nor did aid and credits to Europe help Canada's exchange position.[13]

The establishment of an International Trade Organization (ITO) was contemplated, but the preparations took time. An interim trade arrangement under negotiation in Geneva resulted in the General Agreement on Tariffs and Trade (GATT) in November 1947. Both Canada and the United States secured their minimum objectives in the GATT talks—the Americans the freezing of British preference, which henceforth could only be reduced, not increased. Canada benefited: large tariff concessions were made by others at the cost of very few adjustments to Canada's own high tariff barriers. But there were some Canadian adjustments, and in successive "rounds" during the 1950s, 1960s, and 1970s, the Canadian tariff was eventually significantly lowered. This was a novelty for twentieth-century Canada; perhaps because that was so, the effects were not grasped for some time. The effects, however, included an eventual reorientation of much Canadian trade from inside the country, east-west, toward the United States, north-south.[14]

GATT did little or nothing to unravel the conundrum of hard and soft currency blocs. Indeed, by the time the GATT was signed, the British had been into convertibility and out again, after a run on the pound. The expensive but insufficient arrangements of 1945–46 had run their course. The Canadian government continued to dwell on the importance of a speedy expansion of trade for Canada's internal balance, meaning the divergent trading interests of all regions. Sad to say, trade did not expand as desired. Only in 1955 did export volumes surpass those of 1944. Imports, however, surged, especially from the United States, as a result of the consumer boom of 1945–47.[15] The result should have been disastrous, and initially, it seemed to be. But in understanding what followed, it is important to bear in mind that the doom-laden impressions of the late forties were *not* borne out, and that to a large extent the policies of the period were founded on illusion rather than reality.

Statistics are powerful specters—so real in appearance, so intangible in practice. First, there were happy numbers. Canada, like the United States, enjoyed an economic boom in 1946–47. Record production was achieved, along with record employment. (There was also near-record inflation.) But the statistics that were before the Canadian government in 1947 also showed an intractable draining away of cash to the United States. Imports from the south were 40 percent higher in 1947 than in 1946. It did not matter that Canada was running a trade surplus overall; what counted was that Canada was running out of money to pay for imports from the United States. Some of those imports were luxuries, to be sure. Some might be forgone, and by August 1947, bueaucrats were compiling lists of imported "luxuries" that could be banned or reduced. But other imports—coal and oil for Canadian factories and electrical generators, iron ore for smelters, and up-to-date machinery for industry—were impossible to replace. The economic boom was intimately linked to the availability of American supply, and strangling that supply also meant choking off the economic miracle.[16] Canada would find it difficult to go on without help; but help could come from only one place.[17]

By the fall of 1947, discussions had begun in Washington to discover how the imbalance in Canada's hard currency account could be alleviated. The Americans were told that restrictions on Canada's U.S. purchases were inevitable; at the same time, the Canadian government wanted an American loan to prop up the Canadian dollar. The Canadians had nothing to offer in return. American officials registered dismay. Canadian discrimination against American goods could irritate Congress and impair the prospects for the ITO.[18]

The Canadians had a solution to propose. The Marshall Plan was moving slowly through Washington's administrative and legislative machinery. Its object was to afford enough financial resources to Europe to permit purchases of American goods. If "offshore"—meaning, in this case, Canadian— purchases could be accommodated in the plan, then the problem of the Canadian dollar shortage would be on its way to a solution.

This idea, first presented to the State Department on 18 September, received a cool welcome. The Marshall Plan was months away from congressional approval, and no prudent plan should be founded on what Congress might or might not do. So much the Canadians were told. Behind the scenes, the U.S. embassy in Ottawa vigorously supported the idea of doing something for Canada, either through special purchases by the U.S. government or through the mechanism of the Marshall Plan. (American dispatches from Ottawa in this period closely resemble the internal memoranda of the Canadian government.) Ambassador Ray Atherton urged that something be done or risk impairment to Canadian-American relations "at a time when solidarity is essential."[19]

That was to argue a specific case from general principles. Soon, however, an exciting and quite unique variation crept into the argument. The American embassy reported that Canadian opinion in favor of "a closer integration of the economics of Canada and the United States" had reached "an all time high." This was, in the embassy's view, the best "long term solution" to Canada's paradoxical situation as a member of the British Commonwealth and, simultaneously, "an independent North American nation."[20]

Still, the immediate crisis could not be solved by a nebulous conception like economic integration. As the Canadians had originally proposed, it was dealt with first by Canadian restrictions on the import of nonessential American products; second, by a loan from the U.S. Export-Import Bank; and third, by the agreement of the U.S. government not to complain that the Canadian action clearly violated the existing 1934 and 1938 trade agreements between Canada and the United States.[21] The question of offshore purchases under the Marshall Plan was put over; it was in fact months away from passage by Congress, and its implementation would lag for months after that. In any case, some American officials (Paul Nitze was one) argued that for Canada to benefit from the Marshall Plan, it should contribute as well. Such reasoning pained Canadian administrators, who could barely see how their country could meet its existing aid commitments to the British and other Europeans.[22]

Once the $300 (U.S.) million was pledged, Canada had a breathing space, but not much more, in the opinion of some of its most senior ministers and their officials. There appeared to be no prospect of resuscitating Canada's British trading connection, and no incentive to construct a broader trading area with Europe based on a policy of discriminating against American imports. Rather than accept such a fate, one very senior official stated that he "favored the other 'polar extreme' of much closer continental integration with the United States."[23]

Even at the senior level, most officials did not know that secret discussions were under way for a free trade agreement between Canada and the United States. Memories of 1911 were still fresh in the minds of the Canadians; one of the senior Americans, Jack Hickerson, had spent long evenings while stationed in Ottawa back in the 1920s listening to firsthand accounts of the defeat of reciprocity (the "1911" argument) from the participants.[24]

Acknowledging that the Canadian side was sensitive is not to suggest that there were not sensitivities on the American team as well. State and Treasury officials were described as "personally sympathetic" but skittish: they would have to take soundings in Congress.[25] As the Canadians knew all too well, one reason that Canadian products were not selling in the United States was that they were competitive (and sometimes not competitive enough) with American ones. That was especially true of raw materials and agriculture, but also of certain manufactures.[26] It was not impossible that Canadian factories, once released from the constraints of their tiny domestic market, could expand and compete in the United States; experience in World War II suggested that that was not impossible. This was one reason why the minister of trade and commerce, C. D. Howe, supported as close an integration as possible between the Canadian and American economies. (Howe, born in Massachusetts and a graduate of MIT, had little of the Canadian inferiority complex vis-à-vis Americans. Possibly the Americans also found it difficult to patronize Howe.)[27]

A comprehensive trade agreement with the United States could go beyond the simple abolition of tariffs between the two countries. It might be a customs union, meaning that British preference in particular would be abolished. It might involve monetary union, and in any case it must permit complete convertibility of the two dollars. One American trade official called for a study of "the extent to which political integration is necessary if a customs union is to be established and to be successful," and "the possibility of shifts in the political and social pattern in Canada as a result of economic changes flowing from a customs union."[28]

Canadian officials glumly agreed that the logical price of a customs union went far beyond tariff policy. In 1911, reciprocity had simply meant broadening the area of trade. "Now," a Canadian finance official argued, "we would inherit a vast structure of American government policy. For example, our exchange rate would be tied to the American exchange rate. The western farmer would want the American system of parity prices and support prices." That might well mean "the end of western agriculture as we know it. Policy would be shaped in Washington." Of course, "a customs union . . . may be a fine thing. Some officials in Ottawa still favour it. But let us not blink the price."[29]

Well-informed journalists hinted at what the price might be. "We can't go on as second-class Americans," a Toronto business newspaper proclaimed. The existing situation, with its American branch plants and limited horizons, must be changed—permanently. How, the newspaper did not say. One obvious inference was that Canadians might choose to become "first-class Americans" and accept political integration into the U.S. economy.[30]

By March 1948, Canadian and American trade experts (all of them below the cabinet level) had worked out a sketch of a free trade agreement. It provided for the elimination of tariffs and quotas between the two countries after a five-year transitional period, with a few agricultural exceptions. The Canadians insisted that they be allowed to make a simultaneous offer of free trade to Great Britain so as to appease residual pro-British sentiment at home; the Americans agreed. There would likely never be a more favorable time for such an agreement, the American negotiators argued, either in Canada or in the United States. If higher levels of the administration approved, Truman should meet Mackenzie King promptly for a formal launching of negotiations. For best results, Truman should appoint the Republican foreign policy expert John Foster Dulles to head the American delegation.[31]

So the matter stood in mid-March. On April Fools' Day, Jack Hickerson got a call at the State Department from his friend Hume Wrong, the Canadian ambassador. The Canadian ministers concerned with the negotiations—a group of four or five—had decided not to proceed for the time being. Astounded, Hickerson and his colleagues demanded an explanation, and over time, they got one. It was the prime minister, Mackenzie King, who had decreed an end to the talks: The time was not ripe for such an initiative, he had said. Some of King's ministers, particularly C. D. Howe, went further. "Responsible ministers in Ottawa," including himself, still wanted a comprehensive trade agreement, he told Robert Lovett, the American undersecretary of state. Admittedly, the prime minister was an obstacle, so the two countries should wait until he retired, later that same year.

Unluckily for Howe, this conversation was minuted and returned to Ottawa, where the prime minister read it. Howe was called on the carpet and obliged to grovel for a few minutes until King was certain he had learned his lesson. "In matters of this kind Howe is almost an innocent abroad," he purred to his diary.[32]

Howe was right about one thing: King *was* about to retire. But he was wrong about another: There was no real prospect that a comprehensive trade agreement would be negotiated, even under King's chosen successor, Howe's friend Louis St. Laurent. The issue was not quite dead; it would return the next year and throughout the 1950s, but never again did it achieve such currency as it had had in 1948.

The demise of Canadian-American free trade was conveniently timed. There is no evidence that Truman had known of the project or that he would have approved it. If he had, it might have proved a burden in the forthcoming U.S. presidential election, in which the farm states of the Midwest were crucial to Truman's hopes of victory. Nor would Congress, dominated by the Republicans in 1948, have looked at a Canadian-American economic union with an uncritical eye.

Nevertheless, the State Department's 1948 assessment was perfectly correct. The prospects that year for abolishing the customs frontier were particularly favorable because the Canadians were desperate. Their dollar imbalance seemed to be insoluble, and the measures they had taken to correct it seemed, in the light of the previous three years, to have been futile. For several years Howe had been chatting to American managers of branch plants in Canada about the need to sell more abroad, and long discussions had transpired as to what Canadian products the United States could buy. But as it happened, either the ostensibly "futile" measures worked, or the international economy improved sufficiently to permit a more optimistic outlook. The trade deficit with the United States shrank from C$900 million in 1947 to C$280 million in 1948, while Canada's general trade surplus grew. Its aid to Britain and Europe was cut back. (Most of it had already been drawn.) The increased sales to the United States were mostly agricultural products and various kinds of raw materials.[33]

The Marshall Plan turned out to be just what Canada wanted. The U.S. government—or some of it—was prepared to concede that the Canadians had shot their bolt with their aid program, totaling over C$1.5 billion between 1945 and 1948. When a Canadian wheat sale to the British turned sour (the price was pitched too low), it was recast as an aid program and added to the toll of virtuous Canadian self-sacrifices.

Congress passed the Marshall Plan on 2 April 1948, the day after Canada rejected the trade deal. An Economic Cooperation Administration (ECA) was established in Paris to coordinate aid; shortly afterward, a senior Canadian trade expert arrived there to match American money with Canadian products. This would be done on a case by case basis, and the first case promptly surfaced.

Beginning in May 1948, the British and later other Europeans received authorization to use American aid to buy Canadian bacon, wheat, and flour. Pleased Canadian diplomats reported that the relevant American aid official was of Canadian descent—Loyalist stock—and blessed with extensive business in Canada. That helped; what helped more was that certain commodities were in short supply in the United States. "ECA have adopted as generous an attitude towards Canada as I think we could possibly hope for," a pleased Ambassador Wrong reported on 22 May. By mid-June, of the C$234 million offshore purchases authorized, $133 million had gone to Canada.[34]

With money flowing into Canadian foreign exchange reserves, American officials renewed their blandishments to get Canadian contributions to the Marshall Plan. Their reasoning was straightforward: Canada had been "enormously aided" by the ECA, and the ECA could now be enormously helped by bringing in Canada as a second donor country. It would also have a significant impact in Congress. But the Canadian government was unwilling to agree. Its foreign exchange reserves were not high enough, the officials argued, and American attempts to prove the contrary were wildly optimistic. And so, through 1948, nothing much was done, despite belated advice from the Canadian ambassador in Washington that some concession would help preserve Canada's advantageous position with the ECA and would help the ECA fend off criticism for its offshore purchases.

The Canadians may have had little choice, as J. L. Granatstein and Robert Cuff contend in their study of this issue.[35] Nonetheless, the ECA proved right in predicting that there would be heavy congressional weather for offshore procurement. The United States had a wheat surplus, and Congress was unhappy about ECA-financed acquisitions of Canadian wheat. The ECA therefore announced in February 1949 that it would no longer fund transactions in Canadian wheat.

It was not the disaster it would have been a year earlier. Either the Marshall Plan was taking effect, or European recovery was just that much further along. There were "earned dollars" that could be set aside to buy Canadian wheat or other agricultural commodities. The rapid growth of imports into Canada slowed, while imports from the United States shrank between 1947 and 1948; offsetting trade figures for inflation, they did not recover to 1947 levels until 1951.

There was no great difference between the two North American countries on the desirability of restoring Europe. But the idea that economic aid should promote economic and political unity in Europe was more difficult for Canada to swallow than the United States. Canada had a trading position to defend, and political links, especially with the British; for the United States, trade was proportionately less of a concern, and its "British connection" had long since been abolished. Canada's basic policy nevertheless amounted to resignation to the inevitability of change and apprehension that in any change Canada's existing interests would be diminished if not sacrificed.

In discussing such a subject, providing a certain amount of economic context is necessary. Canadian foreign trade remained relatively constant in volume and shrank slightly in value in the late 1940s, and exports in particular had proved disappointing. Although there was a trade surplus, it too was dwindling; in the 1950s the balance of trade was in deficit most of the time. (It was massively negative as between Canada and the United States every year until 1968.)

One area of the economy that caused concern was foreign—especially American—investment. Some nationalist economists and journalists (Canadian and, more recently, American) believe that foreign investment represents long-term pain for short-term gain.[36] The short-term effects are, however, almost irresistible for an economy gasping for foreign exchange or worried about production and jobs. In the late 1940s the United States had the world's largest pool of available capital and the disposition to put it to use, while Canada was metaphorically lunging for convertible dollars.

American investment in Canada was nothing new. Already large in the 1920s, it grew by 42 percent between 1926 and 1939, and by 29 percent between 1939 and 1945. There were more than 2,000 "controlled businesses" in Canada at the end of 1946; and the total of American-controlled direct investment was C$2.4 billion. American companies dominated the auto industry, as well as rubber, electrical appliances, oil, and nonferrous metals. Between 1946 and 1950, the Canadian economy grew by roughly 50 percent, while direct American investment increased by 40 percent to $3.4 billion. (If portfolio investment is included, the figure becomes $6.5 billion.[37]) The inflow of American investment helped offset the trade deficit and established a trend that was to become much more pronounced in the 1950s. Most of the

"Mais, mon frère, en sommes-nous rendus là?"

"The Pimp": Quebec's nationalist premier, Maurice Duplessis, sells the province's resources to American investors. Cartoon by Robert LaPalme from *Le Canada. Courtesy Robert LaPalme.*

investment was in equity rather than in bonds, where Canada's international indebtedness had declined drastically between the 1920s and late 1940s. In that sector, there was now actually much less foreign (particularly American) leverage over the Canadian economy and economic policy than there had been before World War II.

These statistics were the stuff of dinnertime conversation among intellectuals but their effects were most apparent in Canadian payrolls. Canada and the United States both knew unparalleled prosperity between 1945 and 1950. Production was high and unemployment low. The United States experienced a short recession in 1948–49; Canada expected one but did not get it. A slackening in the rate of growth was not enough to cause optimism and satisfaction to abate. Outside North America, economic conditions also improved steadily, an improvement that was linked to greater prospects of political stability.

In Canada, the Liberals used the economy—and satisfaction with their new leader, Louis St. Laurent—to get re-elected in 1949. In the United States, dissatisfaction was not so drastic as to turn Truman out of office in the 1948 presidential election. The Canadian government, and Canadians generally, breathed a sigh of relief. Not only was Truman a known commodity, he was an increasingly trusted commodity, and that was important because the two countries were linked for the first time in a formal military alliance.

DEFENSE, CONTINENTAL AND INTERCONTINENTAL

Canada's initiation into the cold war was abrupt and dramatic. On 5 September 1945 a cipher clerk at the Soviet embassy in Ottawa walked out of the building with a bundle of papers under his arm. The bundle was, he believed, a ticket to freedom, since it contained details of Soviet espionage in Canada and the United States, including attempts to infiltrate the combined American-British-Canadian atomic bomb project.

The clerk, Igor Gouzenko, underestimated the timidity of the Canadian government. Mackenzie King had no desire to become embroiled in a diplomatic incident that might offend the Soviet Union, and his subordinates had no idea what to do when confronted with a story of spies and secrets. Gouzenko and his family wandered the streets, at one point even threatening suicide unless they were taken into Canadian custody. That idea, at least, appealed to King, who instructed his staff to have the documents picked up, should Gouzenko be so obliging as to do away with himself.

Eventually, however, decency prevailed in the face of the thuggish behavior of the Soviet embassy as it frantically tried to reclaim its vanished employee. Gouzenko was received and interrogated by no less a personage than Sir William Stephenson, the chief of British security in North America. (Stephenson was born in Canada, and anyway the Canadians had nobody with the appropriate expertise to deal with such a case.)

By mid-September, Mackenzie King was finding the experience rather invigorating. He flew down to Washington, where he told a somewhat bemused Truman that an espionage ring existed, directed at the "secret" of the atomic bomb. That piece of information did not in itself impress the American president, who later remarked that the "secret" was at best transitory and that the Russians were likely to produce a bomb of their own within five years. King warned Truman that a high State Department official was said to be implicated in espionage; Truman appears to have done nothing.[38]

King sailed on to London, where the British told him exciting stories about Soviet capabilities. He returned to Canada full of dread, but with no clear idea what to do next. The best that may be said is that with the Gouzenko revelations in the background, the Canadian prime minister and his government were primed to expect no good to come out of Moscow; nor were they disappointed. The contact between King and Truman is also unenlightening. The two men met twice in the fall of 1945—once to talk about Gouzenko, and once to confer with British prime minister Clement Attlee about the future of the atomic bomb. But on neither occasion is there any sense that any far-ranging discussion of the state of the world occurred.

Perhaps there was no need; the two men were united in deploring the stalemate in Europe, the actions of the Soviet occupation forces in Poland and the Balkans, and the intentions of Joseph Stalin. The Canadian and American governments were pursuing similar policies aimed at reconstructing their respective countries after the war, and the foundation of those policies was budgetary restraint and the speedy abandonment of wartime controls and restrictions. Information that might delay the process, or even speed up rearmament, was not especially welcome. But Truman, as the leader of a great power and the sole possessor of the atomic bomb, could not avoid certain responsibilities that King would never be called upon to face. While King devoted his energy, such as it was—he was seventy—to domestic politics and Canada's precarious balance between French and English Canadians, Truman worried about the balance of power. In worrying, he gave no thought whatsoever to consulting Mackenzie King.

Consultation between the two governments was therefore displaced downward. Truman's secretaries of state between 1945 and 1949 had no great interest in Canada; their role was to parrot what their subordinates put before them, should the president ask for it. Among senior personalities in the administration, only Dean Acheson, assistant secretary and then undersecretary of state, took a special interest. He could hardly help it, since his parents were Canadian, he vacationed regularly in Canada, and he maintained a distant curiosity in the affairs of his well-heeled and well-connected Canadian relatives. During the war and after, he worked closely with the Canadian embassy in Washington, where it did not hurt that his father had known the Canadian ambassador's father and father-in-law. More to the point, Hume

Wrong, the ambassador through most of this period, had a waspish and cynical turn of mind that is likely to have appealed to Acheson.

None of this meant that Acheson was pro-Canadian. His Canadian connections liberated him from having to express the normal platitudinous profundities that haunted ceremonies along the famous undefended border; and he knew too much to subscribe to the banalities that constituted Truman's well-meaning understanding of Canada. (Truman had good Canadian friends in Kansas City and wanted the Canadians to make one of them a consul; beyond that, Canadians should be admitted to West Point and Annapolis—an idea that Truman's staff had some difficulty strangling in its cradle.) Canada's distancing of itself from possibly expensive foreign policy responsibilities irritated Acheson, while Canadian preachiness drove him to distraction. In Acheson's world, influence was earned through virtue—intelligence being a very highly regarded virtue—or at worst was purchased by contributions. The Canadian ambassador qualified under the first category, and Canada did not usually dissappoint under the second. When it did, Acheson's wrath was not slow to find an outlet; and Acheson's wrath, on the subject of Canada at least, never really cooled.[39]

But in 1946 most of Acheson's disappointment with Canada still lay in the future. Canada stood well with the administration and the State Department. Canadian diplomats had acquitted themselves well in the confines of wartime Washington. They had shared secrets with their opposite numbers in State, to their joint advantage in the professional diplomats' endless war with the military and its obsessions. Canada had not thrust itself forward at San Francisco, unlike the bumptious Australians, who had vociferously and unsuccessfully defended the rights of small nations not to be pushed around by the greater powers. Canadians and Americans shared the same experiences and the same assumptions about the lessons of the thirties and the dangers of appeasement. When confronted with a problem, the instinct of both was to solve it professionally, not confrontationally—surgically, not with a blast of political anesthetic. Professional fellow-feeling was, in a word, mutual.

If Canadians in Washington and Ottawa felt any anxiety about the United States, it was a dread that the American government might prove unable, if not unwilling, to assume the burdens that its position of predominance thrust upon it. For one thing, there was the problem of the American system of government, which the Canadians considered ill adapted to making foreign policy. Then there were the American traditions of isolationism, and the fear that American public opinion would not sustain the sacrifices required of an imperial power. "The United States," one official wrote in 1945, "with its inevitable minorities, is incapable of following any consistent imperialistic policy."[40]

A modest illustration of this point, as well as an indication of the downward displacement, occurred over the question of continental defense. Air strategists had long argued that the shortest way to North America from the Soviet Union was over the North Pole. During World War II some modest supplies had been shipped to Siberia via Alaska, and with the improvement of aircraft during the war it was reasonable to believe that where air freight traveled, bombs could follow. The Permanent Joint Board on Defense, languishing since 1940 with little to do, now concluded that its hour had struck. But the PJBD had a problem. Nobody had taken it seriously for so long that its circuits and connections had atrophied; it was difficult to make it a conduit for high or even important policy.[41] Nevertheless, the PJBD struggled with the issue of the aerial defense of the continent throughout 1946. Its American members faced a struggle on two fronts. Their fellow Canadians were nervous about the implications for Canadian sovereignty of a joint, long-term defense establishment that took in northern Canada, and their higher authority in Washington, deemed cost-cutting to be more important and more essential to the military's mission than a couple of fighter squadrons floating around the Arctic Circle.[42]

The political process of the discussions is of greater interest today than their military content. The Canadians, it turned out, had virtually no intelligence sources of their own on the Soviet Union. To meet this lack, the Americans shipped their own interpretations north and followed up with their foremost interpreter of Soviet behavior, George Kennan, who addressed a joint meeting of officials in Ottawa in December 1946. Not only were the Canadians relatively uneasy about their own analysis of the Soviet Union, they were remarkably inept in discerning or, especially, discriminating among American intentions, as Joseph Jockel recently noted.[43] American policy was self-contradictory on Arctic air defense. The United States representatives on the PJBD had little to bargain with, but their proposals were taken to be "official" and were treated with appropriate solemnity by Canadian negotiators, who feared, except in the very worst case, to let go of their sovereign authority over an unpopulated and distant frontier.

Eventually all these mix-ups got sorted out. The December 1946 meeting that Kennan addressed concluded sensibly that "all defense plans must be regarded as somewhat utopian and as goals to be attained in the event of an emergency."[44] The emergency did not exist at present. A very mild document was issued by the PJBD, which was publicly restated by the Canadian and American governments in February 1947. Each country retained control over military activity on its own territory; beyond that, there would be exchanges of personnel, sharing of information and plans, and reciprocal, temporary use of such facilities as air bases.[45]

So much for American imperialism. The hesitations and backing and filling of American policy in 1945 and 1946 gave some credence to the argument that whatever objective marxist categories the United States fitted into, its system of government and political tradition prevented it from assuming an imperialistic role. In the late 1940s this realization evoked mixed feelings among Canadian officials and ministers. The British loan episode—too little, too soon—reinforced a sense of unease. Yet for Canadians, there was no alternative to relying on the United States and hoping that something would eventually turn American politics toward a more coherent policy.

What should that policy be? External Affairs Minister Louis St. Laurent tried to set out Canadian assumptions in a speech in January 1947, in which he spoke of the cultural unity that embrraced North America and Europe and defined the defense of Europe, its societies, and its values as crucial to the defense and even the meaningful existence of Canada. Though St. Laurent here bowed in the direction of the United Nations, his subsequent utterances made it clear that he and his officials had given up on the international body as a means of regulating international order. Of course, the United Nations could be reformed by expelling the Soviet Union, a policy favored by some Canadian officials. But that would be a drastic step, a path of last resort. Could not Western Europe and North America be made to see their own duty in a mutual defense system?

Such arguments gathered force as American policy finally took shape in the spring and summer of 1947. The promise of decisive action in the face of the apparently inevitable Soviet sweep across the face of Europe was inspiring, and in Canada it struck a positive chord. The Marshall Plan was never viewed in Canada as a complete solution to the problem of stabilizing Europe. It was seen, rather, as a preliminary to the main event, a theory that was underlined by the continuing communization of Eastern Europe during the fall of 1947 and its culmination in the Czech coup d'état of February 1948.

Official Canadian opinion on political measures to be adopted in Europe closely resembled American opinion, with the same contradictions and ambiguities as in the United States. Canadian dispatches from Moscow from 1945 on took a dim view of the nature of Soviet society, interpreting it as a tyranny devoted above all to self-perpetuation. There was little danger of a Soviet attack on North America or Western Europe, according to Canadian diplomats; on the other hand, the Soviet government was quite capable of exploiting any useful opportunity to extend Communist control into Western Europe. It is tempting to conclude that the closed environment of the Western embassies in Moscow encouraged a certain homogenization of opinion, including skepticism about the Soviet economy's ability to sustain any large military adventure. Nevertheless, Canadian officials were nervous about the possibility of a Soviet misjudgment leading to an unsought war.

In that case, it was clear that the United States, hamstrung by great power rivalry and paralyzed by the Soviet veto, would be perfectly useless as an instrument of security. The Canadian government considered a variety of expedients, including reforming the UN Charter, expelling the USSR from the UN, and finally, forming a separate security organization, as permitted by Article 51 of the charter. External Affairs Minister St. Laurent urged that notion in a speech at the United Nations in September 1947, and Prime Minister King explored it in talks in London two months later.

Two things are remarkable about this sequence of events. One is that Canada's concerns and analysis did not differ greatly from those current in the United States. The other is that official American views had only a trivial impact on Canadian attitudes to larger security questions. The reciprocal—lack of direct Canadian influence on American policy—is also true, but less noteworthy.[46] Canada was not, in security terms, much of a problem for the United States. It did not border on any country occupied by the Red Army. It did not have a disruptive Communist movement. It did not need American military aid and was therefore not usually a major political concern.[47]

At the beginning of 1948 Canada's behavior did briefly worry the United States, when Mackenzie King balked over joining an American-sponsored election supervision team in Korea. This enterprise was at first viewed almost casually; later, as complications developed, undertaking it became pressing on the American part. As it became pressing, it moved up the line until it reached the president. Pearson, who handled some of the consequent negotiations on the Canadian side, even saw Truman on the matter. He reported him "aimless and amiable" and totally uninformed about Korea.[48]

It took threats of resignation from his most senior ministers and a personal intervention by Truman to put King, grudgingly, back on his side. This irruption was influenced by two factors: Mackenzie King's considerable longevity and a growing personal isolationism that was confirmed, in the prime minister's mind, by visits from the spirit world. (Roosevelt's ghost was known to drop by for a chat.) The prime minister fretted that World War III might soon break out, and he had come to believe that it would occur in Korea.[49] As the Canadian defense minister wrote in his memoirs, King's behavior over Korea was merely "the last bellows of the leader of the herd before he cashed in his cheques."

King was more fearful of the general trend of events—impersonal, even mechanical—than he was of the United States or the Truman administration as such. There was some concern among Canadian diplomats in 1947–48 that advocates of a preventive war would gain in influence, but at the same time they agreed that "it is fantastic to assert that the people of the United States or its leaders wish to dominate the world," as leftist critics were beginning to claim. That opinion never altered in the forty years that followed; it was, however, true that Canadians sometimes exaggerated the possibilities that Americans would take irrational or sudden actions. American irrationality—presumed, of course—could always be said to widen the need for Canadian activity and possibly influence in self-defense. A basic pro-Americanism therefore coexisted uneasily with a tendency to pick over the entrails of the right wing in American politics and to worry about what might happen if "inexperience and self-righteousness" prevailed over wisdom and responsibility. Above all, there was concern that fear of communism rather than self-interest or idealism was the foundation of American activity in international affairs. Fear was a dangerous instrument and opened the door to demagogues.[50]

As over commercial union a few months later, the U.S. administration hardly knew what fires were banked inside Mackenzie King's mind or among Ottawa officials over this issue. But Truman and company were not, after all, seeking the prime minister's advice—merely his vote and his money. His country was, on the other hand, a potential provider of significant aid if the situation were sufficiently serious. Such a situation duly arose in February 1948.

On 25 February the Communist party in Czechoslovakia seized power by a coup d'état. Over the next few months, all non-Communists were removed from positions of influence, the most spectacular example being the Czech foreign minister, Jan Masaryk, who was found dead on the pavement outside his apartment. The Czech coup caused a great stir everywhere in the West, including Canada, where Mackenzie King had looked on Masaryk as a particular friend. Official circles anxiously debated whether the Soviets were now finally on the move to the West, but politicians took a more personal interest. The incident was sufficient to stir the Canadian prime minister from the isolationist lethargy into which he had lapsed. When word came that Truman was broadcasting on the crisis, King led his entire cabinet and most of the House of Commons into a radio-equipped lounge to listen.[51]

They were not disappointed. After considerable backing and filling prior to the Czech coup, the Truman administration now finally dared to entangle the United States in a peacetime alliance. How much entanglement remained a matter of debate inside the government, a circumstance that encouraged the Canadian embassy to exercise such influence as it had on behalf of its friends. Those friends included Jack Hickerson, director of the Office of European Affairs at the State Department and a fervent believer in collective security. Fortunately Hickerson's point of view prevailed, though the process took time—just over a year from start to finish.[52] Occasional public statements by Canadian ministers encouraged progress, adding, as George Kennan recognized in April 1948, "a new and important element" to the design of a North Atlantic treaty. "I think," Kennan minuted, "we must be very careful not to place ourselves in the position of being the obstacle to further progress toward the political union of the western democracies."[53]

The start came in March 1948, when responding to a British request, American, Canadian, and British representatives met in secret in Washington. The secrecy was intended to deceive friend and foe alike. By deceiving friends, it doubtless sped negotiations; as for foes, the secretary did not quite achieve its purpose. Since a Soviet spy—Donald Maclean of the British embassy—attended all the most secret conclaves, Stalin had good reason to understand, if not believe, that the three countries' aims were defensive in nature.

The tripartite discussions produced agreement for further talks, also to be held in Washington, but this time including the countries of the Western European Union. The Truman administration conducted these negotiations under the authority of the Vandenberg Resolution. Although the resolution limited the terms and conditions of any future treaty, it nevertheless affirmed the United States' connection to Western European security.

The Canadians argued in the summer and fall of 1948 that the West should not panic in the face of the apparent strength of the Soviet monolith (a word much in vogue in the memoranda). "In our view," Canadian ministers told American defense secretary James Forrestal in August 1948, "there were no limits to the aggressive intentions of the Soviet Union, but for the time being they would not attempt to achieve them short of war." And war, in the Canadians' view, was not "inevitable."[54]

The Canadians early evolved what became a characteristic position on NATO. They opposed a "dumbbell" arrangement, with the United States and Canada on one end and Europe on the other. They opposed unilateral guarantees by the United States. The best way of avoiding war in the longer term, they thought, would be the consolidation of an Atlantic community—a term and an idea popularized by Walter Lippmann and happily adapted by the Canadians. Pearson expounded the Canadian conception in one of the earlier discussions in Washington in July 1948. There would, he said, be "difficulties if North Atlantic defense arrangements were tied too closely to Soviet intentions. This might mean that if the danger were removed, or appeared to be removed, this justification for a collective system would be removed." Rather than basing the future alliance on fear, Pearson and his staff urged hope as a principle—that hope to be embodied in political, economic, and military connections among the North Atlantic nations. The nonmilitary connections were the "dynamic" part of NATO—the part that would counteract the idealistic appeal of communism.[55]

There was another string to the Canadian bow, unmentioned outside Ottawa. The Canadians were attempting to vary their relations with the United States by establishing as strong and multifarious an alliance as possible. Broadening NATO's scope was less of an innovation than it might have seemed: Canada enjoyed close economic and political ties with the British for many generations. In 1949 the end of those ties was not in sight, even though Ottawa recognized that the British were down on their luck. Because that was so, it was clear that the British Commonwealth could no longer be Canada's principal instrument for security—that would now lie with the United States. When ratified, NATO signified the passing of one alliance—as old as Canada—and its replacement by a new, American-dominated arrangement.

The American reaction to this Canadian conception, or to the parts to which the Canadians admitted, was variable. At first, signs were fair. Hickerson liked it. Undersecretary Robert Lovett agreed that a purely military alliance would be "unfortunate," and American negotiators cooperated with Canadians in inserting an article calling for economic and cultural cooperation in the draft treaty, over the objections of the Western Europeans.[56]

There matters stood as Truman's second administration began and Dean

Acheson replaced George Marshall as secretary of state on 20 January 1949. At that time ratification of the treaty seemed assured. But by February, it was foundering in the Senate, and ratification was in doubt. Acheson proposed to jettison excess baggage, and to his mind cultural and economic cooperation were definitely excessive. A last-minute intervention by his friend Ambassador Wrong, vigorously supported by Hickerson, got the secretary to reverse his stand. As Acheson and Hickerson remembered the incident, Wrong and Hickerson invaded the secretary's sickroom and refused to leave until he gave in to Article 2. He did, with sufficient grace; but he anticipated that Article 2 would be a dud, and he was right.[57] But Pearson, who strongly endorsed Article 2 as the best hope for an enduring alliance, was not wrong. NATO's roots in Western public opinion were fed by the military menace from the East Block, but whether they would outlast the menace remained unclear.

The NATO treaty marked the high point of Canadian-American convergence. Irritations between them were few and easily handled. Their agreement was broad, almost all-encompassing. Their diplomats spoke the same language, literally and figuratively, partly because of the recent experiences of war and cooperation, and partly because Canadian and American economic interests were not especially competitive, as offshore sourcing under the Marshall Plan showed. On bilateral questions, misunderstanding did not lead to disharmony. In terms of active diplomacy, the initiative lay with Canada. When Canada faced a crisis in foreign exchange, the Truman administration started to ride to the rescue. An improving Canadian balance of payments and Mackenzie King's misgivings obviated the American effort. The setback, if setback it was, was accepted with good grace and perhaps some relief.

On the larger multilateral questions of the security of North America and Europe, Canadian and American diplomacy worked usefully together. Even Mackenzie King, crotchety and unpredictable as he had become, had no misgivings about falling into the design for NATO. His juniors, both politicians and diplomats, accepted American leadership and adopted the grand design of American overseas commitments with enthusiasm. The convergence was all the more marked because American attention was so strongly focused eastward, on Europe. But what would happen if, once again, America turned west, to the Pacific?

chapter 3

THE COLD WAR: DEPENDENCE AND INDEPENDENCE, 1950–1957

In the last week of June 1950 the Canadian government confronted two unpleasant surprises. The first was the North Korean invasion of South Korea on Sunday, 25 June. There the surprise was in the timing, and perhaps in the blatant method, rather than in the clash between Communist north and Nationalist south. Seen in the long perspective, Canadian officials and ministers told themselves, the absorption of south by north was probably inevitable; given the undemocratic character of the regime in the south, it might not even be all that undesirable in itself. Early reports indicated the North Koreans had the South Koreans on the run. The final victory would surely be a matter of weeks, if not days. After a flurry of rhetoric, mostly for domestic consumption in the Western democracies, things could calm down and the world would go about its business, Canadians assumed. Korea was simply not important enough to go to war for. The Americans—Secretary Acheson in Washington and General Douglas MacArthur in Tokyo—had told the Canadian government so: in MacArthur's case, as recently as February.

THE KOREAN WAR AND ITS AFTERMATH

So matters stood through Monday, 26 June. Tuesday morning brought another shock. The Americans had reversed their earlier position and were going to intervene to stop the North Koreans. They wanted the United Nations to oppose Communist aggression and, incidentally, to ratify American actions. General MacArthur was ordered to see what could be

46

done; reluctantly, he boarded a plane for Korea to make what he could of what was turning into a military debacle.

While the generals worried over the war in far-off Korea, diplomats and politicians struggled with its political dimensions at home. These were two-fold: the nature and membership of the coalition to oppose Communist aggression in Korea, and the limits of the conflict. American leadership of the anticommunist alliance was never in question, least of all by Canada: obviously no other country had the economic resources and military potential to bring to bear. As to the limits of the conflict, there was, from the Canadian point of view, a bad sign: the United States had proclaimed the "neutralization" of the Formosa Straits and interposed the Seventh Fleet between mainland Communist China, and the Nationalist forces on the island of Taiwan. It constituted an intervention in the Chinese civil war, but with what consequences no one could quite foresee. The Canadian government hoped for the best and expected the worst—and kept its opinions to itself.

A first contingent of Canadian ships and planes was sent to Korea, followed, in August, by the announcement that ground forces would also be sent. Through the fall and winter, as the fortunes of war ebbed and flowed, Canadian support for the United States was frequently voiced. In November the two countries pledged to share defense production, as in World War II. As far as the general public could tell, relations were in the best of shape and the best of hands. That was, probably, an accurate reading of the mind of the U.S. administration. But it was not the impression inside the government in Ottawa.

Yet the war did begin well, as far as Canadian-American relations were concerned. Truman's decision to seek United Nations legitimation of American actions was gratifying. Truman reasoned that collective security's hour had struck, and he drew an analogy with the events of the 1930s; Canada's diplomatic establishment found his arguments agreeable and plausible. Nevertheless, official support for a commitment to armed action in Korea was decidedly mixed. Pearson and the diplomats liked the idea, but the cabinet as a whole hesitated. Dedicated to balanced budgets and a minimal military, Prime Minister St. Laurent and his colleagues were reluctant to reconsider their spending estimates.

There was, after all, a difference between Canada and the United States. The United States was a great power (the term *superpower* was not yet in vogue). Not for Canada the debates that had convulsed the American government over the previous year: the fall of China to the Communists, the Soviet atomic bomb, the feasibility and desirability of an American hydrogen bomb, and the estimates of Soviet power and intentions. Despite their differences, American diplomats had an optimistic sense of the state of their relations with Canada. As the State Department's confidential "Policy Statement" on Canada put it, the first objective of American policy toward Canada was "to insure general recognition in the United States and in Canada that a special relationship does, in fact, exist between the two countries, by reason of their geographical proximity, cultural and social similarity and economic and military independence." This was, of course, the lowest common denominator of American policy and was intended to comfort consular officers processing visas and cargo invoices in remote towns with the belief that there was, indeed, a larger meaning to their work. But like most commonplaces, it is indicative of a basic attitude—one that would survive the eruptions of high policy and the complexities of alliance politics. It would even survive Lester Pearson, Dean Acheson, John Foster Dulles—and John Diefenbaker.[1]

The view from the Canadian side was more hesitant. Generally, there was little disagreement, but when it got to specifics, such as the American belief that "the United States and Canada constitute a single unit for hemispheric defense purposes,"[2] the Canadian government became quite skittish. And when it came to American conduct of alliance policy, Canadians watched skeptically—perhaps too skeptically—from the sidelines. They felt uneasy at developments in the United States, even though they recognized the complexities of the American political situation. The China lobby and the administration's inability to bring it under control perturbed Ottawa. How much American policy was being made by Acheson and Truman, and how much by the admirers of Chiang Kai-shek?

Canadians had no desire to make the position of their friends in the administration more difficult, and some fear of provoking the wrath of less amiable elements on the nationalist and isolationist right. The contradictions of American diplomacy, especially at the United Nations, where Canadians reported that American positions changed with the latest wind from Congress, made Canadian diplomats wonder who was in charge. John Holmes, a member of the Canadian delegation at the UN, put it most succinctly in March 1951. There was an "organic confusion" in American policy, he said, exacerbated by the enthusiasm with which American diplomats hawked about every change in Washington's attitude, even when the relevant change contradicted what had gone before. "[A]lthough the great majority of American Government servants with whom we deal are frank and honest and fair-minded," he wrote, "the total effect [of the confusion] is sometimes that of a double-crosser."[3]

Concern for American reaction was seldom absent from Canadian calculations, even when circumstances inside Canada pushed the Canadian government in the same direction the Americans were already taking. Impressions counted, especially when American policy was being driven by congressional pressure. "There must always . . . be in our minds," Pearson was reminded, "the possibility that if we do not demonstrate our fundamental solidarity we should inevitably find it more difficult to get a favourable treatment in procurement and other problems."[4]

Official anticommunism was a case in point. Liberal Canadian politicians sympathized with their American Democratic counterparts over the growing anticommunist hysteria in the United States. An attempt to ride the communism issue by Canada's Conservative party had flopped the previous year, and it was not revived during the 1950s. That did not mean that Canadian politics did not enjoy a distinctly anticommunist tinge. Of the four national parties of the period, all supported NATO, denounced communism, and prevented, if possible, the employment of known Communists in positions of public trust. The electorate rewarded such attitudes: By the mid-1950s, Communists were practically unknown in elected office, and their supporters in the trade unions were on the run. In one case, the Communist-led Canadian Seamen's Union was displaced by the Seafarers' International Union, which obligingly sent up a thug to Canada to direct operations. The government and the Canadian union movement turned a blind eye to the resulting violence.[5] The Communists maintained a toehold in the Mine, Mill and Smelterworkers' Union, another international union with a long leftist tradition in its native United States, and in the electrical workers' union. But the Canadian Communist party was a fringe organization by the late 1940s, and its decline continued during the 1950s. As in the United States, the Canadian Communist party was assumed to consist mostly of police agents.[6]

Mainstream politics, from the socialist Co-operative Commonwealth Federation (always referred to by the abbreviation CCF) to the right-wing Social Credit party (whose beliefs defy brief description), were remarkably harmonious over the fundamentals of foreign policy. NATO was almost beyond criticism. The Soviets were scoundrels. American presidents, both Truman and Eisenhower, were popular. The Progressive Conservative party—the Tories—hankered rather more after Great Britain and British symbols than did the Liberals, but even the Liberals cultivated strong British connections to offset criticism and, as always, to dilute the overwhelming presence of the United States. In foreign policy, on all but a few issues, it was an age of domestic consensus.

Outside the political elite things were a little different. The United States was not an abstraction to Canadians. It was a vivid presence in Canadian life, from tourism to television. This presence tended to increase over the decade. Yet in 1950 British symbols—king, flag, history—were still strong, as royal tours attested. Commonwealth links engaged Canadians' attention, as the British conferred independence on ex-colonies. The commonwealth was regarded, naturally enough, as an avenue to the outside world and as a means whereby Canada could exercise influence independent of the United States. Over the years the importance of the bilateral British connection and of the commonwealth both tended to diminish. They dwindled slowly, imperceptibly, but shrink they did. British cultural models gave way to American ones, just as London gave way to New York as a center for fashion, for publishing, and as a source of ideas.

By 1960, the British connection, still strong, was flagging, and the Canadian affinity for the United States was continuing to grow. To an older generation, the kind of influence the United States was projecting was disturbing. American pulp fiction, comic books, television, and popular music provoked denunciations that were as snobbish as they were ineffective. (The denunciations were closely linked to similar lamentations from respectable Americans at home.) On the other hand, as the link with Britain weakened, some Canadian opinion became alarmed. As American influence grew in every department of life, some Canadians were more likely to assert their differences. In the prism of Canadian-American relations, small problems could seem like large ones.

As the Korean War began, it did not seem that there were many small problems. Ottawa accepted Washington's analysis of events without much question. The north had invaded the south. The fact of the invasion posed a danger to the West as a whole, and it had to be resisted. External Affairs Minister Pearson told the U.S. ambassador that Canada would not "let [the] U.S. down." At the United Nations the senior Canadian in attendance told his American counterpart that the Security Council "might conceivably give its blessing to any military action [the] U.S. was willing to take." He did not say that Canada had absolutely no reservations (it had a few on the wording of the resolutions), but they would not be allowed to stand in the way of support. In other words, the United States would choose a policy, Canada would sustain it, and the UN would likely ratify it. There was no hint that the UN should in any way limit American actions or restrain American freedom of action. The U.S. administration was justified in reding these statements as strong and unconditional support.[7]

Canada voted for the first three UN resolutions on Korea, and it followed up on its vote by sending three destroyers and an air transport squadron to the Far East. This, Pearson proclaimed, was "no mere token support."

"Okay," an American official is supposed to have replied, "let's call it three tokens."[8]

Behind the tokens the cabinet was deeply divided. The ministers wrangled through July and into August. In the press, there was strong editorial support for Truman's Korean policy, but polls told a different story about public opinion. By 39 to 34 percent, Canadians believed that their country should either send only supplies to Korea or nothing at all. There were rumors of unknown origin that the Americans did not want a Canadian contribution. That hopeful idea was laid to rest on 26 July, when the American ambassador indicated to the Canadian government that a contingent of troops would be most welcome. In fact he did more than indicate—he pursued Prime Minister St. Laurent to his summer residence to express official American concern.

That request only added to the cabinet's misery. Korea was a horrible country, according to the only minister who had ever been there. It was a remote place, too close to China and Russia. Would Canadians volunteer to fight so far away? Some ministers could hardly believe that a call for volunteers would be successful. The last war had been only five years back; people were tired of war. During World War II the Liberal party and the country had almost split along English-French lines over the issue of conscription for overseas service. Korea revived the ghost of conscription, and ministers did not take it lightly. The question was not only what Canadians thought but what *French Canadians* thought. Pearson, who strongly supported sending troops to Korea, at one point threatened to resign until the prime minister took his part. But St. Laurent's attitude was never really in doubt.

Finally, rolling over the countryside in a train returning from Mackenzie King's funeral, the cabinet decided to call for volunteers. Canada would send a volunteer brigade to Korea. The prime minister and the defense minister made radio speeches, then sat back to await the reaction. Rather to their surprise, it was favorable. There were more than enough volunteers, not only for a Korean brigade but for Europe as well. And so, militarily and materially, Canada followed the American lead.

Misgivings were not slow to reappear: It was said that Pearson hoped to win Acheson's ear by sending troops. But even a brigade was not a lot, certainly compared to what the United States was having to commit. When defeat turned to victory in Korea, in September, the momentum of events seems to have precluded any serious consultation. The American decision to pursue the enemy across the thirty-eighth parallel perturbed the Canadian government; even more, the Canadians worried that their opinion had not been taken into account. That opinion was based on the danger of provoking Chinese or Soviet intervention, thereby prolonging the war. But although the Canadians questioned the wisdom of invading North Korea, they did not publicly oppose it. There was always the possibility of total victory and the reunification of Korea on American terms; as a recent analysis has shown, that was considered a highly desirable, if somewhat unlikely, outcome in Ottawa. When MacArthur was defeated in November 1950 by Chinese intervention, spirits drooped in Ottawa.

Canadian reactions were divided: when the U.S. ambassador mentioned the possibility of "hot pursuit" of enemy formations into Chinese Manchuria, Ottawa did not at first say no. Pearson himself had by then begun to alter his course. Within a day of the first Canadian reaction, Ottawa joined London and Canberra in discouraging action that might lead to a broader war. In response, the Canadians received reassurances that the United States would not provoke the Chinese by driving all the way to the Yalu River, the Manchurian frontier.

By December, all that was in the past, though it left a bitter residue among Canadian diplomats. By December, too, the Canadian government was reacting to more than just Korea. Pearson and the cabinet were receiving strategic assessments of Soviet military capacity from Washington, as well as speculation about the significance of Korea as part of Stalin's grand design. During December, dire predictions of war across the world were set before the ministers; these warnings were based almost wholly on American intelligence and analysis. The news from Washington depicted a Red Army sweep across Europe to the Channel and the Pyrenees. It was news not shared with the continental European allies, for obvious reasons. They worried about the prospect anyway.

The Canadians decided to abandon their peacetime budget and plan for war—or if not war, then the heightened danger of war. A new budget was drawn up, the military was told to expand, and C$5 billion (Canadian) was set aside for rearmament. The cabinet knew that volunteers would be available, and as they came in, they were formed into a brigade for Europe.

Direct Canadian reports were confined to observations in Washington and at the United Nations. In the American capital Canada's trade minister, C. D. Howe, found confusion and panic. "It seems to me," Howe wrote in December, "that our friends in the United States are suffering from hysteria in a very advanced stage"—this from the most pro-American and conservative minister in the cabinet.[9]

GROWING DISSATISFACTION OVER FOREIGN AFFAIRS

Howe's colleague, External Affairs Minister Pearson, carried the point rather farther. Since 1945 Pearson had taken an urgent interest in the control of nuclear weapons.[10] No Canadian had any particular knowledge of American atomic strategy and certainly no idea of the number of atomic weapons in Truman's arsenal. These were not subjects for consultation, under U.S. law. Though at one point the Truman administration tried to find a middle way, to involve at least some of its allies, it could not succeed: not with the British, because of leaky security; and not with the Canadians, who had no ambitions or capacity in the area.

The lack of consultation fed Canadian fears, and when in November 1950 Truman made a gaffe in a press conference, implying that he might consider using atomic weapons, Pearson took it very seriously. So did the British, who sent Prime Minister Attlee to Washington. Truman was reassuring. He had not meant what he was taken to have said, and in the future he would at least try to keep the British and Canadians abreast of any nuclear plans he might have. All this was better than nothing, but it failed to soothe. As Pearson's undersecretary minuted in January 1951, "the US government have not as yet been very forthcoming in describing frankly and fully their plans and intentions, and still less in giving us any assurances that we will be adequately consulted."[11]

The Truman administration had problems of its own, increasingly centered on the conflict over the conduct of the war between the civilian authority in Washington and its military proconsul in Tokyo. It had an international dimension, because foreign governments, including Canada's, had ceased to credit MacArthur's genius in landing at Inchon and remembered instead his rashness in exposing his army to defeat. Perhaps MacArthur really had meant to secure victory at any price; in an atomic age the price was easy to imagine.

Disquiet and dissatisfaction with American policy generally, and with the conduct of American diplomacy specifically, caused Canadian attitudes to shift. In March 1951 Pearson called for a comprehensive internal review of Canadian relations with the United States. In response, his bureaucrats prepared a set of memoranda on the nature of American relations with Canada.

On the economic front, things were going swimmingly. "Looking over the field," the economists reported, "it seems that the United States deals with us well and generously on a direct country-to-country basis. Whenever Canada can be treated on its own merits, or as a special case, we seem to come off well." Contacts with the U.S. government in this field were excellent—as good as they had been in the palmy days of World War II. Admittedly American behavior in international institutions such as the International Monetary Fund left something to be desired. There, Pearson learned, "everything became a matter, on the one hand, of legalism, and on the other hand, intrigue." Nevertheless, Canada had little to complain of over economics.[12]

Political relations were an entirely different matter. The U.S. embassy in Ottawa did little. Ambassador Woodward was not strong, and most of the burden therefore had to be borne by the Canadian embassy in Washington. On the political level Canada had slight leverage, even less because the Canadian embassy refrained from interfering in American politics by dealing with Congress. Bilateral issues were relatively unimportant, but where issues were active, they were subject to the same congressional pressures that bedeviled larger questions. The St. Lawrence Seaway, a major Canadian objective, was stalled by competing U.S. railroad interests and by U.S. Atlantic ports. Truman and Acheson had done their best, the Canadians believed; and as far as Truman was concerned, they were right.[13]

Where the Americans did not do their best was in managing the alliance, or so Canadian diplomats believed. Eccentric and impulsive policies merged with an imperious disregard for other countries' sensibilities. The imperatives of American politics were assumed to be a sufficient explanation for almost any action, while the idea that other countries might have concerns was considered truly outlandish. "It is customary for the United States Government to spend a long time arriving at a decision on the course of action it should follow in the first instance," External Affairs' American division reported. "However, when this decision has once been taken it expects other governments to agree with the United States point of view without a similar delay on their part and is willing to apply considerable pressure to secure acceptance of its ideas with speed."[14]

As for those ideas themselves, it was hard to tell where they came from: "There is no confidence in the policy pursued by the United States or in United States leadership in the Far East." Even Acheson was not exempt. "For example," Pearson was informed, "it is known that at the time of the

Attlee-Truman conversations [in December 1950] Mr. Acheson was actually advocating what he called limited war with China. At that time more sober counsels prevailed."[15]

Pearson was worried that unlimited war might once more be on the agenda. Relations between General MacArthur and his government were notoriously poor, but the government seemed unwilling or unable to do anything about its Far Eastern commander. But that was only the appearance: On 8 April Truman made the decision to replace MacArthur. For tactical reasons the announcement was put off for several days.

Pearson's timetable ran slightly ahead of Truman's. He wanted to redefine in public, before MacArthur did something else, the bases of the Canadian-American relationship. By differentiating Canadian policy from American and by stressing that Canadian interests were not always the same as the Americans', he was preparing Canadian opinion for a major break with American policy. As he later explained to Ambassador Woodward, "if the fighting in Korea spread to China, [the Canadian] Government might have to reconsider its position with respect to the commitment of troops in the Far East." Woodward continued, "Mr. Pearson said, if General MacArthur could not be controlled, and led the United Nations forces into war on the Chinese mainland, the Canadian Government might well feel that it could not associate itself in such a military venture."[16]

On 10 April, Pearson delivered his reflections on alliance diplomacy in a speech in Toronto. For once—he was not a gifted speaker—he caused a sensation. Canada and the United States had "destinies, economic and political, [that] are inseparable in the Western hemisphere," Pearson reminded his audience, but even close relationships were not always "smooth and easy." They would be easier if the United States accepted that Canada was not willing "to be merely an echo of somebody else's voice." They would be better if the United States "took more notice of what we *do* do, and, indeed, occasionally of what we say." In case the audience had missed the point, Pearson concluded on a strong note: "The days of relatively easy and automatic relations with our neighbour are, I think, over."[17]

Pearson had complained that nobody in the United States paid any attention to Canadians, but this time they did. His speech was widely reported in the United States, and it attracted a lot of attention—almost all of it hostile. Acheson declined public comment, perhaps because by then he had other things to talk about, perhaps because his subordinates warned him not to. General MacArthur's dismissal had been announced at one o'clock in the morning on 11 April; the secretary had phoned his friend, Canadian ambassador Wrong, an hour earlier with the good news.[18]

MacArthur's departure put Canadian-American relations on a sounder footing. Reassured, Pearson did not again raise the possibility of withdrawing from the Korean War. Canadian troops had already arrived there, and they stayed until 1957, four years after the war was ended by an armistice. At its peak the Canadian Far Eastern force numbered about 8,000 men, about half a division—small beer compared with the United States' six divisions. All told, 22,000 Canadian soldiers served in Korea; of these, 309 were killed in action. "By way of comparison," a military historian pointed out, "in 1950, 2,289 persons in Canada were killed in traffic accidents."[19]

The Korean War did not bring the Canadian and American armies closer together. Canadian soldiers in Korea served with a commonwealth division, under British command. The American commanders were not especially excited at their arrival, and the feeling was mutual. When the Canadian defense minister visited the theater of war, he was unimpressed. James Van Fleet, the U.S. Army commander, "did not seem to know what it was all about. His principal staff officers were too old for their jobs. They had all got into the habit of receiving and lying to Congressmen and they put on a similar show for us."[20]

There were other Canadian-American episodes during the Korean War. On the diplomatic front they were not usually harmonious. The two countries differed substantially over the tactics to be adopted in ending the war; as well, Pearson's diplomatic style, conciliatory and nonconfrontational, differed substantially from Acheson's. Pearson concentrated on diplomacy at the United Nations (he was president of the General Assembly in 1952), where his methods persuaded the Americans that he was soft on principle and unrealistic in practice. Pearson, on the other hand, thought Acheson pigheaded and unduly legalistic. At the end of 1952 Acheson took the war to Ottawa, putting his case directly to Prime Minister Laurent. The secretary of state argued, as he had elsewhere, that the United States was making the bulk of the sacrifices in the war and must prevail, even in the face of criticism at the United Nations—to which Pearson was paying entirely too much attention. Acheson later recalled that his mission to Ottawa had succeeded brilliantly; but Pearson remembered the opposite.[21] That the war would eventually end and that it should not expand, both men agreed. As a consequence, there was no formal rupture, merely lingering disappointment.[22]

Friction among ground commanders and their civilian masters did not carry over into the air. Relations between Canadian and American airmen were close and getting closer by the early 1950s, and it was in the air that the U.S. government made its most pressing demands on Canada. The shortest route to the Soviet Union was over the North Pole, and vice versa. The air defense of the United States required an early warning radar system, and it would have to be in Canada. The Canadian defense department agreed, and inside the Canadian government it argued for American radar bases on Canadian soil. The Americans would supply most of the necessary technicians, whom Canada could not in any circumstances provide, and offered to pay two-thirds of the cost.[23]

The reaction in Ottawa was at best diffident. The Canadian government, civilian branch, did not want American troops stationed permanently on

Canadian soil. Those forces, of course, would come under American command and military jurisdiction rather than Canadian law, and for a small country, it seemed rather much to concede. The fact that an arm of the Canadian military had no objection increased the government's nervousness.

Perhaps, as the clerk of the cabinet, J. W. Pickersgill, suggested to his friend the defense minister, the Americans had difficulty in understanding how "disquieting" their request was. "In order to make it abundantly clear to the Americans that these demands for facilities do create real political problems for us," Pickersgill wrote, "it might be worth considering a request for the setting aside for the use of the Canadian Army and Air Force of a training area somewhere in the Southwestern United States, for winter training only, and that in making the request we ask for precisely the same privileges and immunities for our forces as the Americans desire to receive for theirs in Canada."[24] Pickersgill did not add that the Canadian government was embarrassed that it could not itself handle all the financing or the technical details of the radar equipment; by signing on with the Americans, Canada would be admitting that it could not defend itself without help—substantial help, as it turned out.[25]

Eventually the matter was resolved by the successive construction of three radar networks across the continent: in chronological order, from south to north, they were the Pinetree, Mid-Canada, and Distant Early Warning or DEW Lines. The foundations of the DEW Line, the most expensive and complex of the radar nets, were laid under Truman, but the realization was left to the Eisenhower administration. Along with the radar systems came an increasing integration of air defense, which permitted airmen from each country to traverse the other's air space. Throughout, American negotiators did their best to humor Canadian "political" (as opposed to military) concerns, which they considered highly exaggerated. The Canadians reluctantly conceded the point that defense must come before local political problems. Only later would it become clear that the predictions of a political cost had been accurate.

Canadian anxiety over the war in Korea had another and possibly more significant source. Canada's foreign policy faced east, across the Atlantic. While Korea had symbolic importance as an example of the need for collective security, for Canada it was more of a sideshow in the larger theater of East-West conflict. If there were to be a war or a means and place where war could be deterred, it would be in Europe, under NATO. It was to Europe that a permanent Canadian garrison was sent—volunteers like the soldiers in Korea. The Canadian brigade group in Europe became part of the British Army of the Rhine and served with the British until 1969.

In the years after 1953, the Far East continued to be important to Canadians as a constant irritant in Canadian-American relations. Canadians considered their foreign policy in that area to be unreasonably constrained by American prejudices—by American support for Chiang Kai-shek and his

Nationalist Chinese and the concomitant hatred of Communist China. American officials up to and including the president let their Canadian allies know that recognition of the Communist regime in Peking was out of the question, not just for the United States but for Canada as well. The Canadians, weighing the recognition of a government that ruled the largest population on earth against the maintenance of good relations with the United States, acquiesced. They complied with American wishes publicly, even when they judged American policy to be unbalanced, rigidly ideological, and unrealistic, such as over Quemoy and Matsu, two offshore islands that Chiang's Nationalists garrisoned despite heavy Communist bombardment and the threat of an invasion in 1955.[26] The Far East generally came to signify to the Canadian government everything it disliked about the conduct of American foreign policy. Some Canadian diplomats and politicians used the example of American policy in the Far East in their internal debates on other subjects—and not as a compliment to the United States.

The Korean War generated another side effect in Canada. After four post-war years of consumer boom and runaway inflation, the North American economies collectively sputtered at the end of 1949, only to be revived by an injection of government cash with the outbreak of war in Korea. Production rose and unemployment fell. In Canada, virtually all sectors of the economy advanced. Naturally, defense rose farthest and fastest. Agriculture also prospered, but agriculture enjoyed its own rhythm: weather, harvests, and overseas sales. Manufacturing increased, and so did mining, though not by as much.[27]

Canadian exports to the United States might have been expected to soar, but that happened only once, in 1949–50. Imports bounded up the scale, rising in value by a third in just one year, 1950–51. The imbalance was paid for, in large part, by an inflow of investment capital: C$1.3 billion from 1950 to 1953, inclusive. Almost all the inflow was American. The results could easily be appreciated. The Canadian dollar was much in demand and rose in value, overpricing Canadian exports. (Canadians, who took pride in their "strong" dollar vis-à-vis the U.S. currency, usually failed to see its negative economic effects in depressing exports.) In the longer term, however, there were notable changes. Economists pointed out that the trend of trade toward the United States established during and after the war had become permanent. "We are today selling the United States roughly three times the quantity of goods we sold in the best year before the war, 1937," one analyst wrote.[28] What all this meant was that in 1951 Canada sold 59 percent of its exports to the United States; that year, 69 percent of its imports originated in the United States.

American-dominated trade found parallels in other sectors of the economy. In 1948 U.S.-owned investment in Canada totaled C$3.7 billion. In 1953 it was C$6.4 billion, and it rose steadily for the rest of the decade until in 1960 it stood at C$12.1 billion. By 1960, these trends had become a political problem and a sore point in Canadian perceptions of the United States—as had the Far East and the defense systems of the Far North.

That development seemed remote under Truman, but it was in the early 1950s that a conjunction between Canadian nationalism and Canadian anti-Americanism was established. To Dean Acheson, Canadian differences with and resentment of the United States represented a variety of provincialism and bumptiousness; to some of his subordinates, it was the result of Canadian hypersensitivity. "In the field of defense," the U.S. embassy in Ottawa reported in 1955, "the Embassy has had continuously to contend with the Canadian spirit of nationalism and the desire to prevent by all means any United States encroachment on Canadian sovereignty." Yet on this as on other subjects, Canadian opinion was divided.

U.S. investment gave rise to the greatest concern among Canadian nationalists. It flowed to Canada for obvious reasons. Canada was close at hand, easy to travel to, and easy to keep track of. Its majority language was the same as that of the United States, and its legal system was similar. In Canada there were special tax concessions for mining development that mining investors considered a model for the world (and at which tax collectors inwardly groaned). Best of all, Canada had products the United States wanted and needed. In 1952, *Fortune* magazine told its readers that Canada was truly "a businessman's country." The country was run economically by a "stocky, candid, unpretentious 'engineering-type' executive," C. D. Howe. In Canada, Howe had made it to the top of the political heap simply by "behaving like a businessman." Happily for *Fortune* and its mainly Republican readers, 1952 was an election year in the United States, and soon people like Howe would sweep Truman and Acheson and their ilk from office.[29]

THE EISENHOWER YEARS

When the Republicans finally did arrive in Washington in 1953, they had plenty to discuss with Howe. He knew some of them already, "friends of Canada, with a wide knowledge of public affairs in this country," as he put it in November 1952. Some of them, like Treasury Secretary George Humphrey or Defense Secretary Charles Wilson, were investors in Canada, in iron ore and automobiles, respectively. Automobiles were "old money" as investment went, but iron ore was new.

During World War II and as far back as anyone could remember, the United States had been the mineral storehouse of the Western world. Canadian-American trade in minerals favored the United States, which supplied Canada with iron ore for the Canadian steel industry and coal and oil for light, heat, and manufacturing.[30] Canada in return sent copper, lead, and zinc, which competed with American products, and nickel, which did not. During World War II the United States had turned to Mexico and Cuba to supplement mineral imports from Canada, but once the war was over, proximity and scarcity could not be denied.[31]

The Paley Report (the report of the President's Raw Materials Policy Commission) in 1952 drew on this theme. The United States, it concluded, had an "insatiable" appetite for raw materials. It proposed that America procure them wherever it could, as cheaply as it could—a recommendation that was notably *not* followed. The same might have been said for the commission as a whole: its impact on public opinion, including opinion in Canada, was considerably greater than its impact on public policy. In Canada, there were two kinds of reaction. Mining companies and their investors drooled at the prospect of becoming an officially recognized contributor to a notional American mineral stockpile. On the other hand, opinion-makers worried that Canadians were fated to be hewers of wood and drawers of water to the American industrial juggernaut.[32]

American investment in mining was no new thing. It long antedated World War II and its mineral shortages. Historically the Canadian and American mining industries were closely linked by capital, labor, and expertise. (Some of the United States' most prominent geologists were in fact Canadians.) Cyrus Eaton, a Canadian-born Cleveland tycoon (and a man whom Howe detested, a feeling Eaton reciprocated) parlayed government subsidies into an iron ore mine in northern Ontario; unfortunately for Eaton, its reserves and prospects proved limited. Farther west, another form of mineral investment paid off. In 1947 Imperial Oil, a subsidiary of Standard Oil, found an abundant new source of oil in Alberta. To the east, along the Quebec-Newfoundland border, investors eyed iron ore reserves. What followed is a good illustration of the impact of American investment in Canada.

A Canadian company, the Iron Ore Company of Canada, was organized with Canadian and American investment. The principal investor on the American side was the M. A. Hanna Company of Cleveland, directed by George Humphrey, who was already a power in national Republican politics. Humphrey traveled to Canada to meet C. D. Howe and came away impressed. Howe smoothed the Iron Ore Company's path by arranging tax depreciation for a railway from the ore fields, deep inland, to a port on the Gulf of St. Lawrence, Sept-Iles. A grateful Humphrey passed the word: "The stability of the Canadian government" made Canada a marvelous place to invest.[33]

There was a reciprocal to this proposition. Humphrey in later life was proud of what he and his company had done in creating an oasis of prosperity on the remote north shore of the St. Lawrence. He had made "millions of tons of iron ore that lay idle for centuries" available "for the benefit of civilization, not only in the United States, but in Europe." He had exported a piece of the American way of life and in doing so he had immeasurably improved the lives of the people of Sept-Iles and the other towns down the

St. Lawrence river. There can be little doubt that most of the people affected agreed with Humphrey: for them it offered an escape from poverty and monotony—a chance to enter the twentieth century. It is no accident that the most pro-American of Canadian prime ministers, Brian Mulroney, grew up along the lower St. Lawrence in a world where American money and American corporations had made the difference.

Mulroney's experience could be duplicated across the country. Provincial governments, which under the Canadian division of powers control most natural resources, were delighted to import American money, and Canadian jobs. In Alberta, for example, C$300 million worth of new industry appeared in the decade after the discovery of oil by an American-owned company in 1947. It was hard for Alberta or any other provincial government to argue against those figures. And their citizens were, by and large, grateful.

The most spectacular example of the Canadian-American mineral trade was uranium. This dated back to 1942, when the U.S. Army signed up Canadian uranium production (and more important, the Canadian uranium refinery) for the Manhattan Project. This link continued after the war and was enhanced in the 1950s, when the U.S. Atomic Energy Commission offered premium prices for Canadian supplies. Money talked—in this case very effectively, since American uranium contracts were designed to pay off all capital costs in developing a mine, plus a reasonable profit.[34] In 1959, the peak year for Canadian sales, the United States bought C$331 million worth of Canadian uranium; over time, the U.S. government spent well over a billion dollars on Canadian procurement. What it offered Canada, it also offered domestically, with the effect that the U.S. government managed to create two competitive uranium industries inside North America. As uranium grew plentiful and money grew short, it was inevitable that the U.S. government would restrict its purchases to the United States alone; it helped the process along by banning the importation of Canadian uranium throughout the later 1960s and 1970s, greatly to the disgust of the Canadian government.

Uranium was an example of indirect investment; as a matter of policy, all uranium mines in Canada in the period were Canadian-owned. But uranium was a unique case because of its strategic value. Direct investment meant that American-owned firms proliferated and in many cases dominated entire sectors of the Canadian economy. The automobile industry, to take the most extreme example, was 95 percent American-owned in the late 1950s. So was 92 percent of rubber manufacturing, 75 percent of oil and gas, 42 percent of pulp and paper, and over 40 percent of manufacturing in general. Over half of all American foreign investment in the period was located in Canada.[35]

These figures were well known and widely published in the Canadian business press. Why was Canada so dependent on outside capital? editorialists regularly asked. Their answers were not so much unclear as impressionistic. Canadians saved a lot, more than Americans did, but they preferred to put their savings in bonds and banks. On the positive side, this meant that

Canada's fixed debt was largely internally held so that the country was not beholden to foreign lenders. Foreign investment in equity stocks—risk-taking by foreigners—meant that if the economy went down, as it did in the 1930s, the foreign equity investor would be left holding the bag. As time passed and prosperity continued, this argument became less impressive as it became clear, even to Canadians, that investment in Canada was not risky. Those who benefited from such investment by and large lived south of the border. Those who complained lived north of the line.

The U.S. embassy, which monitored the complaints, could do little about the phenomenon. The U.S. government did not control its citizens' propensity to invest abroad, though it was concerned that the investment not mar the United States' image. "Local American businessmen know what is going on," the Toronto consulate reported, "and, generally speaking, they seem to be circumspect and tactful in their personal and professional relationships with Canadians." The expatriate businessmen did not bombard their government with demands for help, and that government, in turn, often had no idea who they were.[36]

There were doubtless genuine Canadian grievances. University presidents complained that American firms did little to support local colleges. Canadian executives complained that they were passed over in favor of Americans for promotion in American-owned companies. Those executives who did impress their American owners eventually found that the road to promotion ran through the head office, out of Canada. And so businessmen joined the brain drain, which, by the 1950s, was again gurgling happily.[37] That too was a subject for lamentations and recriminations. These were listed in the U.S. embassy's periodical reports, a regular feature, of which was headed "Canadian nationalism," meaning some form of anti-Americanism.

To the Canadian government and especially to C. D. Howe, it was not a matter for concern if Americans dominated this or that company, or even this or that sector of the economy. "Why put unnecessary handicaps in the way of our future by adopting narrowly nationalistic and emotional attitudes towards foreign capital?" the minister demanded. In Howe's judgment Canada's sovereignty was not impaired by U.S. investment, nor was Canada's political control of its economy endangered. His own experience as minister proved the point, or so he believed. In the 1940s and 1950s Howe shaped Canada's aluminum industry without reference to American desires or interests by stimulating a new smelter in coastal British Columbia, and by preventing the export of Canadian power to a competing American project in Alaska.

Howe's pièce de résistance was in energy policy, which he also dominated. Between 1953 and 1957 he established an east-west natural gas pipeline from Alberta to Toronto and Montreal in defiance of private investors—many of them Canadian—who would have preferred to supply Toronto from existing American pipelines up the Mississippi valley while bringing gas from Alberta south to Chicago. (Public opinion, incidentally, supported Howe's position—even if not Howe himself.)[38] Ironically Howe used American investment to build his pipeline, whose purpose was to make Canada independent of American energy supply—just in case the Americans were ever tempted to ration their energy to Americans first. Howe was, as the phrase went, a "continentalist"—but only where money was concerned, and only because the United States was where money was to be found. His policies—Canada's policies—were something else.[39]

Howe's approach had coherence and practicality to recommend it, but it must be admitted that it eventually proved a political liability. His imperious style was a problem as far as public perception went—he rammed his pipeline legislation through parliament in the teeth of vocal opposition in June 1956—and even Howe found it impossible to isolate the field of industrial development from other, larger currents in Canadian-American relations. This blending of issues occurred despite the continuing popularity of the United States, its lifestyles, its culture, and even its leader, Republican president Dwight D. Eisenhower.

Polls in the mid-1950s showed a moderate attrition in the prestige of the U.S. government in Canada—at the same time that polls showed that Canadians believed that their way of life was *not* being too much influenced by the United States. Those on the political left—the social democratic Cooperative Commonwealth Federation party—were most likely to disapprove of the U.S. government and its policies; those on the right—the eccentric Social Credit party—were most likely to be in favor.[40]

The Eisenhower administration was not well equipped on the political side to appeal to the Canadian government. John Foster Dulles, the secretary of state, was known in Canada, and for his part, he knew Canada, where he had done business and where he owned property. In testimony before the Senate, Dulles confidently summarized his views on the subject. "He takes a few swipes at Canada," an aide recalled, "their inferiority complex, their ambivalent attitude to the U.S.—but points out that it's a very important piece of real estate and should be humored along." Canada was not alone in the importance of its real estate, according to Dulles.[41]

Dulles's testimony was kept secret, but his patronizing attitude to the lesser allies—including Canada—offended Canadian diplomats' sense that they should enjoy a "special relationship" with the United States. Nor were they pleased that their opposite numbers in the State Department were obliged to suffer loyalty screenings as part of the McCarthyite climate of the day. Dulles's consent to the proceedings indicated that the administration would not be strong in resisting irresponsible pressures at home.

It is true that the timidity with which Eisenhower and Dulles approached domestic political problems allowed them more freedom in the conduct of American foreign policy. The price of strategic freedom, however, was high: tactical concessions to Congress, especially in the economic realm, could easily damage the Canadian interests that so often paralleled and competed with those of parts of the United States. The benefit to specific American interests was offset by damage to overall U.S. relations with Canada.

At first all was rosy between Canadians and Eisenhower. Prime Minister St. Laurent visited President Eisenhower in May 1953 and got a very friendly reception. It was so friendly that when Pearson flippantly remarked that "we" should consider free trade, Defense Secretary Wilson promptly raised the possibility of a customs union of the two countries. That idea was swiftly sidetracked into a State Department study; although Eisenhower mildly supported the concept, it was obvious that the Canadians did not. Instead, the two countries agreed to improve economic cooperation by setting up a joint ministerial committee on trade and economics, to meet every six months. It met for the first time in 1954, and thereafter every six months until it expired in 1969.[42]

After that there was the St. Lawrence Seaway, which the Canadians badly wanted. The Seaway had two main features: a twenty-seven-foot-deep waterway from the St. Lawrence River to Lake Superior, and a hydropower development on the St. Lawrence, to be shared with New York State. The International Joint Commission had had the seaway project before it for years (since 1921, in fact), and there had been an abortive treaty on the subject in 1941. The State Department considered the seaway to be "the most important single facet" of Canadian-American relations, but there were powerful economic political interests to the contrary. These ranged from Atlantic ports to railroads, and up to 1953 they had prevailed despite Truman's best efforts.[43]

Under Eisenhower, the seaway's appeal was broadened. Besides its obvious economic benefits to the Great Lakes states, its supporters argued that it would be a bulwark against communism because it would channel strategic iron ore from the lower St. Lawrence to the steel mills of Cleveland and Toledo, thus enhancing American defensive capacity. The president was still reluctant; as he complained to his brother Milton, the seaway was really a massive political headache. But he complied, and for his pains he got to open the seaway six years later, in tandem with Queen Elizabeth II.[44]

The disposition of the seaway did not deprive Canadian-American economic relations of issues. The Canadians worried that a Republican administration would be protectionist, and they carefully scanned administration utterances for signs of the protectionist virus. Canadian and American concerns in international trade were not far apart, in principle, throughout the 1950s, although in practice they sometimes diverged. In multilateral negotiations under GATT, Canadians and Americans got along, and the Americans did not insist that Canada's general tariff level should decline faster than the Canadians wanted it to. That should have been of some comfort, and it was; but there were always bilateral problems to consider.

These were many. One was the question of Canadian access to American defense contracts. This issue was negotiated by C. D. Howe, who obtained in October 1953 a commitment to "the effective utilization of joint resources" for "the joint defense and the economic strength of both countries." At first selective, the process was broadened in 1958 under the Defense Production Sharing Agreement (DPSA) to mean "virtually total access" for Canadian defense firms in bidding on American military contracts.[45] The agreement reflected the strength of the Canadian government's connections with the State and Defense departments in Washington, which were able to sideline domestic considerations in the interest of a stronger defense relationship with Canada.

Not every issue went as well for Canada. The Eisenhower administration listened to the U.S. mining lobby, and it restricted imports of Canadian lead and zinc. It harkened to Texas oilmen and placed insecure Canadian oil under quota, for national security reasons. This meant that the American oil industry must be supported first, so as to encourage American producers to explore for more. In effect, "national security" meant that American oil was to be pumped first, with all that implied for national insecurity of supply at a later date. Dulles explained to the Canadians that things could have been worse (he was right), but his excuses were coolly received in Ottawa. Ottawa's conception of the "special relationship" did not include the idea that Canadian oil could be truly insecure for American purchasers. In any case, the Americans were also restricting imports of Canadian coarse grains (rye, oats, and barley), so as to appease the American farm lobby.[46] Taken together, these restrictions were a considerable irritant, and there were more to come.

The worst case was wheat. Wheat had not been a problem during the 1940s, when European shortages raised prices and opened markets for everything that could be produced. Wheat production naturally rose on both sides of the forty-ninth parallel, and north and south of the border, farmer voters were, on the whole, pleased. The Canadians were especially pleased because the United States could afford to run far richer farm-support programs, if it chose. And they were not pleased when, in 1954, it did choose.

Public Law 480, passed by Congress in 1954, allowed the U.S. government to buy surplus wheat and distribute it to needy countries. Senator Hubert Humphrey of Minnesota, whose constituents produced a lot of wheat, praised the law as a "new, positive, humanitarian force [in] the ideological struggle." Dulles told Congress that wheat was the key to the Khyber Pass, and more besides. National security was inextricably tied to American farm subsidies—as to Texas oil and the St. Lawrence Seaway.[47]

The U.S. government informed its allies that only indigent countries would get the surplus grain and that existing wheat markets would not be disturbed. Dulles's officials did in fact manage to limit surplus disposals to about 20 percent of American wheat exports, at first. Even these shipments quickly disrupted wheat markets, however, and Canadian sales were displaced. Ironically so were American sales.[48]

The effect in Canada was quite dramatic. Saskatchewan, the principal wheat-producing province, saw its farm income drop 40 percent in a single

Different countries, different customs: in Canadian eyes, their government dominated Parliament, while in the U.S., President Eisenhower was a slave to Congress. Cartoon by Bob Chambers from the *Halifax Chronicle-Herald*. Courtesy Bob Chambers.

year. Complaints to Ottawa followed, with the expectation that the Canadian government would do something—and that it *could* do something—because of Canada's good relations with the United States. This hope proved unfounded.

A year passed, then two. The Canadian-American ministerial committee on trade and economics met, and met again. Protests, formal and informal, were sent and registered. Howe, it appeared, could do little, and his colleagues in the cabinet became restive, especially Pearson and the finance minister, Walter Harris. Taking advantage of Howe's absence on a tour of

Australia, the rest of the cabinet appointed a royal commission (similar to a presidential commission in the United States) to examine the Canadian economy and its prospects—after Howe. To head the commission, External Affairs Minister Pearson secured the appointment of an old friend, Walter Gordon, who was known for his nationalist views and his disapproval of Howe's pro-American policies. By the summer of 1955, Gordon's commission was well under way in its study.

Politically, relations with the United States were neither good nor bad at this time, and from the government's point of view, they would not be allowed to worsen. Canadian policy would continue to follow in the path of the Western alliance, even if the government, especially Pearson, continued to hanker for a more comprehensive North Atlantic alliance that would go beyond military obligations. But such as the obligations were, Canada accepted them. The largest single item in the Canadian federal budget was always defense during the 1950s, and defense never sank below a third of total government expenditure. The source of those funds was Canadian taxes, whose rates were invariably higher than those in the United States.[49] The political cost imposed by the structure of Canadian taxation was not high at that time, but it did represent opportunities forgone in other fields; those fields would not wait forever.

In September 1955 the joint ministerial committee on economics and trade met in Ottawa. On the Canadian side, Pearson, Howe, and Harris sat in; on the American side, Dulles, Humphrey, Commerce Secretary Sinclair Weeks, and Ezra Taft Benson, secretary of agriculture, participated. The sessions were from the American point of view relatively tranquil. First Dulles put American trade in perspective: While international trade was important to the United States, no single bilateral relationship had all that much importance. Nevertheless, the secretary proudly noted, the United States had a "settled liberal policy." This was true as far as it went, but it may have been that Dulles's tone conveyed more than his words. His statement in any case seems to have had less than the desired effect. In his copy of the committee minutes Pearson scribbled, "US immaculate trade policy."

It was true that the United States had recently imposed certain restrictions on imports—lead and zinc, for example—where "voluntary" quotas were in force. This was prudent management; if imports went beyond what was prudent, protectionism would rear its ugly head. Other countries should under the circumstances "show a certain amount of self restraint." Weeks in his statement explained "the political facts of life"; when it came Humphrey's turn, he praised Dulles's "classic statement" of the United States position. As the minutes recorded, "Mr. Humphrey regretted that US policies, and considerations that lay behind them, were not adequately understood abroad." Humphrey expressed some concern about the outflow of gold from the United States but more about socialistic and nationalistic policies abroad that inhibited American investment. Such policies must be changed.

Then it was the Canadians' turn. They seem to have had little to say. Howe brought up trade issues and Public Law 480; to this, Benson comfortably replied that the United States was really maintaining prices, not depressing them. As to its allies, the United States government was already consulting—where it was appropriate. That, said Howe, was news to him.[50]

There was no conclusion. Perhaps from Dulles's point of view none was necessary, and he could be forgiven for thinking that the Canadians were satisfied with the day's expositions. The Canadian ambassador in Washington, Arnold Heeney, who attended, thought that the Canadian ministers—except Howe—had done a poor job of representing their real grievances. "Our ministers were relatively silent," he wrote, "on the central issue and certainly gave the US no reason to think that we were profoundly worried (as we certainly should be) at the course of events." The next day, Heeney lunched with Walter Gordon, who was in Ottawa for his royal commission, and with Pearson's permission gave him an earful. "I fear that I may have increased any protectionist tendencies he may have," Heeney wrote in his diary, "by my account of the U.S. position and my pessimism about the possibilities of change."[51]

The Liberal government was trapped in the contradictions of Canadian-American relations—contradictions that were apparently beyond the ability of any policy to remedy. On the one hand, the Canadian public strongly approved of the alliance with the United States and firmly rejected any suggestion that Canada should wobble in its anticommunist commitment. Of course American influence went well beyond politics, and when asked in 1956 if there was too much, Canadians firmly replied no, 63 percent to 27 percent. On the other hand, certain American policies irritated certain Canadians. Such Canadians were heavily concentrated on the prairies, where wheat farmers were unreconciled to their reduced sales overseas; in the mines, where American protectionism had dealt a heavy blow; in university common rooms, where Eisenhower, Dulles, and American culture (caricatured as low culture) were unpopular; and in certain parts of the civil service in Ottawa.

Events in 1956–57 concentrated these minority feelings and gave them a special resonance. In 1956 C. D. Howe chose to start building his east-west pipeline, with American investment and a government loan. The opposition called the enterprise a sell-out, and the Liberals were unable to counter the charge effectively. Howe got his pipeline, but at a heavy political cost. Next, Canadians discovered the DEW Line, the northernmost radar fence across the Arctic, which was then being built by American contractors with American money. Canadians liked the money, but they objected to the contractors, especially when it turned out that Canadians visiting their own territory required security clearances from Washington rather than Ottawa. The result, as predicted back in 1952, was political embarrassment.

Then there was the Suez Canal crisis. The Canadian government perceived the crisis primarily as a breach in Western solidarity and worked to repair the gulf that had opened between the British government and the American. That involved keeping a judicious distance from the British, of whose conduct the St. Laurent government in any case deeply disapproved. This was interpreted by Canadian Conservatives as a betrayal of Canada's British heritage and as more slavish toadying to the Yankees. This feeling was not, of course, universal, but it damaged the consensus that sustained Canada's foreign policy.

Finally there was the Norman affair. E. H. Norman was a prominent Japanologist who had taken service with the Canadian government and risen to the rank of ambassador to Egypt. Norman, like many others, had been a Communist in the 1930s. When he joined the Canadian diplomatic service, he did not reveal his past, and in the early 1950s, when he was confronted with his youthful activities, he lied about them. Pearson, the responsible minister, deeply disapproved of the witch-hunts ongoing in the United States, and perhaps in reaction he treated Norman very gently, parking him in New Zealand for a couple of years until the heat died down. Unfortunately for Norman, his security record was the common property of three countries— Canada, the United States, and Great Britain. In the United States it came to the attention of the Senate Internal Security Subcommittee.

Norman's past was splashed over the front pages in March 1957. He reacted a few weeks later by committing suicide, jumping off a building in Cairo. The Norman affair then became the property of the opposition in Canada, who exploited it to discredit the government as, once again, slavishly pro-American. The government protested to Washington, where the controversy was treated as just another example of the autonomous power of Congress to do as it wished. Eisenhower's public reaction could hardly be described as an apology or even as regretful. Since the Canadian government was on the verge of calling a general election, the Norman affair did not help its prospects. American "friendship," according to the Toronto Globe and Mail, "seems to take the form . . . of a long series of insults and injuries by those Americans, in Congress and elsewhere, who hold the actual power in the United States, followed by effusive editorials and speeches by other Americans, deploring what has happened and urging Canadians to forgive and forget. It must be the most one-sided love affair in international history." Other Canadians were less restrained.[52] The Conservative opposition exploited the affair in the general election then under way, but it never became what was described as "a major issue" in the campaign, possibly because John Diefenbaker, the Conservative leader, was not sure whether to believe the allegations about Norman or not.[53]

The Liberal government was defeated in the general election of 10 June 1957. The government was old and tired, and it had offended many people. The United States was not the major factor in its defeat—but neither was the United States absent from the hustings. The opposition Conservatives, who narrowly won the election, criticized the government's American ways; they would do better, they promised, and return Canada to its rightful place in the British Empire.

Ironically the 1957 election signified the defeat of a government that had more often than not been critical of the United States government and that had been frustrated in its attempts to obtain satisfaction over a variety of Canadian grievances. The grievances were still there after 1957, but those who had to manage them now were more overtly "nationalist" than their predecessors. Or so at first it seemed.

"Cooperate or else," Jack Hickerson once joked to a Canadian colleague, waving his fist. Perhaps, the Canadians mused, he spoke truer than he knew.[54]

chapter 4

THE TIME OF TROUBLES, 1957–1968

The eleven years from 1957 to 1968 saw a distancing between
Canada and the United States, a remoteness that was different in kind from
what had gone before. Between 1950 and 1957 the two governments had
misunderstood each other, but the two countries had been no further apart—
and were conceivably closer together—than they had been at midcentury.
Disagreement with the United States on particular issues in the Far East and
on the atmospherics of foreign policy had not outweighed approval of and
commitment to the cold war alliance. On every occasion where open confrontation was possible, the Canadian government had drawn back. It knew that
the Canadian people expected nothing less.

That was not true in the sixties. By 1968, ordinary Canadians were notice-
ably less attracted to the United States and its politics than they had been in
many decades. In their rush to judge the United States, they did not notice
that their feelings were shared by many Americans, or that most of their
negative ideas about Americans had come from south of the border.

During this period there were two governments in Canada—one Conservative and one Liberal—and three in the United States—one Republican and
two Democratic. For most of the time the governments, in their larger sense,
got on moderately well. Civil servants continued to be civil. Economists sang
praises to the North American economy, to its American engine, and to its
Canadian fuel tank. Bilateral issues rose and fell. As usual, they were mostly
trade- and investment-related, and figures in both areas rose strikingly in the
1960s. So did prosperity, in both countries. While per capita income increased dramatically in Canada and the United States, Canada began to close

the gap between its standard of living and that of the United States. Not coincidentally, the conditions for trade north and south were much improved by the adoption of a modified free trade regime in automobiles and auto parts—adopted with misgivings and trepidation by Canada. For once, the law of unintended consequences operated strongly in Canada's favor.

All this should have made for an age of good feeling. At best, however, it merely mitigated the increasing divergence in global policies between Canada and the United States. While the United States was spending itself into the space race and conscripting its young men to fight in Asia—always a point of contention between the Canadian and American governments—Canada's commitment to defense expenditures began, slowly, to sag. As the United States turned outward, Canada increasingly turned inward. As the phrase went, what was national security south of the border became social security to the north. In the longer run, that was what would count most.

DIEFENBAKER: STRANGE BEGINNINGS

The point of origin of the time of troubles, if any single day can be so identified, was 10 June 1957. Prime Minister Louis St. Laurent and his Liberal government went to the polls expecting to win, but they lost. The opposition Conservatives prevailed, 112 seats in the House of Commons to 105 for the Liberals, out of a total of 265. On 21 June, John G. Diefenbaker of Saskatchewan became prime minister of Canada.

The news was received quizzically in the American embassy and in Washington. The U.S. embassy was in an upswing at the time. The ambassador, Livingston Merchant, was a professional who was marked for promotion in the diplomatic service. In Ottawa, he was esteemed for his level-headed approach, his liberal disposition, and his evident desire to take Canada seriously. No one blamed the vagaries of American wheat policy on Merchant; he was doing his best, people thought. And he was.

The Liberals, Merchant reported, were in a state of shock at the election results, and the Conservatives were not far behind. Diefenbaker was not precisely an unknown quantity—he had been a member of parliament since 1940—but his energetic performance on the hustings and his evangelical oratory had surprised observers who looked to Canadian politics for calm and sobriety, not to say dullness. In full speech, Diefenbaker specialized in indignation. His eyebrows batted up and down, and his voice quavered as he denounced his political enemies; the words *they* and *them* soon became familiar to Canadians, although the reference naturally shifted with the occasion or the issue. Most of the time he meant the Liberals, but some of the time—or so observers thought—he meant the Americans. To some, the two were indistinguishable. Somebody like Merchant—cool, calm, and patrician— reminded populists like Diefenbaker of the arrogant, self-sufficient Liberals: people like Pearson, who won a Nobel prize in 1957 for his efforts at the

United Nations in the Suez crisis, to Diefenbaker's great indignation. Pearson had left behind the "Pearsonalities" in the Department of External Affairs, so the prime minister believed, supple men inclined to fit in with the American point of view at every opportunity. In any case, Diefenbaker had little time for, or understanding of, diplomacy; as one of the prime minister's staff later put it, "He did not appreciate the environment in which others were operating, and was not willing to give in search of compromise."[1]

The prime minister refused to admit that his prejudices regarding his own civil servants were untrue. Canadian diplomats and officials were profoundly skeptical of many American policies, especially those that threatened to take the United States into confrontation in Asia. They were indignant at American trade policies and resented Dulles's self-satisfied defense of such programs as the wheat giveaway. They also cast an anxious eye at other sections of the Canadian bureaucracy.

They worried that the Canadian military, particularly the Royal Canadian Air Force (RCAF), was too prone to search for grandeur and big budgets in collusion with its American counterpart; for by 1957, it was apparent that both the RCAF and the USAF had come to understand that an international obligation—a commitment to an ally—was much better insulated from budget cuts than an ordinary domestic military program. As those programs grew more expensive and more numerous, procurement officers and chiefs of staff understood that, in a very real sense, true defense began abroad.

In 1957 there were a number of military decisions pending. One was the logical outgrowth of the mounting concern for North America's polar air defenses. To manage North American air defense against what was by 1957 a real threat from Soviet bombers, a joint command was deemed necessary. Officers in Canada and the United States agreed on the point, and so, generally, did the St. Laurent and Eisenhower administrations. Some points of detail still remained to be clarified at the time of the Canadian election, but they were important points to the Department of External Affairs, sufficient to postpone what might have been an opportune announcement before the election.

Next there was the question of weaponry. Part of it was resolved through a Defense Production Sharing Agreement (DPSA, pronounced *Dipsa*), first concluded in 1958 and modified in subsequent years. DPSA provided that Canadian firms could compete for American defense contracts on the same basis as American firms. At the time, it seemed advantageous from both countries' points of view; It allowed the U.S. Defense Department greater competition and variety among its suppliers, as well as dispersing the defense industry more widely at a time when nuclear attack had become a major concern; and economically it was an important boost to Canadian industry.[2] On the other hand, Canada had already bought considerable defense equipment in the United States: C$690 million between 1951 and 1958, compared with Canadian defense purchases in Canada of C$586 million. By itself,

DPSA might not have done much to alter that pattern, as its first couple of years indicated; but the combination of DPSA and the Vietnam War did, producing a cumulative surplus for Canada, between 1959 and 1970, of $500 million. This might not seem like a mammoth sum, but because spending was concentrated in electronics and aircraft, it made a difference to Canadian "high-tech" industries.[3]

Unfortunately for the Canadian government, DPSA did not oblige the Americans to buy products they did not want. Canada had an unsalable supersonic all-weather jet interceptor (the Arrow), that it wanted to sell but that the Americans (and the British) did not want to buy. In continental defense, the Americans were thinking missile systems—which were expensive and vulnerable to technical sniping and congressional criticism. Finally, there was the question of reformulating NATO's military doctrine. Could nuclear weapons be used to make up for deficiencies in military manpower on the continent of Europe? With a Canadian brigade group (equivalent to an understrength division) and an air division in Europe, this issue directly concerned the Canadian government. It too was under study.

The Diefenbaker government was ill equipped to deal with these issues, and in the end it handled them very badly—but not, at first, because its principals were blinded with anti-American prejudices, nor because their grievances, real and imagined, were mishandled in Washington. That had been the case in the past—the recent past—but it was not as true of the late 1950s or early 1960s.

There were good reasons for that, reasons that a professional like Merchant emphasized. "Canada constitutes our most important market," he reminded his colleagues in September 1957, "with about 25 percent of our imports and exports. . . . Our trade with Canada exceeds that with Western Europe and also that with Latin America." Of course, trade with the United States was even more important for Canada, accounting by 1957 for two-thirds of exports and imports. The $1.5 billion balance in transborder trade was in the United States' favor, as it had been for most of the decade. American investment, the Norman case, and wheat subsidies were all lively grievances, and behind them was what Merchant characterized as "a latent but basic resentment against the power and wealth of the US."[4]

It was a situation Diefenbaker could be expected to exploit and that populist politicians anywhere would find congenial. Already Difenbaker had proclaimed his intention of diverting 15 percent of Canadian trade from the United States to Great Britain. It was a fanciful boast, and Diefenbaker was soon denying that he had ever said it, especially when the British seized the opportunity to propose an Anglo-Canadian free trade area. This too was strenuously denied in Ottawa, but like the 15 percent gasconade its memory lingered—a ghost at Diefenbaker's political feast. After their experience the British began to believe that Diefenbaker was no more than a political mountebank; there would be no more help from that quarter.[5]

Instead of taking a tour down memory lane, Diefenbaker acted promptly—indeed very speedily—to settle Canada's outstanding defense questions with the United States. His defense minister, a retired general noted for bravery rather than intelligence, lent a sympathetic ear to his chiefs or staff. They wanted the government to agree to a North American Air Defense Command (NORAD). The Liberals had already approved it, they told their minister; it just remained to conclude the formalities. Thus instructed, the minister saw the prime minister, and when he returned, he plunked a signed authorization in front of his astonished officers.

The North American Air Defense Agreement was announced on 1 August 1957, although a formal agreement was not signed until the following May. A parliamentary resolution approved the agreement; but for the first time an opposition party, the social democratic CCF, voted against. The agreement established a joint air defense command at Colorado Springs, Colorado, under an American air force general, with a Canadian deputy. RCAF fighter squadrons (nine in 1960) were assigned to NORAD "regions," which straddled the border (resulting in some USAF squadrons being placed under Canadian regional commanders, and vice versa). Although the Canadian government equivocated on the issue—or else it was genuinely confused on the subject—NORAD was *not* part of NATO.

But NORAD was only the beginning, not the end, of Canadian-American defense problems. It eliminated short-term decisions and insulated large parts of air defense from Canadian "nationalist" concerns—which was a relief to an overworked American embassy. But problems remained, and nationalism did not vanish as a concern—it simply assumed another form. The new agreement remained subject, in key respects, to political action and consent, for the squadrons dedicated to North American defense needed up-to-date equipment, and the Canadian air force's fighter force was reaching the end of its useful life. The planes to go out of service were Canadian-designed and -made, serviceable and relatively inexpensive. They were a point of national pride. Better still, they sustained a high-cost engineering industry in Toronto and Montreal. No longer did engineering brains have to leave Canada: they could find work right at home. Things were going well for Canadians' sense of themselves, and Diefenbaker, who was triumphantly re-elected with a huge parliamentary majority in March 1958, seemed to embody and express Canadians' pride in their "modern" technology.

Above all, these engineers produced the right plane. That was not true of its destined successor, the all-weather jet interceptor—also Canadian-designed—called the Arrow, or CF-105. The Arrow, so it supporters claimed, was a superb craft, but whether or not that was true, it was hideously expensive. Cursed with no sales abroad and therefore a short production run, the Arrow could have been produced as a sop to the Canadian aircraft industry. Diefenbaker, after hesitating for over a year, finally in February 1959 made up his mind to cancel the plane.

Canada's defense minister, Pearkes, was often caricatured as a pompous anachronism: here he is interviewed in his exclusive club. Cartoon by Duncan Macpherson. *Reprinted by permission of the Toronto Star Syndicate.*

It was a correct decision, but it proved politically deadly. Diefenbaker had struck at a sensitive nerve. Abandoning the Arrow meant substituting for it some other, less costly piece of technology, probably one from the United States. But what made economic sense was psychologically devastating. Many Canadians had come to believe that their country was in effect a little great power, obviously not as large as the United States or Great Britain but with all the same attributes on a smaller scale. Now that was no longer seen to be so. It had never been so.

Diefenbaker's next actions compounded the problem. The prime minister was no expert in advanced weaponry, but the Soviet Union's success in launching a satellite into "outer space"—and the missile that put it there—gave him pause. What if bombers were not the real threat? Or if they were, what if a missile could shoot them down?

So, according to the USAF, it could. The BOMARC (Boeing-Michigan Aeronautical Research Center) missile was being developed to address just this problem. An early model of the missile was coming into service in 1959; a later, more efficient version was promised for 1961. The Americans were deploying BOMARCs across the northern tier of states: a glance showed that they would intercept their targets over Montreal and Toronto. Since they used nuclear warheads, this could have been a matter of some concern to Canadians.

What could have been more natural than to deploy BOMARCs in Canada and move the field of incineration north to James Bay? And what better than to replace an "obsolete" plane with a politically and publicly salable missile system? The heat of modern technology glowed in the government's mind. It promptly applied to Washington for relief from two of its problems: the hangover from the Arrow and the danger that American defense would result in the obliteration of most of urban Canada.

The United States government obliged. A defense production sharing agreement was negotiated, permitting production and jobs to go north to Canada. Two squadrons of BOMARCs would go north as well. They would be manned by Canadian personnel, especially since, as Diefenbaker admitted, they would achieve their "full potential . . . only when they are armed with nuclear warheads."[6]

So Diefenbaker said on 20 February 1959, the day he canceled the Arrow. On 17 March his minister of external affairs, Sidney Smith, died of a heart attack. Smith, a gentle man who had not found politics or Diefenbaker much to his liking, had been a loyal fugleman in the Conservative army; he had not rocked the boat. His successor, Howard Green from Vancouver, was also a loyal Tory footsoldier, and honest and upright to boot. But unlike Smith, who had had his edges polished by decades of service as a university president, Green's attitude to the world had not been tempered by experience. He had last been abroad in World War I, when he had fought for the British Empire. Some believed he was fighting for it still.

That at least was a canard, for Green did not demonstrate much sympathy for Britain or its problems in his time in office. He recognized in the United States Great Britain's imperial successor, and the thought made him bristle. Green was not personally anti-American, and Americans who met him were frequently charmed by his modesty and simplicity. Some wondered, nevertheless, if the simplicity was not outright simple-mindedness. Green believed in listening to the people. A product of an age before polls, he had no very sophisticated grasp of public opinion; if it was wrong, he was prepared to ignore it.

The juxtaposition of Howard Green with the Department of External Affairs caused comment. The department was packed with "Pearsonalities"—people who had worked under Lester Pearson, who had been educated at Oxford or Harvard, brainy types who considered the Conservatives to be "the stupid party." But as it happened, Green's atavistic anti-Americanism found its match in the views of the department—or at least in the views of the department's high command.

The undersecretary for external affairs was one of Pearson's oldest friends, Norman Robertson, a product of Oxford, Harvard and other points south. In the late 1950s Robertson had just returned to Ottawa from postings in London and Washington. In London he had witnessed the estrangement between the Americans and the British in the Suez crisis. His experience in Washington did not reassure him about the wisdom of John Foster Dulles or the U.S. government in general. At every turn he was reminded of American power, and of its nuclear core. Robertson slowly, uncomfortably, came to believe that the balance of nuclear terror was in danger of tipping into mass destruction.

It was time for a change of emphasis, and perhaps more. The late 1950s saw the rise of antinuclear movements in Great Britain and then in Canada, where they were encouraged by antinuclear orators from the United States. An ill-judged public practice alert in 1959 mostly alarmed the public, as it certainly alarmed Robertson. A public opinion poll conducted in September 1961 showed that 60 percent of Canadians assessed their chances of survival in a nuclear war as "poor"; another 30 percent opted for "50/50."[7] People who worried about nuclear weapons began to combine and to organize demonstrations and letters of protest. Such people tended slightly to the political left, polls showed: labor leaders and peace activists as well as "political leaders" believed that Canadian forces should not be equipped with nuclear weapons. By way of contrast, most businessmen, teenagers, and a national cross-section of opinion thought that Canadian troops should acquire atomic arms.[8]

By 1960, Robertson had come to believe that the West's best course was unilateral nuclear disarmament; and his minister agreed with him.[9]

That posed a problem, because the Diefenbaker government, within very recent memory, had agreed to three nuclear-weapons-carrying arms packages. These were the BOMARC, the F-104 fighter with a "strike-reconnaissance" role in NATO, and the Honest John missile, also acquired for Canadian forces in Europe. (A fourth nuclear weapons system, the Genie air-to-air rockets, were acquired much later.) A small breathing space was afforded because purchase and installation were not quite complete and would not be until 1961 or 1962, but there were agreements nevertheless.

Robertson and Green played for time, and they were helped by circumstances. Foremost among these circumstances was the prime minister's tendency to procrastinate. Although he had the largest parliamentary majority in Canadian history and was still, in 1959, leading in the public polls, Diefenbaker was increasingly unable to make up his mind, seemingly paralyzed by the ferocious reaction to his decision on the Arrow. His cabinet met endlessly, yet decided less and less.

Diefenbaker was also getting letters. Letters were important to a man whose political formation predated public opinion polls, and no politician of Diefenbaker's vintage could easily forget the anti-Americanism of the 1911 election and the subsequent events. In August 1960, when Arnold Heeney, the Canadian ambassador to Washington, dropped in for a chat before returning to his post, Diefenbaker told him that anti-Americanism was at an unprecedented high. Heeney was baffled by the news, so Diefenbaker undertook to explain it more fully to him the next day. On that occasion he waved fifty letters at the curious Heeney. According to the prime minister, Canadians were annoyed by distrust of the U.S. military and the Pentagon, "the economic aggressiveness of US interests," "the adverse trading position" (meaning Canada's perpetual trade deficit with the United States), and, generally, the idea that the United States was just pushing everybody around.[10]

Diefenbaker's reading of his correspondence was accurate enough. Unfortunately for his political prospects, he did not read beyond it. Many of his correspondents had been organized to write to him. Those who produced their individual variations on the antinuclear theme were presumably members of a highly literate and politically concerned minority, but they were most active in the concentric politics of the Canadian left. They were not the Conservatives' natural constituency, nor on other issues did they like Diefenbaker. They were most likely to vote for the reorganized CCF, which had just rebaptized itself the New Democratic party, or NDP, although they might in a pinch bring themselves to vote for Pearson and his Liberals, who were passing through an antinuclear phase at the time. Most Canadians stayed aloof: antinuclear some might be, but in the final analysis they were more concerned with good relations with the Americans and with Canada's standing as a respectable member of the Western alliance. Pearson's polls revealed this, but Diefenbaker, as he often said, thought polls were a convenience for dogs.[11]

On Canadian-American relations the prime minister was still "sound," but even there time produced a change. Diefenbaker liked and admired President Eisenhower, another prairie boy from the same generation and from the wrong side of the tracks, and bright in the prime minister's memory as the great leader of the Allied forces in World War II.[12] Diefenbaker liked Eisenhower so much that he hurried along negotiations on a combined flood-control and power project on the Columbia River, straddling the boundaries of British Columbia, Idaho, and Washington. Eisenhower's last international political act was to sign the Columbia River Treaty with a beaming Diefenbaker in Washington on 17 January 1961.

The smiles were deceptive, though not deliberately so on the part of either signatory. Eisenhower may not have known that in response to Diefenbaker's remarks the previous summer, which had been conveyed to the State Department by the Canadian ambassador, his officials had commissioned a full-scale National Intelligence Estimate of Canada to discover why relations were so bad. (Produced too late for Eisenhower, it greeted his successor Kennedy when he took up the study of Canada.)[13] And Diefenbaker assumed that he had the cooperation of the government of British Columbia on the Columbia River Treaty; without its consent his signature was worthless. But British Columbia had not consented to the treaty's terms, nor would it. A second treaty would be necessary, three contentious years later. It would be signed by a government other than Diefenbaker's. An American diplomat called the experience "one of our early lessons on who is in charge of what in Canada."[14]

The new U.S. administration would have something to do with Diefenbaker's departure, though it is important not to overload that fact. Diefenbaker, by 1961, was already in considerable trouble. As an American study put it in 1961, "Canadian uneasiness over Canada's place in international affairs has clearly increased over the last several years." This was natural enough. Europe had fully recovered from the war, and within NATO and at the United Nations, Canada no longer represented a unique island of prosperity in a crumbling world. It followed that for reasons entirely outside Canada's control, it no longer played as large a part in international affairs as it had once done. But as the American study pointed out, Canadians were seeking a cause, if not a scapegoat, and they found it in what they interpreted as increasing American control over their country and increasing Canadian dependence on the United States for such items as military hardware. Any government that confronted such a problem and such a response would have been bound for trouble, and Diefenbaker's was no exception.[15]

More purely domestic difficulties also afflicted the Conservative government. Canada's rate of economic growth had slowed, unemployment was up, Diefenbaker's bombastic political style was becoming embarrassing, and his indecisive government was causing concern. Diefenbaker was starting to look like an anachronism.

John F. Kennedy, the new president of the United States, definitely did not look like an anachronism. His energy, style, and evident intelligence attracted Canadians as they attracted Americans; Diefenbaker was uncomfortably aware that the American president might actually be more popular in Canada than the Canadian prime minister. (Polls taken in Canada in 1962 and 1963 showed this was true: "Kennedy always had a ninety percent approval rating or better," according to an acute observer.) Even before Kennedy took office, Diefenbaker was described as "apprehensive" by his staff and, worse still, as "relishing the more pessimistic omens."[16]

At first Diefenbaker put the best face he could on the subject. He trotted off to Washington in February to see Kennedy and to discuss the current roster of Canadian-American disagreements: trade with Cuba and Communist China, and the problem of nuclear weapons. Green begged Diefenbaker to make no commitment on that score, and he did not; he did, however, leave the Americans with the impression that he would eventually agree to arm the BOMARCs and CF-104s with nuclear warheads. The atmospherics were apparently contradictory. Kennedy did not much like Diefenbaker, considering him insincere and boring. Diefenbaker, while reserving his opinion of Kennedy, thought that the meeting was a success and boasted about it on his return flight to Ottawa.[17]

Kennedy was to return the visit in May. The abortive Bay of Pigs incident (an American-sponsored invasion of Cuba), occurred in the meantime, producing a certain disappointment north of the border, where Green argued that Kennedy was merely driving the island's Communist regime further into the arms of the Kremlin. He told reporters that Canada would gladly mediate between the United States and Cuba, an offer that met "unrestrained sarcasm" in Washington.[18]

Kennedy duly came to Ottawa on 16 May 1961. The visit passed off well as far as the public was concerned. The president brought his elegant wife and delivered an eloquent speech to the Canadian parliament. The crowds cheered. Canadian males adjusted their Madison-Avenue-style suits while their wives sculpted their bouffant hairdos. The national flattery index hit a new level of sincerity.

Things were quite different behind the scenes. There were physical consequences: Kennedy had hurt his back planting a ceremonial tree and thereafter required shots of Novocaine simply to stay upright. He never quite recovered from his Canadian experience, which stayed with him like a nagging tooth. Presumably each twinge reminded him of Diefenbaker, with whom Kennedy again notably failed to hit it off. In Ottawa, however, it was Diefenbaker who was offended for reasons more usually found in the realm of psychology than in that of diplomacy.

In fact, Diefenbaker was jealous, personally and politically. Inmates of his party knew of "the Chief's" resentment toward those who would overshadow him, and while he had been prepared to make a special case of Eisenhower (or Winston Churchill, another of his heroes), he drew the line at Kennedy. Politically, Diefenbaker was prone to take offense at being "pushed around," a trait he shared with other Canadians—even his political rival Pearson, who since 1958 had been leader of the opposition Liberals.

But what did Kennedy want, and how did he seek it? At bottom, the U.S. president was seeking to reintegrate the Western alliance, after what was interpreted as the disastrous mismanagement of the Eisenhower-Dulles years. The mismanagement was much exaggerated, but the idea of reintegration was not. Kennedy expected the United States to bear the brunt of the struggle against communism, but he hoped to rekindle some of the enthusiasm that had created NATO and sent UN troops into Korea.

In Europe this meant that Kennedy, like his predecessors, approved the creation of a united Europe centered on the Common Market. In particular, he wished Great Britain, which remained outside the original Treaty of Rome, to abandon its parochial economic ties with its empire and commonwealth, if that was the necessary price to be paid for a stronger Europe. There were strong arguments behind this view of Britain and Europe. A stronger Europe, better able to share in defense expenditures and NATO burdens, would also be more resistant to the blandishments of communism, East European–style. Ultimately, the onus of defending Europe might fall on the Europeans rather than on the North Americans, and Canada, along with the United States, could hope to bring its troops home.

Pearson, had he been in office, might have been sympathetic to those arguments. Pearson tended to take a longer view of events, and he considered that the British decline in power and wealth was not yet over. Canada's British connection might well turn out to be worth a good deal less than most Canadians were, in 1961, prepared to concede. But Diefenbaker did not see it this way. Canada had traditional interests tied up with Great Britain. Major Canadian exports, especially wheat, traveled east to British ports, where they faced little or no duty. The European Common Market was unlikely to continue such an arrangement; indeed, European agricultural policies virtually guaranteed the disappearance of any market for Canadian wheat.

Diefenbaker did not admit that Canada's refusal to consider British pleas for a transatlantic common market between the two countries had helped propel the British government to seek admission to the European Common Market. He hoped that things would go on rather as they were, and when the British prime minister, Harold Macmillan, stated that they could not, Diefenbaker broadcast his disappointment both at home and in Great Britain. Kennedy's support for Macmillan did not, and could not, appeal to Diefenbaker or his government.

Then there was the Alliance for Progress. Kennedy made Latin America a first target for his enthusiasm, and as a prelude to shoring up American relationships there, he decided to emphasize economic betterment—the Alliance for Progress.

Canada was the United States' only formal ally in the Western Hemisphere, if omnibus treaties like the Rio Pact are excluded. It was also solvent and therefore a potential contributor to Kennedy's plans. To some Canadians, this sudden American interest in their support had the flavor of a deathbed repentance; never before had the US government sought to share its hemispheric concerns. Canadians were doubtful of the character of American–Latin American relations and disapproved of the weight the United States government gave to the superficial willingness of Latin governments to fall in with its wishes. As one Canadian diplomat had bitterly reflected at the United Nations in 1951, "the overestimation by the Americans of the almost entirely rhetorical support which they receive from their

Spanish-speaking friends is one not unimportant cause of grievance on the part of Canada."[19]

Kennedy sought Canadian membership in the Organization of American States (OAS). In visiting Ottawa he expressed this desire privately to Diefenbaker and, after being refused publicly, in a speech to the Canadian parliament.[20] He carried a briefing memorandum designed to remind him of his requirements: he was to "push" the Canadians, it read, for membership in the OAS, contributions to the Alliance for Progress, more aid to India, and a better monitoring of the cease-fire in Indochina. On almost all points Diefenbaker reacted negatively.

He reacted even more negatively when he found a copy of Kennedy's briefing memorandum that the president had forgotten. Although the most the paper recommended was to "push" for American objectives, Diefenbaker interpreted it as another attempt to push him—and Canada—around. He kept the note in his "vault," using it from time to time to stoke the fires of his considerable indignation. In his mind, the note's contents changed form. He came to claim that it described him as an "SOB." And there was even worse, he hinted darkly. As time passed, Diefenbaker seemed to believe that he had a kind of political philosopher's stone in his desk drawer that he could use to counter any attempt by Kennedy to bend him to his will; better still, he could wave it at the Liberal opposition, which his imagination now firmly linked with Kennedy and his circle of northeastern sophisticates. When Kennedy spent an inordinate time talking to Pearson at a state dinner in Ottawa, Diefenbaker had all the proof he needed.[21]

Inevitably the word got back to Washington. Initially, Kennedy was incredulous. He couldn't have called Diefenbaker a son of a bitch, he said; he hadn't known he was one—then. It was, he said, "a species of blackmail," which seems a fair enough comment. From early 1962 relations between Diefenbaker and Kennedy descended into a deep freeze. Kennedy let his staff know that he "profoundly detested Diefenbaker"; worse, he believed he could not trust him. As long as Diefenbaker ruled, Canada could not be regarded as a reliable ally.[22]

The glacial political relations between the Canadian and American governments did not prevent the United States from bailing Canada out of a financial crisis in June 1962, when Canada's foreign exchange reserves dropped precipitously. The United States facilitated credits from the International Monetary Fund, the Export-Import Bank, and the Federal Reserve system. The Canadians imposed a temporary import surcharge, and the Americans did not object. This was done even though the United States' own balance-of-payments problems were not helped by Diefenbaker pegging the Canadian dollar at a rate that was bound to promote exports and diminish imports. If that would lend stability to the Canadian economy, then apparently it was worth the price.[23]

It was not a bad bargain. The Canadian financial system steadied, and

"MY FRIEND AND I WOULD LIKE TO CONSOLIDATE OUR DEBTS"

The nationalist Diefenbaker and his finance minister petition Kennedy for a quick loan. Cartoon by Duncan Macpherson. *Reprinted by permission of the Toronto Star Syndicate.*

Canada embarked on an economic boom, with per capita income (in real terms) rising for the first time since 1956. But the economy was considerably more stable than the Canadian-American political alliance. This Kennedy would now discover. In October 1962 surveillance disclosed that the Soviet Union was installing missiles in Cuba. Kennedy decided that he had to get them out, even at the risk of war, and as a first measure he imposed a naval quarantine on Cuba to prevent any more missiles from getting ashore. Before he announced this action, in a television address on the evening of 22 October, Kennedy sent personal envoys to each of his major allies, including Canada. Canadian cooperation would be useful, if not essential: if there were a Soviet military response, it would likely come over the North Pole. NORAD was therefore the first line of detection and defense.

The United States' other allies—Britain, France, and West Germany— received word of Kennedy's intentions calmly and promised support. Diefenbaker, with Howard Green, did not. "Kennedy wants his own way," he told his secretary. "He wants the Russians out of there, and then they'll bomb us." Would the Canadian cabinet have time to get to its VIP bomb shelter? Kennedy, who phoned Diefenbaker during the crisis to ask that Canada's NORAD forces be placed on alert, complained about the prime minister's "negative rasping."[24] But the rasping had few practical consequences. Diefenbaker refused to order "Defense Condition 3" when asked, but his defense minister and his generals put Canadian forces on alert anyway. "I decided I would put the troops on alert without making any announcement," Defense Minister Douglas Harkness later said. It was in any case impossible under NORAD to have American forces on alert when the Canadians working in the same room were not.[25]

Diefenbaker's public statements conveyed, accurately enough, his hesitations. They did not adequately convey or explain his dismay at Canada's slight influence over Kennedy's management of the crisis—a dismay that inadvertently revealed the hollowness of Canada's pursuit of influence in NATO or with the United States by military expenditures. But that was something for the long term. In the short term Diefenbaker's political problems were greatly increased by the Cuban crisis. He did not receive public approval for his inaction. Most Canadians were appalled: 79.3 percent, according to a public opinion poll, supported Kennedy in the crisis. There were rumblings in the Conservative party, with predictable consequences. The prime minister, according to one of his ministers, "became so incensed he lost his reason completely. . . . [There] was an absolutely ghastly scene."[26]

Events were closing in on Diefenbaker, and for the first time his government was politically vulnerable. In a general election in June 1962 the Conservatives lost their majority in the House of Commons, receiving 116 seats out of 265. To prevail over the Liberals, Diefenbaker needed the support of one or another of the third parties—the NDP with 19 seats or Social Credit with 30. By the fall of 1962, the Liberals had the edge in public opinion polls, and it seemed clear that they would win the next general election. The smaller parties would, under those circumstances, share defeat with the Conservatives, so they were understandably reluctant to precipitate a political crisis.

They did not count on John Diefenbaker's ability to provoke one. The Cuban crisis concentrated American attention on the polar gap in their defenses. The question of arming Canadian forces with nuclear weapons acquired renewed urgency, and that in turn precipitated bitter quarrels inside the Canadian government. The Canadian Defense Department supported taking nuclear weapons on a "two-key system," with American authority and Canadian permission necessary before use. The minister of external affairs and his undersecretary took the opposite tack, and the prime minister veered back and forth between the two. In public the government waffled, claiming now one thing, now another, and fudging the issue of whether Canada had actually made a commitment to arm its BOMARCs, Honest Johns, and CF-104s with nuclear warheads. Howard Green and Norman Robertson were satisfied to let this situation continue indefinitely; Defense Minister Harkness was not, and by the turn of the new year, 1963, he spoke for others besides himself.

Christmas 1962 produced one last present for the prime minister. Hearing that British prime minister Macmillan and President Kennedy were meeting in Nassau in the Bahamas, Diefenbaker invited himself to the party. Macmillan, as host, found it hard to refuse and coerced Kennedy into staying to an unwelcome lunch. "There we sat like three whores at a christening," Kennedy would tell his friends. Lunch over, the president headed home, leaving Macmillan the disagreeable task of briefing Diefenbaker. Diefenbaker's presence had been entirely political, designed to enhance his own standing at home. He enhanced it further by issuing his own interpretation of the Kennedy-Macmillan talks; not surprisingly, he told the world that the whole shape of Western defense was being reconsidered, and with it Canada's nuclear role. Diefenbaker's statements were as unwelcome as they were inaccurate, and they further damaged Canadian-American *and* Anglo-Canadian relations.

The final crisis began on 2 January 1963, when General Lauris Norstad, the retiring NATO supreme commander, paid a farewell visit to Ottawa. At the airport he was met by a junior minister and the Canadian chief of the defense staff, then faced a scrum of reporters anxious to get footage on the issue of the day—Canada's commitment to acquire nuclear weapons.

> Q: General, do you consider that Canada has committed itself to provide its Starfighter [CF-104] squadron in Europe with tactical nuclear weapons?
> Norstad: That is perhaps a question you should direct to the Minister rather than to me, but my answer to that is "Yes."[27]

It takes a great deal to place Canada on the list of urgent problems that confront the president of the United States. But by January 1963, Diefenbaker had managed to do it. Getting rid of the Diefenbaker government did not become American policy, but it was widely known in the White House and the State Department and beyond that Kennedy would be only too pleased if Diefenbaker tumbled from power. In the 1962 Canadian election Kennedy's pollster, Lou Harris, went secretly to Canada to work for the Liberals; Harris checked first with the president and got a cheery "good luck."[28] In 1962, Kennedy had no thought of helping out himself, but by 1963, he was ready and anxious to do whatever he could. That much was personal, because it was not clear whether the United States would secure any policy advantage even if Diefenbaker were defeated. The Liberal opposition had very mixed views on nuclear weapons, and Lester Pearson, the Liberal leader, was widely regarded as "soft" on the great issues of East-West confrontation. (In a television interview Pearson brought down wrath from the right wing in Canada and the United States by allowing that if he had the choice, he would "rather be red than dead"—and would use the fact of being alive to fight on against the reds.)

On 12 January 1963 Pearson changed his position. His supporters had persuaded him that a formal commitment to procure nuclear weapons had been made. And so Pearson told a Liberal audience that if he became prime minister, Canada would take two steps forward and one back. Canada would honor its pledges and take nuclear weapons; then it would negotiate to get rid of them. On the issue of the day Pearson had nonetheless taken a clear stand, and according to the polls it was a winning one. Asked in November 1962 whether Canadian forces should be armed with nuclear weapons, 54 percent of English Canadians and 59 percent of French Canadians said yes.[29]

Diefenbaker had not yet given up. When Parliament reconvened after its Christmas recess, he issued another confusing statement on the state of Canada's nuclear commitments. It would be his last.

In Washington, Diefenbaker's latest obfuscation was badly received. It distorted Canadian-American negotiations on nuclear warheads by giving them a far more optimistic cast than could possibly be justified. Combined with Diefenbaker's opportunistic misinterpretations of the Nassau conference, it was more than could be borne. The new American ambassador to Ottawa, Walton Butterworth,[30] whom even his colleagues considered rash and overbearing, urged Washington that enough was enough. It was high time to put Diefenbaker in his place by issuing a formal démenti and telling the world that Diefenbaker was, in effect, a liar. "If you want to play rough," Butterworth said, "then we'll play rough too."[31]

The State Department agreed with Butterworth. By 30 January, a draft was ready and passed through the hierarchy, where acting Secretary of State George Ball and McGeorge Bundy, the national security adviser, had the final word. Kennedy did not see the draft, but given his feelings about Diefenbaker, his approval could be assumed. The statement was accordingly issued at 6:15 P.M. on 30 January. It stated unequivocally that Canada had made commitments and that negotiations for honoring those commitments had had no issue. Though Diefenbaker's name was not mentioned, it was obvious that he was the target.

Back in Ottawa, Diefenbaker was pleased rather than outraged. He wanted an escape from his political dilemma at home, and Kennedy had just handed it to him. "We've got our issue now!" he gloated. "We can call our general election now!" It would, he confidently believed, be 1911 all over again.[32]

But it wasn't. More Canadians believed Kennedy than believed Diefenbaker. Diefenbaker's defense minister, after a futile final attempt to bring the prime minister on board, resigned. The opposition, even the antinuclear NDP and Creditistes (Social Crediters from Quebec) combined against him, arguing that Diefenbaker's indecision and untrustworthiness counterbalanced even the acquisition of nuclear weapons. Canadians would not stand for

Diefenbaker anymore. The Conservative government fell on a vote of no-confidence on 6 February, and a general election was called for 8 April.

Kennedy was delighted. He offered what aid he could to Pearson and the Liberals—it was tactfully declined—and followed the campaign closely. The State Department stimulated consuls across Canada to come up with estimates of the final results, and desk officers in Washington supplemented their efforts with their own informal opinion sounding; as Willis Armstrong of the Canadian desk later reminisced, they came very close to the actual totals.[33]

Diefenbaker had begun the campaign far behind in the polls, but he ended it short of absolute disaster. His party chieftains kept his anti-American enthusiasms under control, though the campaign did feature in its final stages a bogus letter from the American ambassador in support of Pearson. On 8 April the Liberals secured 129 seats to Diefenbaker's 95. Pearson, a notoriously poor campaigner, had almost snatched defeat from the jaws of victory—but not quite. Diefenbaker had to resign, and on 22 April Pearson formed a government.

PEARSON: HOPES DISAPPOINTED, 1963–1968

On 10 May 1963 Pearson and his entourage helicoptered into Hyannis Port, Kennedy's vacation compound on Cape Cod. They were well received. Prime minister and president hit it off, and the prime minister demonstrated the knowledge of baseball that had made him a credible minor league player 40 years before. When discussion turned to diplomacy, the harmony continued. "The honeymoon was on and everything which had been sour was sweet," the Canadian ambassador, Charles Ritchie, recalled.[34]

Kennedy was prepared. "The advent of a new government in Canada has naturally stirred nearly all branches of the government to new hope that progress can be made in effective negotiations with this most important neighbor on all sorts of problems," McGeorge Bundy wrote. "It is the President's wish that these negotiations should be most carefully coordinated under his personal direction through the Department of State."[35]

Progress was made on a range of outstanding issues: the Columbia River, oil imports, the balance of trade, and even transborder flights. He and Kennedy confirmed to their mutual satisfaction that "their views on international affairs are not widely different," allowing for the differences between a great power and a middle power. And of course on the subject of Diefenbaker, they were as one; much of the evening of 10 May was spent reconstructing Diefenbaker's bizarre relationship with Kennedy. When Kennedy gaily asked if the State Department press release had been of any use in the campaign, Pearson somberly replied, "It probably cost me fifty seats."[36] That was an exaggeration, but it had a large kernel of truth.

And so Canada got American nuclear weapons—four systems of them over time. Some were deployed in Canada under NORAD, and others in Europe under NATO. They were supposed to be temporary, but they did not leave until 1984. The troops in Europe got warheads for their missiles and aircraft on a less lasting basis; the strike reconnaissance role was eventually negotiated away, and obsolescence took care of the rest of the problem. Other issues, like the Columbia River Treaty, took longer to resolve, but in the end they too were taken off the active agenda.

The compatibility between Pearson and Kennedy masked certain less compatible facts. Pearson himself was by no means an uncritical admirer of the United States. When he was in government in the 1950s, he had greatly resented John Foster Dulles's overbearing insistence that American allies dance to a single tune. Several of Pearson's Liberal party colleagues qualified as Canadian "nationalists" of the kind the American embassy had denounced ten years before. In particular, Pearson's campaign organizer, Walter Gordon, the man who had hired Lou Harris, was determined to resist what he saw as the takeover of the Canadian economy by its giant neighbor. Gordon was particularly concerned by the impact of branch plants on Canadian society, arguing that when it came to a crunch, branches in another country would always take second place to the interests of the country of ownership. Not every Liberal shared Gordon's views, but in the aftermath of the election victory the prime minister could hardly deny Gordon his choice of cabinet portfolio. In 1963, Pearson made Gordon finance minister, and in June, Gordon produced a budget.

The budget took aim at foreign (American) investment in Canada, another issue of the fifties that Diefenbaker's aberrant behavior had temporarily concealed. Gordon proposed a takeover tax for new foreign purchases of Canadian firms. But his takeover tax proved at least as unpopular on Canadian stock exchanges as it was on Wall Street, and within days Gordon climbed down. Other parts of his budget also fell victim to criticism, not all of it from outside the Liberal party. Gordon suffered a major political defeat both outside and inside the Liberal party. For the next five years Pearson's party and his cabinet rumbled with disputations between "nationalists" and "continentalists," the latter being a term that the nationalist faction applied rather promiscuously to its enemies, especially Trade Minister Mitchell Sharp. Whatever Pearson's initial promise, the United States remained an issue in Canadian politics; and after a little while it became even more of an issue than ever before. In Washington the State Department took the opportunity to remind the White House that Canada was, after all, a foreign country, no matter how "special" the relationship.

In Canada, the American question went beyond mere politics. It affected jobs, economics, and general culture. American styles were everywhere. American television, popular music, and literature enjoyed huge popularity, to the disgust of their native Canadian competitors. Canadian television viewers could select their American content either directly—by tuning in an American station (25 percent did that, in English Canada, in 1967)—or by proxy, by watching American shows carried on Canadian television networks. In March 1964, on any given evening, 57 percent of Halifax viewers (who could not receive direct U.S. signals) and 74 percent of Toronto watchers (who could) were watching American shows. Canadian regulators worried and, worrying, experimented with various forms of introducing "Canadian content" into Canadian broadcasting. These forms were, of course, compulsory. Newspapers and other forms of publishing escaped the phenomenon. In any case the Canadian best-seller list continued to resemble the American one, with certain local variations.[37]

This aspect of Canadian life was novel for Kennedy's officials. "I didn't realize that they felt we were a monstrous, mammoth obliteration of their own identity and of their own arts and of their own culture," the American chairman of the International Joint Commission reminisced.[38] But who, exactly, were "they"? In 1963 the short answer would have been, "an embattled minority." By 1968, however, the minority was starting to grow. For under Pearson, ironically, Canadians began to turn away from internationalism and from cooperation with the United States, to concentrate on themselves.

And so there is another aspect of the Pearson government that requires comment: its internal policies. Until 1963, the social programs in place in the United States and Canada were not profoundly different. Both countries had varieties of social security programs, pensions for the disabled and the elderly. Both countries also practiced a form of medical care that was essentially private, charitable, and entrepreneurial by turns, with little or nothing in between. The Pearson government, which lasted until 1968, changed all that. Under Pearson, the Canadian social security state—which liberally ladled out money to education, the elderly, welfare, and, finally, free medical care (generally called in Canada medicare, a very different beast from its American homonym)—came to fruition.[39]

This development had obvious implications for the way in which Canadian budgets were constructed. In Diefenbaker's last fiscal year, 1962–63, 22.3 percent of the Canadian federal budget had been spent on defense. By 1967–68, Pearson's last year in office, it was 16.1 percent. And three years later, 1970–71, it was 12.9 percent.[40] Of course, since 1945 Canada had never spent as much, proportionally, as the United States on its military effort, but during the 1950s and early 1960s Canadian governments had struggled to keep up appearances. One of the lessons of the Cuban missile crisis was that appearances counted for very little in the real world of superpowers. And so, gradually, appearances drooped. "The politicians started to regard us as little more than ornamental luggage," one defense official complained. "So they tried to make us as light as possible."

Social policy and defense were areas of major concern in Canada in the 1960s, but overshadowing both was the rise of a different kind of nationalism in Canada. The Province of Quebec was Canada's only officially bilingual province, a testament to its French-speaking majority, but also to a vigorous and active English-speaking minority, which was concentrated in and around the city of Montreal. The governments of Quebec jealously guarded their own autonomy, but government's writ did not go far in a society where the Catholic Church played a dominant role in social policy and education. This left the English-speaking minority its own schools and institutions, as well as the running of most of Quebec's large corporations and banks.

In the 1950s and 1960s this relatively stable situation began to come apart. Fear that the French language was being submerged by English-speakers in culture and in business stimulated a linguistic and territorial nationalism in Quebec that aimed to promote, improve, and entrench the French language and French-speakers and that would use the authority of the provincial state to do it. The simultaneous decline of the Catholic Church forced the province to expand its jurisdiction into areas of social policy, just as the reforming Pearson government in Ottawa was constructing its own, Canadian, national version of the welfare state.

The result was a clash between the Canadian and Quebec governments, and between English Canadians—who were simultaneously a majority and a minority vis-à-vis Quebec—and "Québécois." There were varieties of Québécois nationalism, of course, but they all proposed to limit the power of the Canadian federal government, either by confining it to "political" foreign policy and defense or by abolishing it altogether and seizing independence for Quebec. In 1965 the Quebec government advanced the theory that it possessed foreign policy jurisdiction in areas such as education and social policy, an argument that would have bifurcated and then truncated Canada's own foreign policy. The government of Canada suspected, with some reason, that this was the thin edge of the wedge and that Quebec would use its constitutional theories as a means to gain independence, gradually. Ottawa therefore did its best to circumvent, divert, and eventually outflank the Quebec government's constitutional position. Quebeckers—French and English—were divided among themselves on the issue. Ottawa's line had strong defenders among French-speakers: the undersecretary for external affairs, Marcel Cadieux, and Pearson's minister of justice, Pierre Trudeau, among others. The dispute moved from administration to politics almost immediately, and it would stay in the political realm until the majority of French-speaking Quebeckers made up their minds on the subject. In the meantime the government of Quebec built up its own expertise in international affairs and began to seek allies abroad.

Two aspects of Canada's internal affairs therefore entered the realm of Canadian-American relations: Canadian nationalism, taken on its own, and the clash between Canadian nationalism and Quebec nationalism, with all that that might mean for the stability of the United States' northern neighbor. Worse still, de Gaulle's France showed a marked interest in the possible independence of Quebec. Could Europe, through France, be returning to North America? From the mid-1960s on, the possibility that Canada might break apart or be disrupted could never be absent from American calculations of policy.

The Quebec issue had to be left to the Canadians to solve. But Canadian nationalism, because of its importance in the Canadian government's approach to the world, required attention from the United States. Its first manifestation, in Walter Gordon's June 1963 budget, stimulated protests that American business in Canada was being denied equal treatment. But Gordon's budget was short-lived, drowned in a torrent of domestic protest. Even before it was buried, the tables were turned when the U.S. government proposed an interest-equalization tax that would have raised the costs of loans in New York to Canadian lenders. In short order Canada was in Washington asking for an exemption, which was granted on 21 July. One of Gordon's senior officials complained to his American counterparts that Canadians were "seriously disturbed by this reminder of dependence on the USA."[41] Disturbed or not, they needed the money, and Gordon had to seek another field of action.

He found it in a battle with the National City Bank of New York over its purchase of the Mercantile Bank, a small Dutch-owned enterprise headquartered in Montreal. The Mercantile was the only foreign-owned bank in Canada and was considered an anomaly by the Canadian government, which jealously guarded the ownership of the banking system by Canadians as a guarantee of "Canadian control over banks." The Netherlands was small and distant, and the Mercantile itself was not large. But the United States was large and close at hand, and National City proposed to use the Mercantile as a base for expansion. On the other hand, Canadian banks had carried on large and profitable operations in the United States for over a hundred years, and a certain principle of reciprocity applied. Despite discreet advice from experts in the United States and over protests and threats by Gordon, "who said purchasers would be taking risk of unfavorable Canadian action," National City went ahead.[42]

A battle royal later developed, as the Canadian government made good on Gordon's threats by restricting the ability of foreign-owned banks to function in Canada. This was done even after Gordon left government, suggesting that some at least of his nationalistic ideas had a stronger base in the government than his critics or his devotees had supposed. Eventually a compromise was worked out, granting temporary relief to Mercantile but no lasting exemption.[43]

The Kennedy administration gave prolonged thought at one level or another to avoiding nasty disputes like the one over the Mercantile Bank. Perhaps it would be useful to turn a collection of working groups loose on Canadian-American problems, one official wrote in the summer of 1963. Clearly they required more than the periodic joint ministerial meetings, which were still going on, could manage. Agreement on a set of principles governing Canadian-American relations would help. Such principles could then shape "an organizational structure for continued discussion and resolution" of ongoing problems; but even without the principles, the working groups would be a good idea. One would cover energy, meaning U.S. oil and natural gas imports, and a greater interchange of electric power. Another would work on the vexed question of American investment in Canada, with a view to amending the behavior of American subsidiaries so as to make them more palatable to the local community. Other working groups would consider balance-of-payments issues and the extraterritorial application of U.S. law, which had been an occasional irritant in Canada since World War II. A working party to tackle other trade problems, with an eye to "establishing some sort of formal trade relationship, possibly approaching a limited free trade area or customs union," was rejected as too disturbing to the Canadians. The idea was, nevertheless, again in the air after almost ten years' repose.[44]

Both ideas—the statement of principles and the idea of working up better trade arrangements—actually bore fruit. The idea of establishing principles was put on the agenda of the next ministerial meeting and of the next meeting between prime minister and president, in January 1964. That meeting announced the establishment of a working party of two ex-ambassadors, Livingston Merchant for the United States and Arnold Heeney for Canada. The two men knew, liked, and respected each other, and they also found that they had an unusual propensity to agree. They worked away for the next year and eventually produced a document that attempted to analyze problems of bilateral consultation using case studies from the previous four or five years.

The Merchant-Heeney report was duly approved and issued in July 1965. It tried to square Canadian independence with Canadian-American partnership, and to accomplish that end it recommended a variety of sensible procedures. Among them was a suggestion that problems between Canada and the United States should be settled as far as possible "through diplomatic channels." That did not strike the right note, and Heeney was roasted in the Canadian press for what was taken to be his timidity in the Canadian press for what was taken to be his timidity if not his cowardice. "The bureaucrats' dream. Keep it quiet boys," one reporter wrote. To another, the report confirmed "our lackey status." It was an extraordinary outpouring. Ironically, the critics of the Merchant-Heeney report zeroed in on the area in which Canada was strongest. According to one American diplomat, "We regarded the Canadian diplomats as among the world's most tenacious, informed and competent."[45] Many Canadians obviously had a different opinion. The report—principles, structure and all—expired under the onslaught.[46]

By 1965, Canadian-American relations were again taking a downward turn. Kennedy, who had taken such a keen personal interest in Canada and its exotic politics, was dead, assassinated in November 1963. His successor, Lyndon B. Johnson, knew little or nothing about Canada and cared less. The machinery underneath ground on, from cabinet committees down to bureaucratic contacts, but there was no longer any desire to manage Canadian-American relations as a whole or to clean the slate of problems. Under Johnson, it was back to ad hockery.

The results were not always bad or even unimpressive. One of Walter Gordon's objectives was to locate more industry and jobs in Canada and to repair the leakage of Canadian funds to the United States through an imbalance of trade. He created incentives for locating industry in Canada, and as a result several auto parts manufacturers and one auto company, Studebaker, moved to Canada or expanded their operations there. The big U.S. automobile companies—General Motors, Ford, and Chrysler—cared very little, but small American parts manufacturers did. They complained to Washington that Canada was subsidizing the competition. Under the law, and after investigation indicated the case was true, the United States government was obliged to impose countervailing duties.

The American treasury secretary explained the problem to Gordon over the telephone. Those in the room in Washington later claimed they could hear the shouting in Ottawa five feet away from the receiver. Despite the noise, Gordon got the point. Out of the discord emerged a new negotiation, and from the negotiation an agreement governing trade in automotive products. The agreement's usual name is the Autopact, and within certain limits it prescribed free trade in automotive products between Canada and the United States. The limits were designed to protect the smaller and weaker Canadian automotive industry, and it was agreed that they would be reviewed at a later date. The agreement's American progenitors hoped that they had discovered a way to secure the dream of eventual free trade, a slice or a sector at a time.

It may be wondered if Canadian nationalistic considerations did not enter into the negotiation of the Autopact; after all, Walter Gordon was still finance minister. In Pearson's opinion, there was no point in worrying about ownership in a business that was already about 99 percent American-owned. The fact that the industry was American-owned and its unions American (international) unions was a great help in securing the Autopact's passage. President Johnson happily backed the bill: according to one story, he believed that Pearson had done him a favor over Cyprus—which was then erupting in civil war and requiring United Nations attention—and Johnson believed in paying his debts. In the end, the only nationalistic considerations that applied to the passage of the Autopact were American ones.[47]

The agreement was signed at the Johnson ranch, where Pearson and his external affairs minister, Paul Martin, were being entertained for a few uncomfortable days. Pearson did not like Johnson, but he was obliged to get along with him. The two men met from time to time, twice in 1964 and then again in January 1965 for the signature of the Autopact. Johnson cheerily greeted Pearson as Harold Wilson, the recently installed British prime minister, and then took the Canadians for a terrifying ride around the ranch.

Siamese twins: President Johnson explains continental economics to Prime Minister Pearson. Cartoon by Duncan Macpherson. *Reprinted by permission of the Toronto Star Syndicate.*

Good relations survived the Johnson City summit. Johnson cooperated economically the next month, when the issue of Canadian borrowing in the United States reappeared. In the view of the U.S. Treasury, Johnson was trying to avert real limitations on Canadian loans; Pearson believed that it was all part of a grand quid pro quo and that Johnson was again rewarding him for sending Canadian peacekeeping troops to Cyprus.[48]

Johnson apparently liked to tour the diplomatic horizon with some of his guests, and with Pearson he touched on a variety of subjects: France, de Gaulle, China, and Indochina, as Kennedy had done before him. Pearson had an interest in the last-named subject. He had been Canadian delegate to the Geneva conference of 1954 that had secured French withdrawal from Indochina and established a kind of peace in Laos, Cambodia, and Vietnam. Canada sat on truce supervisory commissions for all three in the 1950s, committing a fair proportion of its diplomatic manpower to the task; by 1963, the only one left was for the divided country of Vietnam.

BOGGED DOWN IN VIETNAM

The International Commission for Supervision and Control in Vietnam (usually abbreviated as ICC) had three members: Poland, representing the Communist interest, Canada, representing the West, and India, holding the neutral balance. All three were supposed to look out for truce violations by either side and to offer remedies or at least issue complaints. It was a precarious balance, since the perceptions and opinions of the Indian delegates varied directly with the Indian government's conception of the likely outcome. Pearson, for his part, was never enthusiastic about Canadian participation in the process but saw it as a necessary part of Canada's duty in the cold war—defusing a dangerous conflict and preventing worse from happening, perhaps even nuclear war. On a smaller scale, Canadians on the commission saw it as a moderating influence whose mere existence was a bulwark against aggression from the north. Such a view disposed them on occasion to compromise with the Indians—despite their role as defenders of Western interests.

The ICC's first tasks—supervising the French evacuation of North Vietnam in 1954–55 and securing safe passage for Vietnamese who wished to move south from the north or vice versa—was not controversial in Canada. Canadian sympathies were with the refugees fleeing communism, and this was especially so for Canadian officials helping with these tasks on the ground, who often found it a definitive experience of Communist brutality and chicanery. The Canadian governments of the 1950s and early 1960s, both Liberal and Conservative, supported the formation of an anticommunist state in the south and preferred to believe that Ngo Dinh Diem's southern regime, propped up by American aid, could survive indefinitely. Although the Diem government was itself repressive and brutal, Canadian observers considered it by far the lesser evil, compared with the Communist north.[49]

The nature of American aid to Diem's government was something of a problem. The Geneva agreements prohibited the importation of arms with some qualifications. The United States, on the other hand, had supplied the South Vietnamese Army with enough arms by late 1957 to defeat an invasion on the scale of the Korean War. This free hand with military supplies gave the Canadians some qualms, but the qualms never compensated for their broader conviction that the South Vietnamese cause was just and that American behavior was justified.

Diefenbaker had never upset the Vietnamese applecart. The scale of the conflict and the size of the American military mission in Saigon grew considerably between 1957 and 1963. Diefenbaker knew generally what was happening, but his own considerable fund of anticommunism and the conservative views of his people on the spot kept him sound. In any case his attention was engaged elsewhere.

Although Vietnam worried Pearson, it was overshadowed by more urgent problems in 1963. Subsequently Pearson indicated that he had some fellow feeling for Kennedy's dilemma in Southeast Asia. He quoted Kennedy as asking, "But how do we get out of there?"[50] It was not a question that Johnson would repeat—at least, not to Pearson.

The basis of Pearson's concern about Southeast Asia was the reverse of Johnson's. Where Johnson worried about the credibility of American power, Pearson worried that American power would become less credible, not more, if the United States became bogged down in a land war on the continent of Asia. When the land war became a fact, Pearson offered sympathy and encouraged withdrawal. It was a posture not calculated to win many friends in Washington, and it was a difficult position to argue. The consequence of withdrawal would, of course, be defeat, with all that that implied for the people left behind in South Vietnam. That consequence Pearson seems to have regarded as a necessary evil, compared with the greater evil of a war that the Americans would probably not win. That a northern victory would be evil was a proposition sustained by Canadians on the ICC, who reported in March 1965 that the South Vietnamese guerrillas were "a creature of the ruling party of North Viet Nam" and that the south was facing "an insidious form of aggression."

The Canadian government allowed Canadian diplomats on the ICC who traveled regularly to Hanoi to act as go-betweens for the Americans. Their reports showed that there was no hope of any kind of peaceful compromise and that the North Vietnamese were not about to be impressed by American firepower. That firepower included a bombing campaign of formidable proportions—and less-than-formidable results. It was with that in mind that Pearson traveled to the United States in April 1965 to receive a World Peace Award at Temple University in Philadelphia.

In measured and somewhat oblique language Pearson told his American audience that the bombing campaign was not working. Why not stop the bombing and see if that worked instead? The message got through, but not quite as Pearson would have wished. An American ally was being critical of American policy on American soil.

Pearson was asked to visit the president at Camp David before he left the United States. What followed was designed to be unpleasant. "What did you think of my speech?" Pearson asked. "Awful." Johnson was incensed that a foreign leader would criticize him "in my own backyard," and he told Pearson so at length. The Canadian's protestations were swept aside by a flood of emotional rhetoric. Afterward, Pearson tried to explain what he had meant in a letter, but it made no difference. From that point on he, and with him Canada, were in the presidential doghouse.[51] Johnson liked to talk, in public at least, about "those clever Canadians" who were "screwing us with the

Autopact" and offering unhelpful advice on a war they would not themselves fight.[52]

Johnson's remaining years in office were cursed by Vietnam, and Canadian-American relations suffered for it. Pearson was criticized at home and even in his cabinet, by Walter Gordon, for taking a feeble attitude toward U.S. policy in Vietnam. The left condemned him for continuing the defense production-sharing agreement with the United States, a profitable item in Canada's balance of payments.

Diefenbaker's bitterness and resentment finally caused his own party to turn on him, but not before he had helped wreck Pearson's career too. Pearson announced his retirement in December 1967. A convention was assembling to choose his successor just as Johnson, also fed up and defeated by the war in Vietnam, told the American people he would not seek to run again.

chapter 5

CONTINENTAL DYSFUNCTIONS, 1968–1974

Many young Americans' first acquaintance with Canada began with a letter from the United States government. The "greetings" conveyed by Uncle Sam stimulated reflection. With over five hundred thousand U.S. troops in Vietnam by the end of 1968 and every indication that more were needed, many male Americans of draftable age piled into the family car or headed for the nearest Greyhound station. Hours later, they were crossing the border.

"I was twenty-three when I reached Canada in April 1969," one draft-age refugee later recalled. "I knew nobody here. I didn't know what to expect." Canadian immigration officers, schooled to deal kindly with American tourists and the dollars they brought, on the whole treated the young Americans correctly if not warmly.[1] Canadian public opinion would have supported a great deal less warmth: a poll in 1968 indicated that 51 percent of Canadians would have banned any and all American war resisters; only 28 percent wanted to let them in. The Canadian government, however, sided with the latter.[2]

A *Manual for Draft-Age Immigrants to Canada*, widely distributed in the United States, gave tips on cleanliness and proper dress to would-be border-crossers. "Applying for status is a shirt-and-tie affair," readers were told. "Get a good night's sleep, bathe, shave and get a haircut."[3]

Most draft-age immigrants to Canada headed for Canada's larger cities, Toronto, Vancouver, and Montreal—none more than two hours' drive from the border. Because the economy was booming, they generally found jobs; these varied by experience and education, as in the United States. "If a guy's got a BA in political science, then he has a rough time," one complained. On the other hand, plumbers and electricians were in demand.[4] Some clustered around "American exile" centers (there was even a magazine, *Amex*); others melted into the community. So effective was the melting that nobody knew precisely how many draft dodgers or military deserters from the United states there were in Canada. The total number of American immigrants to Canada between 1965 and 1974 was not quite 175,000, and estimates of the draft dodgers and deserters range from 50,000 to 125,000.[5]

The immigrants believed they had little hope of ever coming home. (A poll in 1970 showed that only 21 percent thought they could ever go home.) For many, perhaps most, this was not an immediate burden. The language and often the accent were the same. Certain reference points had changed, perhaps forever, but some had not. The standard of living was somewhat lower, but not very much lower. Median family incomes rose 55 percent in Canada between 1955 and 1976; in the United States in the same period, they grew by only 10 percent. Statistics showed that the Canadian median income was now higher than the American, although Canadian tax rates were higher. Personal consumption in Canada was, perhaps as a consequence, lower.[6]

Despite occasional problems with Canadian immigration, many felt that Canada welcomed them, personally and collectively. "Canadian society is very easy to adapt to," one immigrant claimed. "For some reason you can make friends with Canadians very easily, and I have a close relationship with a Canadian girl."[7] Others were surprised to learn that as Americans they might never be wholly accepted in Canada, that there was a difference between a born Canadian and a legal Canadian.[8] They might also have been surprised to learn that most Canadians did not want draft dodgers admitted to their country. It was a slice of opinion the Canadian government ignored.[9]

Canadian politics were different, though how different was at first hard to detect. Certainly Canadians worried about some different issues: the French-English, or Canada-Quebec, problem, for example. There were conservatives and liberals in Canada, as there were in the United States, but also socialists and exotic beings called Social Crediters. Further left was the Canadian radical fringe, who initially welcomed the draft dodgers as living proof that the citadel of imperialist capitalism was finally crumbling. Later, however, there was irritation that the draft dodgers were not "ultra-militant, superlunary being[s], but merely . . . deeply offended, middle-class moralist[s]." As it turned out, the supermilitants were even less to the Canadian left's liking because they preempted native Canadian issues with their own. This, according to one disillusioned Canadian radical, was merely "American imperialism of the left."[10]

There was certainly an air of romance to the exiles and their beliefs. Canada was romantic. It was more traditional, perhaps more backward than the United States. It had a bachelor scholar-prime minister who drove a

Mercedes convertible—a far cry from Richard Nixon or Hubert Humphrey. It had a tiny army and no draft. It had a kaleidoscope of politics and even socialist governments in two provinces. American libertarians were charmed.

But they were less charmed in October 1970 to discover that the Canadian government had sent the army into the streets of Montreal and Ottawa, that a Quebec cabinet minister had been murdered by terrorists, and that some five hundred radical suspects had been put in jail without benefit of habeas corpus. President Richard Nixon phoned Prime Minister Pierre Trudeau to express sympathy and support. Shaken, some Americans began to think of going home, and gradually, through the 1970s, many trickled back. Perhaps the Canadian state was not so different from the American state after all. Or worse still, perhaps it was: What American president would have dared to lock up hundreds of citizens on the pretext of suppressing an insurrection and be supported by 80 percent of public opinion? On the other hand, what American president faced Trudeau's problem of thwarting the disruption and fragmentation of his country by a group of extreme ethnic nationalists?

If the draft dodgers had delved further into Canadian politics, they might have discovered some other uncomfortable facts. The Canadian government was not truly opposed to the war in Vietnam—at least, not in the simple and direct way that the draft resisters hoped. Trudeau regarded Vietnam as a disaster, certainly: "it had divided the United States from almost all its allies with respect to some aspects at least of Vietnam policy [, and] it had created a monetary crisis in much of the western world."[11] But Trudeau knew there was not much Canada could do about it. On the day he became prime minister, in April 1968, calm descended over the Vietnam desk in Ottawa's Department of External Affairs. From that point on, it was a matter of wait and see: waiting for the end of the war, and seeing whether at that point Canada could help with the tidying up.

PIERRE TRUDEAU AND RICHARD NIXON

"No more helpful fixers" was the motto of the moment in Ottawa, and it applied as much to Canada's relations with the United States as to its dealings with the United Nations. Instead of preaching to the Americans, under Trudeau Canada would concentrate on its national interests and on keeping its own house in order. The Canadian people apparently agreed. In June 1968 they conferred a parliamentary majority on Trudeau and his Liberal party, confident that he would use it wisely.

For Trudeau the beginning of wisdom was defining it. The Canadian government was convulsed with task forces dedicated to reinventing the wheel. In March 1969 the cabinet spent a whole weekend discussing whether it was truly in Canada's interest to be aligned in the cold war; if so, whether NATO was the proper instrument; and, as Trudeau insisted to his colleagues, whether Canada's armed forces were really intended to impress "our enemies, or our friends." If the latter, they were not doing a very good job, as measured by Canada's nonexistent influence in Europe. "By noon we were aligned," one minister remembered, "and by four o'clock we were in NATO." But not wholeheartedly: the Canadian contribution to NATO was halved to 5,000 troops, who spent the next ten years trying to find a viable task they might carry out in case war ever did break out.[12]

The American government paid little attention to these developments. In 1968 the Johnson administration was on its prolonged way out of office. Nixon was new and fresh; he seems to have been satisfied that Trudeau posed no threat to American interests. Nixon's national security adviser, Henry Kissinger, brushed aside suggestions from one of Trudeau's old professors (the Canadian prime minister had once spent a year at Harvard) that Canada's head of government leaned too far to the left. When Trudeau first visited Nixon in March 1969, he mentioned that a reduction in Canada's NATO commitment was in prospect. Nixon responded "in strict confidence," according to Trudeau, that "he too hoped to bring troops back in time."[13] Even after the Canadian withdrawal was announced, adverse American reaction had a ritualistic quality, which was not in itself sufficient to stimulate any reconsideration on the Canadian side.

Nixon's attention, like Johnson's before him, was firmly fixed elsewhere. The president instructed Kissinger to divide foreign policy items into three slices. The first slice consisted of items that required immediate attention; the second, items of occasional interest; and the third, items that were seldom if ever to be brought forward. That included most of Africa, Asia, "and all of Latin America and all countries in the Western Hemisphere with the exception of Cuba. . . . This," Nixon added, "is going to require a subtle handling on Kissinger's part."[14]

The handling might have had to be even more subtle if strong differences had emerged between Canada and the United States over broad policy. On the external side, there was no great reason for concern. Trudeau was not disposed to say or do much about Vietnam, but he did move to break the logjam in Canada's Far Eastern policy by recognizing the People's Republic of China. This was duly denounced in Washington, where Nationalist China's flame was carefully tended—but not in the White House, where parallel preparations for an opening to Communist China were already under contemplation. Nixon's subsequent trip to China removed not only a current issue between Canada and the United States—much to the chagrin of Nationalist Chinese supporters in Washington—but a problem of much longer standing, dating back to the 1940s. Canadian concern for American Far Eastern policy would be taken off the agenda, at least as soon as the Vietnam War was finished.

If Nixon thought that Trudeau had little positive to offer him, even over China, he knew that the United States had nothing to fear from Canada in the immediate future. Trudeau set Canada's foreign policy agenda firmly in economic mode, and in that sphere the United States had a certain bargaining advantage. After the financial crises of the 1960s, it is not surprising that the Canadian government focused on its balance of payments and on Canada's perennial trade deficit with the United States. The Canadians wanted a continuation of the Autopact, which in the early 1970s produced an unexpected (and short-lived) surplus for Canada. They wanted to ship more oil, which had been limited by American quotas since the mid-1950s. They would have liked to ship some uranium, whose import the U.S. government had banned on the expiry of purchase arrangements made in the 1950s.[15]

There were agricultural problems, too, that switched back and forth depending on which farming interest was most recently outraged. But there was nothing that Canada could do for the United States over Vietnam, and nothing that Canada wanted to do in perpetual crisis areas like the Middle East—nothing that could act as a political bargaining counter. Yet it was politics that engaged Kissinger's interest, and Nixon's. ("Only later," Kissinger was to write, "did I learn that the key economic policy decisions are not technical, but political."[16]) When the Canadian-American Joint Ministerial Committee on Economics and Trade met in 1970, its American members were unburdened by extensive preparation. To the American embassy staff, no meetings at all were preferable to another encounter where the Canadians had all the facts and the opportunity, however slight, to do something with them. So the joint committee perished, and another "management" device disappeared.

The joint committee on defense had already disappeared, but defense relations went on nevertheless. As for the PJBD, its chairman confessed in 1970 that it "has not been very active" but should be kept in reserve, just in case "conventional channels" became clogged.[17] On the other hand, Canada regularly renewed the NORAD agreement and remained in NATO. If draft dodgers came up as an issue, they left no trace in Nixon's briefings on Canada.

Nixon needed to have only the slightest concern about public opinion in dealing with Canada. There were regional pressures, such as from the mountain states on uranium or from Texas on oil, but no large worry or concern penetrated public discussion of foreign affairs. There was, nevertheless, the problem of Canada's internal stability.

Since the early 1960s a legal movement for political independence had emerged in Quebec. Until 1968, it was fragmented although vocal; in 1968 it acquired its first credible political figure, a former provincial Liberal cabinet minister, René Lévesque. Lévesque organized his own independentist ("separatist" was the local term) political party, the Parti Québécois, which argued for "sovereignty-association" with Canada. Quebec would get political sovereignty, and Canada would get economic association. In the provincial election of April 1970, it won a quarter of the votes, even though the provincial Liberals under Robert Bourassa carried the day and a majority in the Quebec legislature.

These events were all reported back to Washington by consular staff and by the embassy in Ottawa. Staff had more than the legal activities of Lévesque and his associates to report on. Since 1963 a series of terrorist cells had appropriated the name Front de libération québecois (FLQ) and had conducted sporadic terrorist actions against the Canadian state. Because these were left-wing terrorists, inspired by Algeria and Latin America, they warred on the state's capitalist lackeys as well. In the winter of 1970, for example, one well-placed bomb caused chaos in the Montreal Stock Exchange. The FLQ had further plans in 1970: to kidnap the Israeli consul general in Montreal (FLQ members trained alongside the Palestine Liberation Organization, a feat recorded and broadcast by a pliant press corps) and then, when that proved impracticable, the American. Since the American consul was too well guarded, they turned to his British counterpart and kidnapped *him*, on 5 October 1970.

This caused a stir. The U.S. government naturally wanted to know what was going on; because of the FLQ's links with American groups such as the Black Panthers, there was already common cause between the FBI and the Royal Canadian Mounted Police. Now these links were drawn tighter, and the next news caused them to be made tighter still. A second FLQ "cell" kidnapped Quebec's minister of labor, Pierre Laporte. The two hostages, held separately, were used to pressure the Canadian and Quebec governments to free imprisoned terrorists and to reward the current kidnappers with gold and a flight out of the country. There was considerable excitement in Montreal as a result. Such excitement had in the recent past led to riots and looting; under the circumstances it became possible to believe that Canada was in a "prerevolutionary" situation. The two governments, federal and provincial, responded by calling in the army and invoking a state of emergency that gave them the power to arrest and imprison without warrant and without habeas corpus. That action did not save Laporte, who was murdered on 17 October by his kidnappers.

The next day, a Sunday, Richard Nixon called Trudeau to offer his sympathy and support. If it could happen in Canada, he told an audience in Grand Forks, North Dakota, it could happen in the United States. Under the circumstances, there was in Washington "no appreciable sympathy" for Quebec independence, and considerable admiration for Trudeau's firm and energetic response to terrorism.[18] Having bolstered public opinion with the state of emergency, the government used the imperfect police resources at its disposal to find the two sets of kidnappers. One set were still holding their hostage and got a free flight to Cuba; the others had murdered theirs, and were tried and sent to prison.

Throughout the October Crisis, as it was called in Canada, the American government cooperated as best it could with Trudeau. There were rumors at the time of CIA involvement, of plots in which American spies toyed with disrupting Trudeau's nationalist-leftist regime. To date, none of these stories has any foundation.[19] The United States was not about to complicate its life by cultivating the separatist side in the debate between Quebec and Canada. Nixon's interest in Canadian-American relations was at home.

CANADIAN PRIORITIES AND AMERICAN INTERESTS

The Canadian prime minister faced two publics in conceiving and then balancing his American policy. Canadian public opinion in general was going through a nationalist phase: the further left it was the more acute the concern it expressed about the United States, its government, its policies, and its multinational corporations. What preoccupied the Canadian nationalist left was replicated, in a minor key, inside Trudeau's second public, the Liberal party. The Liberals almost defined centrist politics in Canada, but in the 1960s the center moved left, and with it the Liberals. They knew they were facing heavy criticism from the left for what one leftist academic labeled "silent surrender"—the capitulation of Canada and its largely Liberal governments to American multinationals. In English Canada, at least, the Liberals wanted to corral as much of the nationalist vote as they could; in French Canada they wanted to redefine Canada in such a way as to attract and then retain public opinion away from the *Quebec* nationalists, Trudeau's deadly enemies. So the Liberals moved to reinforce identifiably *Canadian* institutions, to counter Quebec separatism with Canadian statism. Yet with Trudeau there were limits to the lures of even Canadian nationalism. According to the Canadian deputy chief of mission in Washington, even though "a lot of 'idiotic' statements have been made in Canada regarding American investments . . . 'the Prime Minister is not an idiot.' "[20]

Idiot or not, Trudeau had to take Canadian sentiment into account. It was a sentiment that was listening far more to Walter Gordon, who was out of politics but still a force in Canadian life, and his disciples than to Trudeau. Opinion polls defined a public that believed that Canadian dependence on the United States was increasing (March 1970) and that Canada should "buy back" its economy from foreign corporations, despite a warning from Trudeau that such action would drastically lower the Canadian standard of living. The money, the prime minister said, would be far better spent elsewhere.[21] One of Gordon's favorite nostrums, a government-owned Canada Development Corporation devoted to increasing Canadian control over the economy, won favor with 80 percent of Canadians in January 1971, while over 60 percent stated that there was already enough American investment in the country.[22] Later that year, the Canada Development Corporation was enacted by the Canadian Parliament. Its object was to seek out good domestic investment opportunities and, by the bye, increase Canadian control of Canadian industry.

The government was also seen to be investigating the question of regulating foreign investment. A government-sponsored task force produced a lengthy essay in 1968 known from the task force chairman as the Watkins Report, that questioned the performance of foreign-owned firms and suggested a number of mild remedies. A parliamentary committee with a Liberal majority delved into the question and in August 1971 recommended a screening agency to scrutinize foreign takeovers of Canadian industry. As everyone knew, *foreign* meant American. Finally, in 1971 Trudeau's minister of national revenue, Herb Gray, sponsored an investigation of foreign investment. The resulting document was known as the Gray Report, for though Gray did not write it, he certainly agreed with its conclusions. The Gray Report was highly doubtful of the value of foreign investment; its strident tone commended it to the left, which found in it another stick with which to beat the "complacent" Trudeau government and its supine attitude to the United States.[23]

For critics proof of the government's un-Canadian character resided in the statistics that showed foreign investment growing. At the end of 1972, U.S. residents had C$38.6 billion in long-term investments in Canada, 77 percent of the foreign investment total. Government supporters replied by noting that 77 percent was down from 81 percent in 1967, and that U.S. investment was growing more slowly than investment from other countries. Foreign control of industry was also down, from 61 percent to 58 percent in a single year, 1971. Sometimes administrative decisions helped. In 1971 the International Nickel Company was reclassified as Canadian rather than foreign by the government; as a result, "foreign control" of the Canadian mining industry dropped from 71 percent to 58 percent. Statistics are, after all, "State Arithmetic."[24]

Canadians were clearly coming to believe that they did not want or need to be dependent on the United States, particularly for investment or for other forms of special treatment. Some Americans, especially in Washington, agreed with them. During the 1960s the United States had given Canada special consideration on the Autopact, on tariff negotiations under GATT, in the Canadian-American Defense Production-Sharing Agreement of 1958, and on access to American capital markets. Yet quarter by quarter, year by year from 1968 to 1972, Canada showed a surplus in trade with the United States. While the American index of industrial production remained stagnant, rising only in 1972, Canada's rose steadily between 1968 and the end of 1972. Moreover, Canada enjoyed a favorable trade balance overall (that is, with all countries combined), as it had since 1961, although that surplus was offset by external payments so as to produce a general deficit on current account. It was the weakness on current account that proved crucial in negotiations between Canada and the United States during the 1960s and that accounted for American reluctance to insist on exact reciprocity.[25] With the United States running an annual trade deficit of about US$5 billion, that reluctance was vanishing.

There was another factor that entered the equation. Canada was no longer, in the late 1960s and 1970s, the most favored location for U.S. foreign investment. Between 1966 and 1974, U.S. investment in Canada rose in value by 81 percent; the comparable figure for Europe was 172 percent. At the same time, the rate of increase for American exports to Europe grew faster than that for Canada. That, in turn, reflected a faster rate of economic growth in Europe than in Canada—even though Canada's was not unimpressive.[26]

Canadian nationalism and increasing American irritation were on a collision course, or so it appeared. Canadian officials traveling south found a cool reception as they tried to negotiate various deals. Canadian attempts to expand investment in Canada, especially in regions with low employment where subsidy made the difference in choosing location, were treated with suspicion.[27] There was little to show in the summer of 1971, when Nixon's treasury secretary, John Connally, decided to reconsider the United States' foreign economic policy. As Nixon would later put it to his staff, "we have too long acted as Uncle Sugar and now we've got to be Uncle Sam."[28]

Being Uncle Sam meant surveying and unilaterally altering policies judged disadvantageous to the United States or its balance of payments. The resulting package was presented to Nixon and approved. It proposed wage and price controls, temporary import surcharges, and help for American exports. It also proposed the cancellation of the Canadian-American Autopact.

On Friday afternoon, 13 August, the president and his advisers debated the shape of things to come. Connally was belligerent. Recalling that Canada had recently floated its dollar, the treasury secretary argued that cooperation with that country, or any other, should have little or no priority.

> Connally: "So the other countries don't like it. So what? Why do we have to be 'reasonable'—Canada wasn't."
> Arthur Burns: "They can retaliate."
> Connally: "Let 'em. What can they do?"
> Burns: "They're powerful. They're proud, just as we are."[29]

What followed illustrated not the weakness but the strength of Canadian-American relations. Though Connally viewed Canada with disfavor, Canada was not his principal target. There were those on his staff and in the State Department who did not regard Canada as very much of a problem and who considered the Autopact a major triumph for American economic diplomacy. As the secrecy around Connally's bundle of economic delights gradually unraveled—as it had to because of the number of officials required to put Nixon's decrees into proper form—the Autopact's inclusion came to the attention of those who had negotiated it six years earlier. Soon the Autopact had landed on Secretary of State William Rogers's desk; shortly afterward it was safe, reprieved by Rogers's intervention. Connally does not seem to have cared much. Only the White House press secretary was put out, because he had to unstaple his carefully prepared packages of press releases, renumber them, and only then release them to a famished press. Ironically, when some of the Americans responsible for the coup told their Canadian colleagues, they were met with blank disbelief. Not for the first time, Ottawa remained comfortably obtuse.[30]

Nixon announced his economic measures on Sunday evening, 15 August 1971. They caused a stir, and nowhere more than in Canada. Trudeau was off on vacation, basking on a yacht in the Adriatic, and so were most of his senior colleagues. Among the emergency team hastily assembled to respond to Nixon and Connally, the general feeling was that there must have been some mistake. Surely Canada had been included only by accident in Nixon's measures. A timely reminder of Canada's special status and all would be well, as it had been in 1962, 1963, and 1968.

But all was not well. Through the last two weeks of August, the height of the Washington summer, Connally carefully stage-managed a pageant of repentance in his elegant office in the treasury building. Sitting behind Alexander Hamilton's desk, the secretary coolly received a parade of erring nations and laid down the terms of their salvation. Canada's representative, a sweating and rumpled finance minister, was no exception, though the scripting failed when the secretary began to read from the briefing notes intended for Japan. The minister got the point nevertheless: Canada was part of the problem, in Connally's eyes, and there was no convincing him to the contrary.

The August encounter set the stage for notably unsuccessful negotiations that lasted all fall. In Canada even nationalist newspapers trembled at the presumptive effects of Nixon's measures, his unilateral impact on the world economic system. It was remarked that the leader of the free world did not realize that *Canada* and not Japan was the United States' largest trading partner. Was it a measure of Canada's real status, its invisibility in American eyes? Perhaps the Americans were just taking Canada for granted again. Fantastic predictions were made of the probable effects of Nixon's attitude, and his economic tactics. The federal government's negligence was blamed for allowing such a dreadful situation to happen, and two provinces, Ontario and Alberta, threatened to open their own offices in Washington. It was a sign, and not a good one, of Canada's shifting political balance and how it might affect relations with the United States.

Finally Trudeau was enlisted to visit Nixon in December 1971—about the time that Kissinger began to realize that Connally's economic measures were affecting the United States' good political relations with its various trading partners.

Perhaps as a consequence, Trudeau's meeting with Nixon was accounted a success. Trudeau was at his didactic best, carefully explaining that unless Canada were allowed to earn money from its trade with the United States, it could hardly afford to go on buying American products. Did the United States perhaps plan to keep Canada forlorn and dependent? Naturally Nixon denied any such intention. He did not wish to treat Canada in any specially positive or negative fashion, but merely as another foreign country. We have the statesmen's word for it that the conversation in fact surpassed these stupefying banalities, but that seems to have been the gist of their remarks. They emerged for a jolly dinner, and Trudeau flew home.

With relations apparently on an upward curve, preparations began for the visit of Nixon and his court to Ottawa the following spring. The White House prepared carefully, circulating draft after draft of the presidential speech to the Canadian Parliament. In Ottawa members of the U.S. embassy equally carefully took Nixon's portraits out of their desk drawers, dusted them, and set them up for temporary display in case their commander in chief stopped by. (He didn't.) If the embassy staff's hopes were disappointed, Nixon and his speechcrafters were not. He delivered a notable oration and delivered it well. After disposing of some of the clichés of Canadian-American after-dinner speeches, Nixon proceeded to argue that there were real problems to confront, and he proposed to confront them. He would respect "Canada's right to chart its own economic course," rejecting "the false impression that our countries are essentially alike." This, he added, was the essence of the "Nixon Doctrine," which had recently been proclaimed. (The doctrine in fact dealt with the United States' desire to offload some of its overseas responsibilities on consenting allies, such as South Vietnam, but like all useful doctrines it could be expanded to fit awkward cases.)

The visit was remembered for the speech and for the circumstances surrounding it: a would-be assassin lurked in the crowd in Ottawa but found no opportunity to attack the president. Meanwhile Nixon's entourage made known their impatience as they waited for presidential authority to pursue the latest urgencies in Southeast Asia.

The Nixon visit's rhetoric found an echo in the Canadian government's own analyses. The implications of Nixon's trade policy seemed to undermine the secure economic foundations of Canada's foreign policy, based as it was on the presumption of special treatment from Washington in times of crisis. The external affairs minister, Mitchell Sharp, asked his officials to suggest a solution to the problem, and within a short time he was presented with a paper arguing three options. These were, first, the status quo, which many judged unsatisfactory; second, closer relations with the United States, which no one found attractive; and third, what was described as a combination of strengthening the Canadian economy and reducing Canadian vulnerability to the United States. This was the "Third Option," and to the officials who drafted it, it was designed to make preeminent sense.[31] It was presented to cabinet in November 1971 and, after considerable debate, accepted.

The Third Option had limits. Sharp discussed these in a position paper in April 1972, at the time of Nixon's visit. "Option 3 . . . if it is to make sense and to be feasible, must be conceived as seeking important but limited relative changes in some dimensions of our relationship with the United States, which continue to involve extensive interdependence." At the same time,

YET ANOTHER RAID TO THE NORTH.

Nixon visits Ottawa. Cartoon by Aislin from the *Montreal Gazette*. *Reprinted by permission of the Toronto Star Syndicate.*

Canadian policy should seek to create the widest possible freedom for Canada to pursue new policies in "social justice" and other domestic fields.[32]

Over the next six or seven years the Canadian government sought to implement the Third Option, only to find that trading partners other than the United States were hard to come by. The Europeans and the Japanese showed polite interest but equally politely declined to create a special relationship with Canada that would needlessly offend the United States. The Canadian business community declined to reorient its sales practices. Geography and custom made it far easier and cheaper to market in the United States. Timidity and language barriers reinforced this tendency.

The U.S. embassy, whose job it was to analyze this new departure in Canadian policy, was unimpressed. According to the economic counselor, "We'd look at the trade figures and say, 'Lots of luck, Canada.' " As far as the embassy was concerned, the death of the special relationship was much exaggerated, and Nixon's speech therefore "a stupidity."[33]

The Third Option would ultimately have little effect on Canadian-American trade and even less on Canadian-American relations. Its eventual failure would eventually have a considerable impact on how Canadians dealt with the world, and the United States, but that failure would not be apparent for another decade. In the meantime there were more pressing problems, and the most important of these was Vietnam.

THE VIETNAM PEACE PROCESS

The United States would need Canada before long in Vietnam. There the Canadians persisted as part of the moribund ICC, permanently paralyzed as between its Canadian, Polish, and Indian members, who were unable to agree on anything. Nixon and Kissinger intended to have peace in Vietnam by election day, and as part of the peace package it was convenient to create an international peacekeeping force. Canada, which had experience in such forces, was a logical candidate to express Western interests.

Trudeau's government dusted off its plans for Vietnam. The Americans, busy with negotiations with North Vietnam in Paris, did not seem especially interested. Peacekeeping, though important, was subsidiary to the main issues of peace—and Nixon's reelection. Nixon left nothing to chance in his drive for reelection. Trudeau, campaigning under the uninspiring slogan, "The land is strong," did. The result was an apparent reversal of their political fortunes, with Nixon domestically strong and Trudeau, for the time being, politically weak.

Nixon was triumphantly re-elected in November 1972. Trudeau, who went to the polls a week before, barely survived. Canada once again had a Parliament of minorities, with the Liberals only two seats ahead of the opposition Conservatives. The balance, as in the 1960s, was held by the NDP and the Creditistes, the surviving French-speaking wing of the former Social Credit party. Neither the NDPers nor the Creditistes were especially enamored of the United States, its president, or the Vietnam War.

This was made plain when Nixon opened a Christmas bombing offensive to persuade the North Vietnamese to bargain more realistically and grant the Americans "peace with honor" in Vietnam. For Trudeau, the timing was inconvenient. He had to face a new Parliament on 4 January 1973, and in that Parliament his object was to survive the first vote of nonconfidence from the opposition. It was virtually certain that the opposition would make a motion condemning the U.S. air attacks, and if the government resisted, it would be defeated. And so the government pre-empted the motion on 5 January, denouncing the prolongation of the war in Vietnam.

Trudeau's parliamentary maneuvers did not win him friends among the Nixon administration. Though Canadian embassy officials hastened to explain that the parliamentary resolution was merely a cynical political ploy designed to dish the opposition, Nixon was furious. Except for one subject, the Canadian embassy was put in purdah. Canadian officials were not to be received by their administration counterparts, and Canadian invitations to the embassy were to be refused. The official exception to the rule was, ironically, Vietnam, where Canada was still needed as part of a tripartite peacekeeping team (the other two were Indonesia and Hungary). The unofficial exception was that American officials now met their Canadian colleagues over lunch. Life went on.[34]

On 27 January 1973 the Vietnam peace accords were signed in Paris. Canada rather grumpily agreed to follow Kissinger's desires and his timetable and join a peacekeeping expedition whose chances of success were practically nil. External Affairs Minister Sharp announced that the Canadians would be joining for 90 days, subject to renewal if nothing went awry. It was short notice, designed to put pressure on Canada's peacekeeping partners and on the North and South Vietnamese to cooperate. The short term was all that counted: time to get the remaining American troops out of South Vietnam, time to turn over arms to the South Vietnamese, and time to get American prisoners of war out of North Vietnam. Admittedly, 90 days was rather fleeting even for the short term.

A modest contingent of Canadian troops was hastily assembled and flown to Vietnam. Canadian aircraft picked up the U.S. POWs in Hanoi and flew them out of the country. And on the ground Canadian officials tried to separate Communist from capitalist as each army scrambled to occupy as much territory as possible.

Ninety days passed, and Canada renewed its stay for another 90. The second 90 days were, however, the last. Although the U.S. government would have preferred to see the Canadians remain longer, there was no overwhelming pressure to keep them. Most of the Americans were out of Vietnam by then, and Nixon had troubles of his own at home.

Nixon's determination to defeat his political enemies at home had produced the Watergate crisis. As a result, by the summer of 1973 his administration was hobbled by congressional investigations and special prosecutors, whose pursuit of the truth was likely, so it was believed, to take them to the door of the Oval Office. All this was being played out on television, daily, religiously watched in Canada as in the United States.

Meanwhile Trudeau brought Parliament under control. His political agenda was not what it once had been. Instead, this most intellectual of prime ministers led his party troops in daily political streetfighting in the House of Commons, passing popular legislation he would have disdained only a year before. Inevitably, given the complexion of Canadian public opinion and the necessity, politically, of outflanking the left-leaning NDP, the new Liberal program was high-spending and nationalist in fact and in tone.

The Liberals legislated against multinationals by introducing a bill for a Foreign Investment Review Agency (FIRA), which, after prolonged debate, was supported by all parties in Parliament and passed into law in November 1973. The agency would regulate both the acquisition of Canadian firms by foreign companies and the establishment of new foreign investment in Canada. A national petroleum company was proposed, publicly, by Trudeau in December 1973. It responded to special conditions at the time (see Chapter 6), but its ancestry had a strong trace of populist resentment of large, American, multinational companies.

Trudeau took some time to follow through on his promise of a national Canadian oil company. In the spring of 1974 the polls told him it was time to act. He provoked a parliamentary defeat, called an election for July, and won it this time, with a majority of seats in the House of Commons. It was therefore as prime minister that Trudeau gazed on the last phase of Richard Nixon's presidency, culminating in Nixon's resignation on 9 August 1974.

The Nixon presidency, Trudeau might have reflected, had spawned a series of paradoxes in Canadian-American relations. On the global scale relations were better than they had been in years, probably since the 1940s. This happy result had been obtained without the benefit of Canadian advice, pressure, or complaints. There was, under Nixon and Kissinger, less consultation between the topmost levels of the governments of Canada and the United States on world issues on global problems than ever before. When Trudeau went to Washington or when Kissinger came to Ottawa, there were briefings, and Trudeau was apparently content to listen to Kissinger analyze and expound his vision of the world. That vision, involving a balance of power and detente between the two superpowers—and an absence of saber-rattling—was congenial to Canada, where a lessening of tension was considered a notable good by and for itself. The settlement of the Vietnam War removed a domestic headache in Canada and may ultimately have set the stage for a decompression of Canadian nationalist sentiment. In 1974 such a development remained far in the future.

All this was achieved without the slightest personal rapport between president and prime minister. Trudeau and Nixon were not similar, either in background or attitude. Trudeau had a rich father and had gone to Harvard—not to mention the London School of Economics and the Sorbonne. He dressed well and enjoyed a flamboyant lifestyle. Trudeau, not Nixon, dated Barbra Streisand. "That asshole Trudeau," Nixon ground out to his cronies in 1973, and was taped for the benefit of posterity.[35]

The animosity mattered very little, which defines a second paradox. Trudeau and Nixon both made much of their break with the past in 1971–72 and of the ending of the "special relationship" between Canada and the United States. The death of the "special relationship" and the creation of the Third Option policy that accompanied it had the character of a charade, though probably not intentionally. There were too many factors in Canadian-American relations that were truly unique, from personal links in labor, business, government, and academia to the detailed calculations necessary to keep a 3,000-mile border functioning and appropriately porous.

The detailed nature of Canadian-American relations gave the subject an eternal—and eternally frustrating—character. When Trudeau and Nixon met, the great attraction for the Canadian was to receive a briefing from Henry Kissinger, whom the Canadian prime minister greatly admired. Trudeau did not want to spend the time dealing with the Autopact or the Atlantic fishery; he wanted to make the most of his unique opportunity. When Ford succeeded Nixon, Trudeau and Kissinger carried on, and so did Canada's various ministers of external affairs. Time with Kissinger was quality time, to be passed in a *tour d'horizon*. In August 1976, for example, the discussion began with Korea, carried on to South Africa and Namibia, then turned to the current Conference on International Economic Cooperation. The meeting was more than half over before any strictly bilateral subject was raised.

To Kissinger that was as it should be. When the Canadian ambassador came to see him one day carrying a thick briefing book, Kissinger, who was by then secretary of state, looked up. "I hope you have't come to lecture me about the sex life of the salmon," the secretary intoned. To his own officials dealing with Canada, Kissinger was equally off-putting. When the assistant secretary for economics finally got the secretary's attention and time for a briefing on outstanding Canadian-American issues, Kissinger listened impatiently. Finally he ended the meeting: "These are small problems," he told his staff. "Solve them."[36]

What the politicians didn't know presumably didn't hurt them. When Nixon temporarily "froze" Canadian-American relations in 1973, his own civil servants made light of his decree. They had, after all, business to transact. Nixon's abrupt departure made little difference to this business.

The first and most urgent topic to be discussed with the new Ford administration was energy. As the discussants would discover, it had a long history.

chapter 6

KEEPING WARM, 1974–1984

The ninth of November 1965 was a banner day for statisticians and demographers. Just after seven o'clock that evening, the lights failed—not just in a few localities, but all over northeastern North America. The power outage stimulated a surge in the sale of candles and flashlights, as well as a flood of articles in the next day's papers—after the lights went on in the composing rooms. In the aftermath, demographers discovered a startling but short-lived rise in the birth rate in the summer of 1966. Ordinary citizens learned that much of North America was linked in regional electricity grids that crossed state lines and international boundaries. The great power failure of 1965, which affected millions of Americans and helped produce thousands more, in fact occurred in Canada, at Ontario Hydro's Niagara Falls generating plant.

It was a measure, small but significant, of the importance of the continental energy trade and a reminder of what could happen if that trade were interrupted. Energy exchanges between Canada and the United States were nothing new. In the nineteenth century Nova Scotia bituminous coal had been shipped south to Boston, and Pennsylvania anthracite had traveled north to central Canada. Starting in 1880, Canada had imported oil, including from the United States; imports remained substantially greater than domestic production until 1953, when Canadian oil finally became available in quantity.

Coal and oil are nonrenewable resources, but the establishment of a market in those commodities nevertheless creates a continuous expectation, not to say requirement. Oil and gas supplies are therefore a sensitive item in international trade. During World War I and World War II the Canadian and American governments cooperated in insuring that enough coal and oil went north; in exchange, Canada found it appropriate to guarantee electricity exports to the south.

The boundary-makers of the eighteenth century had been strongly attracted to lakes and rivers as devices for separating Canadians and Americans. As a result, the international boundary follows the Greak Lakes system from its source to the St. Lawrence, passing by a number of rapids on the way. Those rapids attracted American investors who were looking for cheap and accessible power in the late nineteenth century, and the resulting generating stations were hooked into Buffalo or other towns in northern New York State. This circumstance did not sit well with potential Canadian consumers of hydroelectric power. A public power movement in Ontario undertook to return Canadian resources to Canadian consumers and as a first step created a provincially owned electric system, Ontario Hydro, in 1906.

The emergence of government-owned utilities limited foreign ownership and control by definition. The reason for their emergence had less to do with another phenomenon—the much lower Canadian price for electricity, which derived from the abundance of hydroelectricity in central Canada and British Columbia.[1] Although utilities fell under provincial jurisdiction in Canada, the export of power was appropriated by the federal government in 1907; thereafter, the export of power required an annual permit. The intention and effect of this were to minimize the flow of electricity to the United States; in 1955 only 5 percent of Canada's electricity production was exported there. But the temptation existed nonetheless. Hydro projects—and even more, nuclear power stations when they came onstream in the 1960s—were capital intensive, and exports were a good way of amortizing their cost. This argument, intriguing in the 1950s, became overwhelming twenty years later. Technology was another factor: supply was simply more secure when electrical systems were linked in regional grids. Links over the border expanded for that purpose, and short-term energy sales to meet peak demand north or south of the border became customary.

Although Canada and the United States cooperated in securing energy supply of all kinds during World War II, the end of the war witnessed electricity rationing and brownouts as supply failed to keep pace with demand. As a result, the Canadian government took a leading role in energy supply management in the 1950s and 1960s; equally, Canadian nationalists turned an anxious eye on American investment in the Canadian energy sector.

OIL AND GAS

That sector, apart from electricity, was dominated by the foreign-owned firms that in the late 1940s and 1950s had had the capital and the technology to develop the oil and gas fields of Alberta. Sixty-nine percent of the Canadian oil and gas industry was foreign-owned in 1954, and the figure rose to 75 percent in 1968. (The proportion was so high, disgruntled Albertans argued, because central Canadians would not invest the necessary funds.) The effect was to establish a strong connection between the oil companies, and oil fields, of Texas and Alberta; and it created a new wave of American influence and style in Canada's foothills province. "Wanted by American oil executive large attractive house—price no object," ran an advertisement that was lovingly quoted by envious Calgarians.[2]

Government policy—provincial and, until the 1960s, federal—encouraged investment. Investment meant jobs, a better balance of payments, and revenues for governments, both provincial and federal. Expanding the investment and exploiting it for the profit of Alberta and Canada also created a strong incentive for the Canadian government to export oil and natural gas south. A peculiar American import policy encouraged this, for although Canadian imports were limited under pressure from Texas and Louisiana, cheaper Middle East oil was excluded as well.

American restrictions on oil and gas imports were justified in terms of national security. In the event of a war, the United States did not wish to find itself at the end of a long seaborne supply line. Better by far to have domestic producers in place and to encourage them, even if in the process the United States had to pay a slightly higher price for energy supply. This argument was, however, difficult to apply to Canada, and even more difficult when a vast petroleum reserve was discovered on Alaska's north slope in 1968. Alaskan oil and gas could be shipped to the lower 48 by sea; this was hazardous because of the danger of spills but desirable because of pressure from west coast ports and the American shipping industry: or it could be shipped by pipeline through Canada. It was not hard to guess which alternative the Canadian government endorsed, especially because the construction of a pipeline might well prove a bonanza to Canadian suppliers and construction workers. Better still, there was oil on the Canadian side of the frontier, in the ocean northeast of Alaska. A pipeline would help Canada develop its northern petroleum reserves in the Beaufort Sea. The Canadians stressed the environmental hazards of West Coast shipping, too, but in the late 1960s the environment was not yet a fashionable cause, and such warnings carried less conviction than they would later. Nevertheless, the environmental argument, once introduced into Canadian-American relations, did not depart.

American oil companies were inclined to downplay the difficulties of delivering Alaskan oil to market. Enterprise and technology would overcome all barriers, or so it seemed. Why not ship Alaskan crude to the East Coast as well as the West? True, there were thousands of miles of ice-clogged straits in between, so that some experimentation was necessary. A reinforced tanker, the *Manhattan*, was outfitted by the Humble Oil Company and dispatched north. An international incident soon followed.

Powerful maritime countries have an interest in securing unfettered navigation for their ships and subjects. So it had been with Great Britain in the eighteenth and nineteenth centuries; so it was with the United States in the twentieth. The U.S. Navy had a particular interest in asserting freedom of passage through various straits around the world. Until the 1960s, it had not applied the doctrine to the straits north of Canada, since they were virtually unnavigable except for submarines. Those few ships that had traversed the Canadian north had taken years to do it; the navigation season north of the sixty-fifth parallel was at best eight weeks long and dangerous even then because of ice floes. Canadians took comfort in the impenetrable isolation of "their" north, and so did their government, which preferred to spend money anywhere but the north.

The *Manhattan* proceeded across the Arctic from east to west in September 1969. Its owners did not ask Canadian permission, and the Canadians did not have the means, legal or physical, to stop it. It was a record voyage: 15 days. Granted, it had to be assisted by Canadian icebreakers, but the feasibility of navigation was established. The *Manhattan* did other things too. It jolted a century of complacency and neglect in Ottawa. It stimulated a strong and wholly adverse reaction among nationalists and environmentalists. They in turn pressed Ottawa to do something. The Canadian government decided that it had to respond and that it would proceed through law.

It began by taking a step backward. Canada accepted the jurisdiction of the International Court of Justice in the Hague for international disputes, but the cabinet decided to limit that acceptance, excluding Arctic navigation from the structure of international law. Surely, the argument ran, waters that were actually frozen and connected to land for ten months out of twelve were "special," not subject to the usual international rules and customs. The fragile Arctic ecosystem deserved exceptional protection—protection that Canada was prepared to extend via an Arctic Waters Pollution Protection bill, introduced in Parliament in April 1970.

The United States government and President Nixon were displeased. Nixon is said to have refused an explanatory phone call from Prime Minister Trudeau, and in any case the American government declined to accept the legality of Canada's actions. Trudeau's Arctic initiative was, on the other hand, highly acceptable at home. He never retracted his position, although in later years Canadian governments found it difficult to enforce Canada's jurisdiction over Arctic navigation in a manner satisfactory to Canadian nationalists. On issues of law of the sea generally, Canada took a separate course from the United States throughout the 1970s and 1980s—in the process winning the support of the Soviet Union, which, like Canada, had a long Arctic coastline.

The Arctic nevertheless remained rather arcane. The *Manhattan* may have established that Arctic voyages were possible, but it also proved that they were expensive and impractical. Boating expeditions on the Northwest Passage remained an affair that principally interested lawyers and eccentrics.

They did not cast too much of a shadow over Canadian-American relations, even in the field of energy.

Between 1968 and 1972 energy, especially oil and gas, was something that the Trudeau government wished to sell to the United States. The United States, whose petroleum reserves had been declining for some time, on the whole wanted to buy, but not badly enough to come to a hasty agreement. A study by George Shultz, Nixon's labor secretary, argued that a continental energy agreement was desirable, but that first the United States should get the Canadians to provide against the unhealthy dependence of their eastern provinces (including Quebec) on cheap overseas oil. ("In fact," a November 1972 emergency preparedness study suggested, "[the] Canadian storage situation is probably better than the US East Coast."[3]

The Canadian government, as it turned out, liked cheap imports for one of its poorer regions. Quebec was politically volatile, and any move to deny Quebec access to cheap energy might have a negative effect on the province's appreciation of the economic benefits of remaining in Canada. So nothing was done.

Canadian ministers and officials meanwhile paraded through Washington hawking their energy wares. They enjoyed mixed success. A Canadian pipeline would have its advantages, Nixon administration officials conceded, but it would be politically delicate to oppose a trans-Alaska project. As for what was termed a "common continental oil policy," it was a good idea, but not if the Americans insisted on diverting surplus Canadian oil to eastern Canada instead of allowing it to flow south to the United States. In George Shultz's view, the United States would be trading access to "the high price of the U.S. market" for "definite assurance in times of emergency that the flow of Canadian oil continues."[4] But that assurance was not immediately forthcoming. There matters stood in mid-1971, as negotiators on both sides struggled to put together a package that Nixon and Trudeau could sign when the president visited Ottawa.

They failed. Nixon's visit was postponed, and after the *shokku,* there were other things to talk about. The U.S. government finally revealed its support for an Alaskan pipeline, postponing Canada's dream of Beaufort Sea oil riches. A belated offer of security of supply and extra Canadian crude attracted no interest.[5] For a while Canadians visiting the United States made hopeful public noises about Canada's boundless energy reserves, and American imports of Canadian oil continued to rise. While exports rose, Canadian reserves started to decline, in 1970, 1971, and 1972. The rate of discoveries had already peaked, in 1967. Previously solid forecasts drifted downward as production followed reserves into decline.

The continental energy policy drifted into limbo during 1972. On the American side, the United States' ability to offer the Canadians offsetting supplies from the gulf states (Gulf of Mexico, that is) was becoming questionable. The Canadians could no longer offer security of supply, and neither could the Americans. "In summary," an official wrote in November 1972, "viewing the uncertain future, it is difficult to appraise the security difference between *no* formal agreement and the maximum formal understanding the U.S. and Canada might attain."[6] As it later turned out, Canadian oil production would peak in 1973. It declined drastically thereafter.

THE ENERGY CRISIS

In October 1973 war in the Middle East set in train a great oil crisis. An Arab oil embargo aimed at states friendly to Israel cut supplies to the United States and certain of its allies and threw international oil markets into chaos. The price of oil doubled, and supply appeared to dwindle. Canada's easternmost (and most economically disadvantaged) provinces faced winter with only 80 percent of their fuel supplies guaranteed.

The Canadian government had another concern. The crisis, like that of 1971, stimulated Canada's provinces to ride off in all directions at once. British Columbia made noises about consulting its own interests. Quebec talked about a special deal with Iran. The Atlantic provinces conferred with neighboring New England. For reasons of Canada's political balance, if for no other, a strong policy was called for from Ottawa. Other reasons, however, were not lacking.

Ottawa, like Washington, was unprepared. The very idea of oil scarcity was strange, after a generation of abundance. The Arab oil embargo made Canada's energy nightmare come true: Canada was at the end of a very long supply line, behind the United States. Worse, from a political point of view, Canadian access to international oil supplies was still funneled through the great multinational oil companies, causing Canadians to suspect that in a pinch Canadians rather than Americans would be allowed to go short by head offices located in New York or Houston. That particular sentiment was unique to Canada, but another was shared north and south of the border: a deep suspicion that the oil crisis had been fabricated by the great oil companies so as to gouge profit from helpless consumers.[7] The oil crisis therefore helped confirm a Canadian nationalist scenario, and that in turn influenced the policies put into place by the Canadian government in 1973.

A government-owned oil company was the least Trudeau could offer his worried electors, but it took time to establish one. A pipeline to the East Coast from western Canadian oil fields was another, but it would take longer still. More immediately, he tried to balance increased eastern Canadian import costs with rising prices for western Canadian oil. The difference would be made up by *American* consumers through an export tax, and the export tax turned into a subsidy to ease the cost of imported oil to the impoverished Maritimes. Meanwhile the Canadian government instituted export controls on petroleum products.

Trudeau's action was understandable. His civil servants estimated that unless immediate controls were placed on exports to the United States, "Canada itself will be short 3 million barrels" over the winter of 1973–74. To meet Canadian supply, exports to the United States were cut back by at least 10 percent; in those uncertain times more cutbacks were a possibility. In the longer run Trudeau's emergency oil policy established a two-price system for Canadian oil; repaid the producing provinces with prices under the world market price, thereby stimulating regional discontent; and failed to afford Canadian consumers much incentive to conserve supply. Having created a clientele for subsidy in eastern and central Canada, it proved politically onerous for the government to escape the effects of its generosity.

The oil export tax and even more the export cutbacks did not please the United States. As the State Department pointed out to a Canadian diplomat, the Canadian decision would "not be well understood" in the American Midwest and the New England states, "both heavily dependent on imported fuel oil and propane." Was there no possibility of rectifying this policy? To this the Canadian could only reply that "it would be futile to seek Canadian reconsideration."[8] As for the export tax, the U.S. administration was taken aback. William Casey, then undersecretary for economic affairs, told one of Nixon's aides that "he wished he could think of some way to counter the Canadian action of putting $1.40 export tax per barrel of oil"—but he couldn't.[9]

There is no doubt that these Canadian actions violated the continentalist expectations that the government of Canada itself had helped stimulate not more than two years before. They may even have transgressed the "special relationship." On the other hand, the United States had itself frozen prices from time to time and had not passed on the saving to its customers abroad. A convincing argument was made that Canada's supplies were relatively small in the larger American picture. That argument seems to have persuaded Nixon's temporary energy "czar," William Simon, when coupled with an assurance that border state Americans dependent on Canadian crude oil supplies would get their supplies that winter.[10] Success may have been its own justification when, in the opinion of Canadian officials juggling oil imports, Canada escaped serious oil shortages by the skin of its collective teeth in 1973–74. Natural gas, where there were long-term supply contracts covering 40 percent of Canadian production, was not included in the cutbacks.

There may nevertheless have been a long-term price to be paid by Canadians for consulting Canadian interests first, and exclusively. Politically the oil crisis brought Canadian-American energy relations from the purview of the executive into the domain of Congress. Congressmen and senators from the northern tier had in the past usually been boosters of good feelings along the border. It took little effort, required no knowledge, and exacted no pain to do so. Now it appeared that contrary to expectations the Canadians were being unreliable, if not unfriendly—foreign, in fact. If that were so, did it make sense for Canada to receive special or even favorable treatment? It was John Connally's question in 1971; others would echo it in the years to come. Some would go farther, clamoring for retaliation against Canada and its oil cutbacks.

The Trudeau government concluded that while its policy was self-evidently justifiable, it had not done enough to explain itself to Americans. Trudeau himself, on a visit to President Ford in December 1974, took time to mollify senators, including some of those who supported retaliation. The shifting balance between president and Congress after the Vietnam War suggested that direct diplomatic attention to congressional needs was advisable, and in the late 1970s, some was supplied. Such attentions would become a much more important factor in Canadian-American relations in the 1980s.

Between friends: Pierre Trudeau and Gerald Ford in Washington. Cartoon by Duncan Macpherson. *Reprinted by permission of the Toronto Star Syndicate.*

In other areas Canada sustained American energy initiatives. The Canadians supported the creation of an International Energy Agency in Paris, which Kissinger intended as a general staff for the developed countries in bargaining with the Organization of Petroleum Exporting Countries (OPEC). There was further bargaining over pipelines because of Canadian hopes to use Alaskan supply to piggyback Canadian long-distance wells. Nor was it forgotten that while oil reserves were falling, reserves of natural gas were rising, and with them Canadian hopes once again for a trade bonanza with the United States. There were complications between eastern and western Canadian provinces, as Ontario in particular sought its own assurances on security of supply and price, after which exports to the United States could be considered. There was even an agreement on pipelines in 1977, this time for a natural gas conduit along the Alaska Highway. It came to naught in a welter of complications, but not before Nixon had passed into Ford, and Ford had given way to Carter.[11]

Oil and gas were but one aspect of the energy question. There was still electricity, nuclear or hydroelectric. The first was the specialty of Ontario, the second of Quebec. Overall, electrical exports increased considerably in proportionate value, by 500 percent and more between 1965 and 1975.[12] Most of these figures were generated by short-term, peak-load contracts with American utilities, but by the later 1970s something new was creeping in.

The Liberal Bourassa government in Quebec undertook to expand the province's economy through electrical megaprojects in its underdeveloped north. Collectively known as the James Bay hydro project, Quebec's dams and generators produced electricity far in excess of the province's ability to use it. In 1965, Canada sold C$14.3 million worth of electricity to the United States; in 1975, C$104.3; and in 1985, C$1,408 million. Even allowing for inflation, this was a tidy sum, and much of it was accounted for by long-term contracts. Those contracts were largely Hydro Quebec's, the electricity arm of the provincial government and the standard-bearer of the modernization of the French-speaking sector of the province's economy. The flow of American dollars, Quebec's various governments believed, paid for the province's economic future and established an autonomous link between French-speaking Quebec and its American neighbors, a link that might just acquire political importance at some unspecified future date.

When, in November 1976, a separatist government was elected in the Province of Quebec, setting that date acquired a certain importance. It was the task of the Liberal government in Ottawa to prevent the date from ever occurring, and the object of the Parti Québécois government in Quebec City to bring it forward, as fast as possible. The United States could be of assistance to either side. Once again the attitude of the United States became a subject of the first importance in Canadian politics—or in Canada-Quebec relations, if Canada indeed fell apart.

THE UNITED STATES AND THE QUEBEC CONUNDRUM

Pierre Trudeau did not believe that Canada *would* fall apart. Separatism was a dead issue as far as he was concerned; it was important to get on with the real business of the country.

But observers were not so sure. Before 1976, the separatist Parti Québécois (PQ) was the official, legal opposition in the Quebec legislature, with a strong popular vote. It had every prospect of taking power as, in 1976, it did. Even relations between the pre-1976 Liberal government in Quebec City and the Liberal government in Ottawa were punctuated by jurisdictional battles. Relations between French- and English-speaking Canadians were uneasy. Many English Canadians feared that the federal government's policy of bilingualism in the civil service would deprive them of jobs and opportunity, while many French Canadians feared that even the French majority in Quebec would be drowned in a sea of English-speaking immigration. Quebec premier Bourassa passed through his legislature a law limiting the use of English and forcing immigrant children to attend French-language schools, but he neither calmed the fears of French-language nationalists nor soothed English-speakers. He

The language issue in Quebec. Cartoon by Aislin from the *Montreal Gazette.* Reprinted by permission of the *Toronto Star Syndicate.*

had other troubles as well, especially with a militant labor movement; 1976 was largely spent legislating disgruntled Quebec workers back to their jobs.

Bourassa feared for the future. Dreading what 1977 might bring, he called an early election for 15 November 1976 and lost. The separatist Parti Québécois became the government of Quebec. The PQ leader, René Lévesque, did not campaign on a platform of immediate secession from Canada. Instead, he promised good government, relief from Bourassa's troubled regime, and then a referendum to give the government a mandate to negotiate "sovereignty-association" (see Chapter 5) with the rest of Canada.

The prospect that Canada's second-largest province might secede or that Canada might collapse altogether had immediate repercussions. The Canadian dollar fell on international markets. Prime Minister Trudeau issued reassuring statements. It soon became clear that nothing sudden was about to happen. Lévesque would first consolidate his position with his own electors, in part by demonstrating that Quebec would be readily welcomed by the world and even by English-speakers as a newly sovereign state with no disruption to the province's economy and standard of living.

The United States was Quebec's second-largest trading partner, after the neighboring province of Ontario, and its principal source of funds. The construction of Hydro Quebec's northern megaproject, James Bay, depended on large amounts of American cash raised through bond issues in New York. Until 1976, Quebec's investment prospects were rated good, with apparently never a thought that the province might want to change its political status. Consequently Quebec and Quebec Hydro enjoyed an AA credit rating and paid a favorable rate of interest on their borrowings. The attitude of New York money managers would be important in the aftermath of the PQ victory.

So would be the attitude of the government of the United States. If Washington tipped its hand toward Quebec and indicated that a separate French-speaking state would be an acceptable outcome of the Canadian crisis, then Lévesque's prestige and prospects would soar. If, on the other hand, Washington remained aloof from Lévesque's cause or indicated a preference for Trudeau, the PQ's chances would diminish. Caution remained the hallmark of Quebec politics. As Lévesque and his advisers recognized, their voters would not be inclined to take too many chances, or risk too many changes.

There was some concern in Ottawa that the United States might not find a separate Quebec unwelcome. Some of Canada's policies in the 1970s had caused concern in Washington, and Trudeau's Liberals liked to think of themselves as fiercely independent of American pressures. Ottawa was quarreling with *Time* magazine over its tax status and warring with American border television stations over the appropriation of their programs, free of charge, by Canadian cable TV companies. The Foreign Investment Review Agency was screening American (and other foreign) investment for advantage to Canada. Logically (and Trudeau was logical) it would be easier for the United States to have its way with a disunited Canada. The Canadian government therefore sought reassurance in conversations with the United States ambassador, Thomas Enders, immediately after Lévesque's victory. "Does the United States really think a united Canada to be in its own interest?" the prime minister asked. Enders promised to seek instructions and report back.[13]

In Washington, the question was already being studied. Its conclusion, speedily arrived at, was that the partition of Canada was definitely not in the American interest. Quite the contrary: Its impact would be most unfortunate. Even if, in the outcome, the United States were able to pick off the best pieces of real estate (British Columbia and Alberta were sometimes mentioned), there would still be the question of what to do with the rest. In the late 1970s speculation about the absorption of Canada was not absent: how many states would Canada comprise, and what would it do to the Electoral College? Alternatively, Canada could emerge with two to ten independent ministates. And what if Canada proved to be not merely an unstable and quarrelsome series of ministates but a destabilizing example to *American* regionalists?

It was a consideration that had occurred to Enders, and it impressed others as well. "I even raised the question of whether the American union might not be adversely affected," Enders later explained. That was in addition to the loss of a stable and democratic ally, a force for security in the North Atlantic area, and the damage that separation would cause to a dynamic economic partner to the United States. No, Enders concluded, Quebec's separation was plainly not in the interest of the United States.[14]

The ambassador's view found no dissenters in the State Department. The question could now properly be referred to the political level, which in November–December 1976 meant the incoming Democrats, and Jimmy Carter. Carter was, Enders said, informed, and he approved an American policy that did nothing to encourage Lévesque or Quebec separatism. Publicly, nothing whatever would be said. Behind the scenes, Enders passed the word that the United States would be ill served by support for Quebec. He found fertile ground, especially at the *New York Times*, where James Reston, its Washington editor, proved to be an old friend of Canada and, by extension, of Canadian unity.[15]

Fortunately for Enders's analysis, Lévesque and company did little to encourage American support. A visit by the Quebec premier to New York in January 1977, during which he met bankers and investment dealers and addressed the Economics Club, was a bomb. Lévesque managed to convince his audience that in his hands Quebec would be a bad investment; Quebec bonds already cost 50 basis points more on the New York market than other Canadian securities. Although Quebec securities eventually recovered,[16] Lévesque learned that he and his government should not try too much. Perhaps as a result, the left wing of the PQ was considerably muted in the years to come.

Trudeau also paid a visit to the United States. In his case, he was received at the White House and addressed a joint session of Congress, arranged at the behest of President Carter. The speaker of the House of Representatives protested that the previous foreign orator, the president of Mexico, had attracted barely a couple of dozen listeners. His objection was met by a strenuous White House campaign to turn out the congressional troops for the occasion.

Carter and Trudeau got on famously. Both men liked to master their briefs; as autodidacts they could trade information and expertise and commune over policy questions. The president's entourage were lavish in their praise of the Canadian prime minister, who had, it seemed, struck all the right notes of modesty and frankness—and possibly flattery, since Trudeau had learned a good many lessons in that line since becoming prime minister in 1968.[17] Carter's secretary of state also took a helpful attitude—friendly to Canada, admittedly without knowing too much about the subject. That may have been one of Canada's strengths, according to the Canadian desk officer at the National Security Council: "you don't get taken too seriously," and therefore you did not raise expectations that could not be sastisfied.[18]

The head of the National Security Council under Carter, Zbigniew Brzezinski, knew considerably more than average about Canada. His father had been prewar Poland's consul general in Montreal, and young Brzezinski had been raised there. He had ambiguous feelings about Canada as a result. He had witnessed at first hand English-Canadian snobbery and superiority vis-à-vis French Canadians, and he understood French Canadians' sense of grievance at their place in Canada. As a Pole, Brzezinski had a lively appreciation of the power of nationalism; unlike Trudeau, he saw it as a positive force.

Brzezinski never seems to have exerted his feelings about Canada, or the inevitability of Quebec separation, to the point of influencing official American policy. He had, after all, other, more urgent preoccupations, and Canada was an area that set outside all but the most general "national security" considerations. Carter's own apparent liking for Trudeau and his preference for stable federal states (as a southerner he shared folk memories of unstable federal unions) in any case pushed policy to the point of all but explicit support for Trudeau's counterattack on René Lévesque and Quebec separatism. If he were a Canadian, Carter told the press, he would of course support a united country; but he wasn't, and he would never think of interfering.

Trudeau doubtless judged American interference on his side to be a double-edged sword. He was content to see the Americans rebuff Lévesque's attempts to make "official" or state visits to the United States, or to open quasi-diplomatic offices. Quebec had to be satisfied with what other provinces had—what was officially a tourism and trade promotion center in New York—even though it as staffed at a level that went considerably beyond the norm for Canadian provincial delegations.

The U.S. government, for its part, took a remarkably dispassionate long-term perspective on the problem of Canada and Quebec. Quebec nationalism was deep-seated, the State Department argued in August 1977. There was little that Trudeau could do to overcome it, and for Quebec to stay permanently in Canada, he or his successor would have to compromise, possibly by offering Quebec more powers or by devolving power to all ten Canadian provinces, so that Quebec would be no better treated than any other unit in the Canadian federation. Of course, such a solution might fatally weaken Canada without appeasing Quebec.

If Quebec did separate, both Washington and Ottawa would face a dilemma. In Washington's case, a new relationship with Quebec would have to be worked out, preserving as much as possible of the United States' existing interests in Quebec territory. As for the rest of Canada, the State Department was not so sure. The departure of Quebec might stimulate a drawing together of the remaining, English-speaking provinces, but it might also act as a signal to some of those on the periphery to pull out. "Once started, it is questionable whether the process could be stopped. Some of the provinces or regions would try it alone, some would seek some form of association with the U.S. The effect would be that the U.S. would be faced with either new responsibilities and/or opportunities, or a number of small and weak, although probably friendly, countries to the North."[19]

It was a prospect that Carter himself did not have to contemplate. In the short term, the existence of the Quebec problem in such an acute form probably dampened the Trudeau government's enthusiasm for further nationalist initiatives in its relations with the United States. Official summaries for the period are virtually unanimous that Canadian-American relations were good, even very good. Trudeau strongly supported the thrust of Carter's foreign policy, looking to further detente with the Soviet Union and a diminution of American exposure in sensitive areas, such as the Panama Canal treaty. When Carter negotiated and signed a Panama Canal treaty, Trudeau journeyed to Washington to be present at the ceremony—a tangible sign of appreciation and support.

A CONSERVATIVE INTERLUDE

At home in Canada, the 1976 election temporarily raised Trudeau's standing and popularity, but only temporarily. In 1979 his government, exhausted and paralyzed by internal and external problems, was defeated in a general election. It seemed that Canadians were tired of Trudeau and his confrontational approach to problems, whether it was Quebec or the economy or even the nature of Canadian federalism. The opposition Conservatives promised to do better, to turn Canada into "a community of communities." Their leader, Joe Clark, became prime minister in June 1979 at the head of a minority government. The balance of power was once again held by the NDP and the Creditistes, but the Conservatives expected it to be a short-term balance. People were so sick of Trudeau that Clark imagined they would soon turn his way. The Conservatives decided to go ahead and implement their platform as if they actually held a majority.

In Canadian-American relations the Clark government took no great initiatives. Clark was told that there were no truly serious problems between the two countries, although there were a great many minor ones. A dispute over maritime boundaries and fish on the East Coast had supposedly been solved by the signature of a treaty, but the treaty was being blocked by the U.S. Senate, where the senators from Rhode Island and Massachusetts had exerted their influence. Canadian energy supply remained tight, and Carter was warned not to expect much Canadian oil, despite the Iranian crisis. On multilateral topics, Carter could assume Canadian support, whether on strategic arms limitation, the Middle East, or Southern Africa.[20] Carter had nothing much to worry about from Canada; Clark, however, had to be concerned with Carter's declining political stature and his inability to manage Congress.

But Clark worried too much about the mote in his neighbor's eye. He had a beam in his own, as was shown when his government was defeated on its budget in the House of Commons in December 1979, at a time when the Conservatives were considerably behind the Liberals in the public opinion polls. Trudeau, who had resigned the Liberal leadership shortly before, returned to lead the Liberals in a general election set for February 1980.

While the campaign was on, a bizarre episode furnished the greatest publicity in a decade in Canadian-American relations. The Canadian embassy in Teheran gave shelter to six American diplomats who were fleeing their own embassy when Iranian militants stormed it. The Canadians disguised the Americans as Canadians, complete with passports, and smuggled them out of the country. Canada prudently closed its own embassy at the same time. The escape was almost the only good news for Carter in the whole Iranian crisis, and it briefly gave Canada a great deal of friendly publicity in the United States.

Canada's Iranian caper did not affect the outcome of the Canadian election. Joe Clark lost and Pierre Trudeau won, with a majority. The Liberals were back, without serious opposition in Ottawa, until 1984. The opposition, Trudeau knew, would come from outside, from his disgruntled opponents in the provinces. It would come, especially, from René Lévesque in Quebec, who had finally scheduled his referendum on "sovereignty-association" for May 1980.

Trudeau threw himself and his forces into a second election campaign, and he won, 60 percent to 40 percent. More comforting still, a bare majority of French Canadians had voted for Canada and against René Lévesque. The PQ would go on to win another provincial election in 1981, but its heart—its sovereignty policy—had been cut out. In the short term Canada was safe from Quebec separatism, and the United States would not have to dust off its scenarios for an independent French-speaking state north of Vermont.

CANADA'S NATIONAL ENERGY POLICY

Trudeau's Liberal government in Ottawa from 1980 to 1984 was determined to make its mark. The prime minister and his supporters were depressed by the thought that his first eleven years in power, 1968–79, had changed little. Now was a time for serious initiatives, and the Trudeau government had two in mind. The first was a serious reform of the Canadian constitution, to give Canadians for the first time an enforceable, constitutionally protected bill of rights (called the Charter of Rights and Freedoms) on the American model. The second was a reshaping of Canada's energy policy. Announced on 28 October 1980, the National Energy Policy (NEP) promised to reverse foreign ownership in the oil and gas industry, promote exploration and development in northern Canada, and secure a made-in-Canada oil program. It would also bring Canadian-American relations to their lowest ebb since 1945.

The roots of the NEP were anchored in the Canadian nationalist movements of the 1960s and 1970s. Suspicion and resentment of multinational corporations, especially in the oil and gas area, made the government yearn for a Canadian-controlled and Canadian-domiciled industry that it could more readily rely upon, and influence. Petro-Canada, the national oil company, was a step, but only a step.

The rise in oil prices during the 1970s and the apparent success of OPEC made the Canadian government—or at any rate certain planners within that government—think hard about ways and means to capture economic rents from oil and gas. The abrupt rise in prices in 1979 and 1980, from US$20 a barrel to US$32 a barrel in 1980 and even US$40 a barrel in 1981, sharpened the desire to catch up on the oil bonanza.

In the NEP, revenues from oil production would be redistributed, with the federal government getting more (29 percent) and oil companies and producing provinces getting proportionately less (36 percent and 35 percent, respectively). The existing oil companies would mostly be unhappy, because foreign-owned companies would be treated differently from Canadian-owned firms, which were given an inside track on special development grants. Moreover, the federal government proposed, retroactively, to assign itself a 25 percent interest in oil properties on federal lands. Only companies with 50 percent Canadian ownership would be allowed to produce oil on such lands. And the oil companies' grief would be nothing compared to the rage of the producing provinces, British Columbia, Saskatchewan and most important, Alberta. Their governments regarded oil revenues with a solitary, possessive eye. They had also elected no Liberals in 1980, a fact that apparently impressed Trudeau and his ministers not at all. Inside the Liberal cabinet and caucus, it meant that a possible brake, a safeguard, was missing.

The fact that the NEP was part of the Canadian budget may have guaranteed that it would reach the public in a relatively pristine form. The Canadian budget process is kept extremely secret, to eliminate any possible suspicion of leaks and insider information. It is not usually discussed even by the cabinet. While this process safeguards the purity and integrity of the resulting document, it also avoids positive political inputs and timely warnings of trouble to come. If a government is in a minority, it runs the risk of defeat or at best a humiliating compromise, such as occurred in 1963 over the nationalist proposals in Walter Gordon's budget; Joe Clark's government fell on its budget in 1979. But Trudeau, with a reliable majority, had no such fears.

What is certain is that those parts of the Canadian government that dealt regularly with the United States had no knowledge of the NEP before it was read out by the finance minister. Accounts differ as to whether anyone in External Affairs, apart from its minister, knew what was afoot, and even the minister was advised very late in the day. Some diplomats were distressed. Discrimination against foreign firms simply because they were foreign was not an easy position to defend.

Wall Street reacted first. "The recent budget set off a wave of hysteria on Wall Street, especially on the American Stock Exchange where energy stocks loom large," an American observer wrote.[21] The *Wall Street Journal* spoke darkly of a Canadian attempt to "hijack the Canadian investments of American oil companies."[22] Nor did the NEP impress the United States government. When the program was announced, the American embassy was in the hands of a lame duck, Kenneth Curtis, the Democratic ex-governor of Maine. Curtis, unlike Enders, was not a forceful presence in Ottawa; and since the Quebec referendum, circumstances had changed somewhat. Although the timing of the Canadian announcement was probably coincidental—it was part of the federal budget—it was convenient. President Carter himself was only days away from defeat in the presidential election, and it was altogether probable that the United States would be unable to come up with a coherent response for the next three months, until Carter's successor was inaugurated. American diplomats in Ottawa fumed, honed their arguments, and thought of better days. The arguments would be ready and waiting in January for the new administration.

What they had to say would certainly not have pleased the Canadian government. Canada, a developed society and a member of the summit seven club, was a paradox: the phrase of the day was "an industrialized country with third-world policies." They might have added, "with *popular* third world policies," because polls showed that 64 percent of Canadians approved Trudeau's policy of Canadianizing the oil and gas industry.[23]

Ronald Reagan's administration was prone to contradictions in its Canadian policy. The president himself liked Canadians without knowing much about them or their policies. His officials—cabinet officers and civil servants both—were aware that the president would not needlessly seek a quarrel with Canada, and that at one stage he even made establishing a tripartite relationship with Canada and Mexico a priority for his administration. That project, the "North American Accord," went nowhere in particular, except as a barometer of Reagan's general attitude to Canada. As a barometer, however, it had its uses, especially with those in Washington who stressed Canada's importance and uniqueness—its "special" character. Reagan in fact believed it *was* special—and that helped make it so.

Those uses negated the other fork of Reagan's Canadian policy, its ideological aspect. Right-wing Republicans were thicker on the ground in Washington than at any time since Herbert Hoover. They did not like Trudeau. Treasury Secretary Donald Regan considered the Canadian prime minister a socialist or at best a social democrat. The right-wing *National Review* denounced him as a leftist ideologue devoted to undermining international capitalism—and Reagan read the *National Review*. Even classical liberals had their doubts about Trudeau and Canada because of their attempts to twist the international system away from equality or treatment of investors, while benefitng from the unequal advantages of the Autopact—the Canada-as-a-"Third-World"-country syndrome.[24]

The first clash between pragmatism and ideology occurred early on. Reagan wished to make Canada his first visit abroad, and he wanted the visit to be successful or at least pleasant. The State Department had already been firing off letters of complaint to Canada about the unwholesome features of the National Energy Policy, with bits of the Foreign Investment Review Agency thrown in for good measure. The imminence of the Reagan visit was useful in getting a particularly strong note withdrawn—but only as to tone, as Secretary of State Alexander Haig carefully explained.

Reagan's visit to Ottawa went without a hitch as far as the president was concerned. He and Trudeau seized photo opportunities, with the prime minister characteristically confronting anti-Reagan demonstrators in front of the Canadian Parliament. All this was good footage on the American evening news. Behind the scenes, Trudeau concluded that a meeting of minds with Reagan was impossible since the president slid away from any serious policy discussion. When the Middle East situation was broached, for example, the president launched into a lengthy joke about two Israeli soldiers capturing the Egyptian Army (the punch line was, "Look, we're rich!"). "You should have seen Trudeau's face," an onlooker reported.

But it could have been worse—and as the summer of 1981 wore on, it got worse. When Ottawa proved stubborn, the State Department and other agencies began to consider, and even to preach, retaliation against Canada, perhaps by negating Canada's prized membership in the summit of seven leading industrialized countries. Consideration of a free trade offer to Canada, which had resurfaced inside the U.S. government, was postponed or canceled. The atmosphere between Washington and Ottawa got so bad that Reagan's ambassador, a political appointee from Chicago with good connections in the White House, personally appealed to the highest political level to allow things to cool down. He was successful; some minor Canadian concessions and the beginnings of a downturn in the price of oil did the rest.

There were a few more problems that surfaced because of American political animosity toward Trudeau. Some senators remembered and resented Trudeau's Canada-first policies in energy in the mid-1970s; the NEP was even more deplorable. They invited down to Washington one of Trudeau's most formidable domestic opponents, the premier of Alberta, to address them on his problems and then, at the instigation of the very right-wing Senator Jesse Helms of North Carolina, Trudeau's particular political rival, the separatist premier of Quebec, René Lévesque. Helms was a partisan of decentralization in the United States, and he may have felt an attraction toward this ultimate decentralist. Lévesque, who was once further to the left than Trudeau, took advantage of the occasion to explain to the American financial press that the Canadian prime minister was no better than an economic vandal. Americans could do much better, he explained, with him and his "continentalist" colleagues in Quebec, who believed firmly in a more closely linked North American economy. He did not add that they believed in such a link because it offered a salable alternative to an economic connection with the rest of Canada.[25] To Republican senators he allowed that Trudeau's energy policies were idiotic, and he promised that if Quebec became independent, it would join NATO. The visit complete, Lévesque returned to his northern fastness. There were no policy consequences, and little impression was made on the administration, but a certain poiint had been made that Canada's internal divisions could in some circumstances be exploited by American politicians.

The great issue of 1981–82, the NEP, soon lost its impetus. During 1982 the price of oil began to slide below the OPEC cartel price. This was bad news for Canada and for the Canadian investors who had put their faith and money behind the NEP. The NEP would work only if oil prices rose; if they fell, it became a kind of galloping disaster. They fell, and with them plummeted the fortunes of the Trudeau government. Inside the State Department, the mood was now to wait for events to take their course, as they did.

They did more. 1981–82 saw not only the reversal of OPEC's fortunes but a severe economic recession, the first Canada had known since the 1950s and the worst since the 1930s. Canada's gross national product declined by C$11 billion (constant dollars) between 1981 and 1982. Interest rates reached an all-time high, and Trudeau's voters began to look elsewhere.

Thoughtful observers in the Canadian business community took a hard look at the fruits of the Liberals' economic policies. Since 1980, and to some extent since 1970, Canada had tried to navigate its own course in the international economy. Relying on multilateral trade under GATT, Canada also sought to pursue its Third Option, the expansion of trade and trade contacts with the European Economic Community and Japan. Above all, the Third Option aimed to avoid too much reliance on the United States in trade. This was coupled with nationalistic policies designed to recapture control of strategic economic sectors, such as energy, from foreign investors, and to insure that Canadian resources, such as oil, served Canadians first.

By 1981, the Third Option was an admitted failure. The proportion of Canadian trade going to the United States rose, not fell, between 1971, the year of the Nixon démarche, and 1981. Canadian business showed little interest in stretching its resources to service a distant and doubtful European market. Officials felt that Canadian business was lamentably unenterprising, and business responded that government was regrettably academic and schematic. Both sides may well have been right. As one observer wrote, "Canadian industry is not generally competitive on a world scale . . . and thus there is no ready substitute for the U.S. market." Yet Canada depended on exports: 70 percent of its total industrial and agricultural production was exported in 1980.[26] The only clear result was embodied in the trade figures: 70 percent of Canadian exports flowed to the United States, and 68 percent of imports came from there. (The comparable American proportions were 16 percent and 17 percent.)

The NEP had done a little better in terms of its goal of raising the Canadian content of the oil and gas industry. There, 24 percent was Canadian-controlled in 1971, 62 percent in 1981, and 64 percent in 1984. With oil prices ratcheting down and Canada's high-cost oil sands and frontier oil fields passing beyond the realm of economic possibility, this was only a slight consolation. It was more than offset by the strain on Canada's balance of payments caused by financing the takeovers; this had a significant negative impact on the value of the Canadian dollar.

In 1980 the Trudeau government promised to expand FIRA's authority over new foreign investment. It was a controversial pledge, which made Canadians in investment-poor regions such as the Maritimes and Quebec nervous; their view, sustained by some academic studies, was that Canada might well suffer more economic loss in terms of forgone investment, rather than gain benefit from the FIRA process. Foreign direct investment had in fact plummeted after the implementation of investment review in 1974, and although it had recovered, there was concern that FIRA's effects were being seen in a lower price paid by investors for Canadian assets.[27]

The promised to beef up FIRA was short-lived. Under pressure from the United States, the Canadian government agreed that it would not expand FIRA. Nevertheless, the United States took Canada to the GATT tribunal in Geneva seeking remedies for concessions extracted from American investors in return for permission to expand or relocate in Canada.

In fact, the specter of foreign investment was becoming tired of its Canadian address. In 1981, C$3.56 billion returned to the United States from Canada, and in 1982, C$2.3 billion. The NEP made its own contribution to this by driving Canadian exploration rigs out of the country to the United States, but there was more to come. In an ironic reversal, in 1981 more money began to flow into the United States than poured out. Canada contributed C\$2.2 billion in 1980 and C\$3.1 billion in 1981.[28] It continued to flood in every year thereafter. Canadian money was in the vanguard, seeking more and better opportunities than were available at home. As foreign investment in the United States rose, Americans worried about their sovereignty and their immunity to foreign influences, just as Canadians had ten or twenty years before.

These figures made a powerful impression. In trade, the Trudeau government reversed course, starting in 1981. The Canadian government worried not only about the Canadian economy but about the American. Persistent American balance-of-payments problems, not to mention the blast of overseas competition, raised the possibility that American trade legislation would be tightened up. It might be a matter of prudence to slip under any future legislative net that Congress might devise to exclude foreign goods. It was still too much to contemplate asking the Americans for free trade, but Canadians began to study the possibility of sectoral free trade with the United States, starting in 1981. Sectoral free trade used the model of the Autopact, which was regarded as extraordinarily beneficial to Canada. The trouble was that the Autopact was the only example of sectoral free trade, and it existed only under a waiver from GATT that dated back to 1965. Nor was there any particular incentive for the United States in a sectoral free trade arrangement with Canada.

Nevertheless, sectoral free trade was tried on, almost as an intellectual exercise, in 1983–84. Canadian and American negotiators attempted to match American advantages with Canadian demands, only to draw a blank by June 1984, the month in which Trudeau finally retired. Sectoral free trade was stillborn, but it had a continuing influence. It symbolized a turning away from multilateral approaches and a return to bilateralism. More to the point, it signaled the bankruptcy of an entire set of policies that had characterized Canadian economic policy since the 1960s. As the State Department had predicted, it was a conclusion the Canadians had been able to reach entirely on their own. That they had done so was a measure of the leakage of confidence from the Canadian economy and the Canadian political system between 1980 and 1984. Canadians, it seemed, no longer had quite the faith in themselves and their autonomous destiny that they once did. That this was so offered the United States an unusual latitude in its policy options in 1984. While it held out the possibility of benefit, there was also the possibility of political risk if not instability if Canadian self-confidence continued to dissipate. But that would be a matter for the Canadian government after Trudeau—and Ronald Reagan's second administration—to decide.

LOVE THIS PLANET

The 1970s and 1980s witnessed the growth in importance of a number of apparently novel issues in Canadian-American relations. There were disagreements enough, particularly between 1980 and 1984, on a wide variety of topics, from Third World developments to Central America to the Law of the Sea to disarmament and peace. Just at the end of his term, in 1983–84, Pierre Trudeau even took to the skies in a last-minute fly-around designed to promote world peace, which he judged was in danger from Ronald Reagan, Yuri Andropov, and Star Wars. (He still found it possible to authorize American cruise missile tests over Canada's icy landscape, so similar—it was hoped—to Siberia.)

These developments took their toll. Each issue had its constituency, both in Canada and in the United States, but in the end singly and collectively they were relatively abstract. Far less abstract, but just as intractable, was a set of difficulties that fell under the general heading of the environment.

The emergence of an environmental movement in Canada was closely modeled on—and even derived from—similar movements in the United States. A sense of a shared heritage and shared values found expression in the national parks systems in both countries and in parallel concerns for conservation north and south of the border. The International Joint Commission created in 1909 had established a joint responsibility for managing the environment along the border. As early as 1918 the IJC had pronounced on the seriousness of pollution in the Great Lakes basin and had proposed an ambitious transnational regime to clean it up. The idea was so ambitious that it was promptly buried, and pollution went on unchecked. Further west, in the 1930s, the United States was able to prove that airborne damage had been caused to American property by a Canadian polluter, the smelter at Trail, British Columbia. Damages were awarded, and a precedent created. Yet Trail was a particularly flagrant and apparently isolated example.

Pollution of the less immediately visible kind was tolerated in the interest of the greater good of the greater number—a good that was usually interpreted to favor industrial growth. Victory in war, progress, and jobs all depended on accepting a certain amount of pollution, and measurements of pollution were limited, crude, and imprecise. On the Niagara frontier, to take one example, chemical companies buried their byproducts while the products went on to feed the war effort or the postwar industrial machine. Explosives, pesticides, and fertilizers were the currency of the industrial age; their necessity was measured by cost-benefit ratio. Workers who were paid from the proceeds built their homes on top of the dumpsites by the Love Canal. All of this took place inside the boundaries of the United States (or elsewhere along the border of Canada) even if some of the consequences were separated from the international boundary by only a few yards of earth, concrete, and luck.

The publication in 1963 of Rachel Carson's *Silent Spring*, on the unintended effects of pesticides, set enthusiasm for the environment in motion, along different lines from the past. Canada established a Department of the Environment in 1971; the United Nations pondered the subject in a conference in Stockholm in 1972; and other events, official and unofficial, sped the movement along.

Two aspects of pollution came to concern Canada and the United States. The airborne variety was well known, but it had been assumed to be limited or specific in source and effects. Waterborne pollution had many parents, communities and industries up and down the Great Lakes basin, or along the many streams snaking across the forty-ninth parallel or the Maine boundary. The pollution could be spectacular, most vividly when a river in Cleveland, Ohio, actually caught fire. The two forms of pollution were not far apart: it was widely known that what traveled in the air must eventually come down, in the form of rain—acid rain.

The term first appeared in general use around 1975. According to a 1977 magazine article, "It dissolves concrete, rusts cars, kills fish and stunts tree growth by up to 60%. And it comes disguised in gently falling rain. . . . *It is acid rain, the latest environmental shocker.*"[29] Acid rain derived from coal-fired thermal generating stations, mostly American, and smelters, mostly Canadian, and was produced by the combination of water with sulphur oxide or nitrogen oxide. Falling on freshwater lakes or northeastern forests, it destroyed vegetation. It was not hard to project a future without fish or forest or, in economic terms, without tourism or lumber. That linkage was firmly made by the late 1970s, and from that point acid rain had a growing negative constituency in the northeastern states and eastern Canada. By the same token, the issue attracted no support in states that produced coal. Overall, the public was undecided; the very novelty of the subject made it difficult to remedy by the usual political means.

Water pollution, the more traditional nuisance, was dealt with under a Great Lakes Water Quality Agreement, signed in Ottawa in 1972 and updated in 1978. The agreement established a Great Lakes Water Quality Board with representatives from adjacent states and provinces, as well as the two federal governments, with an office in Windsor, Ontario. The agreement, in conjunction with the American Water Pollution Control Act, seems to have been efficacious. By 1975, 60 percent of the population on the U.S. side of the Great Lakes was served by "adequate" sewage treatment facilities, and 97 percent on the Canadian side—up from 60 percent in 1971.[30] A dispute between president and Congress over funds delayed progress somewhat: only after Nixon's departure from office was the necessary money made available. The very extent of Great Lakes pollution made solutions expensive and time-consuming, always subject to budgetary vagaries. But on the whole, progress was made, and the Great Lakes "lived" long after several of them were considered "dead."

A second water pollution issue was equally time-consuming because it involved several novel concepts for which it proved hard to find a satisfactory solution; and because of the local interests involved, a remedy was long delayed. The Garrison Water Diversion project, as it was known, proposed, among other things, to bring water to parched areas of North Dakota by linking the Red River (flowing north) and Mississippi River (flowing south) systems. According to environmentalists, that posed a hazard to the purer

The water pollution issue along the border. Cartoon by Ed McNally.

northern stream by introducing southern organisms. North Dakota supported the idea, while neighboring Manitoba opposed it. Presidents dithered, boards investigated, and time passed; a solution was not found until 1984, when it was decided that Garrison could be partly built, but not so as to affect the ecosystem of the Red River basin. Between 1975 and 1984, the Garrison Dam appeared ominously on most high-level agendas between Canada and the United States. That it was eventually solved, and under Reagan, was a triumph of a sort.

That left acid rain. The midwestern states, coal producers and utilities, and their friends in Congress displayed an entirely understandable nervousness on the subject. Like the St. Lawrence Seaway thirty years earlier, acid rain pitted the interests of one region against another's, with stalemate as the result. The Reagan administration was doctrinally as well as politically reluctant to act; the president was even said to believe that trees were more the cause than the victims of pollution. ("Look, killer trees," his press secretary cried out as the campaign plane flew over Colorado forests.)

Since the American administration was disinclined to move on the subject, the Canadian government decided to appeal to the American public and to its friends in Congress. But while Canadian ministers—particularly John Roberts, minister of the environment—made friends and established alliances, they were never enough. By 1984, acid rain had not moved off dead center, and in the east the rain continued to fall. This was a topic that had to be taken up by the next government.

FAREWELL TO TRUDEAU

"We put up with Trudeau for so long," one American official lamented. But Trudeau went at a time of his own choosing, after a walk in a February blizzard in Ottawa. He left behind a mixed record in Canadian-American relations. He had managed well enough with three out of the five presidents with whose terms his term overlapped. Johnson had barely mattered; Nixon he had regarded, finally, as impressive; Ford and Kissinger had been an active pleasure; and Carter was a made whose policies he respected, although he had found the personality difficult. Even with Reagan, for whose intellect Trudeau had no respect, the record was neither bleak nor unfruitful. Trudeau was professional enough to do his duty when required, or reminded; his officials and their American counterparts made sure of that.

"We got a problem," Reagan's aid Michael Deaver once told the Canadian ambassador, "Your guy and my guy are not getting along." Since it was important that they "get along," Trudeau promptly issued the requisite reassurances to Reagan, or perhaps more important, to Reagan's immediate entourage. With that wrinkle ironed out, relations could proceed, as they had for the previous fourteen years, cordially but at arm's length.

Circumstances dictated no less and no more. In Trudeau's time in office, Canadian self-perception fluctuated wildly. As always, Canadians fashioned their vision of themselves and their country in relation to the United States. The 1970s were a period when Canada was self-consciously "different" from the United States, when Canadian preoccupations and politics sought alternatives to the model offered by Americans. The result was, in many ways, quite distinct. Canadian politicians spent their money differently—on social welfare—not to mention their time, frequently quarreling among themselves as to what kind of society an independent Canada really ought to be.

No American government of the period made Canada a priority; even for Carter, relations with Canada meant that he wanted to keep his attic and perhaps his upstairs guest room ship-shape. Occasional guests from Canada were welcomed, but also kept distant and pleasant, like third cousins once removed. As a consequence, there was little pressure on Canada to conform to American wishes or American models.

Yet at the end of the Trudeau period, Canadians were beginning to think that for too long they had ignored what the United States might have to offer. That was to some degree because Canadians lost confidence in themselves and in their country during the 1981–82 recession. Trudeau's policies— nationalist and statist—had been tried, and the results had been found wanting. It was, possibly, time for something new.

chapter 7

FREE TRADE AND ITS DISCONTENTS

In September 1985 the Canadian cabinet held a planning session at Meech Lake, a government conference house just outside Ottawa. The house was grand, a millionaire's cottage from the turn of the century, but grander outside than in, where whatever charm it once had gave way to civil service durability. Collapsible tables, coffee urns, plastic, and Naugahyde set the tone. It was, however, both convenient and isolated, and Conservative Prime Minister Brian Mulroney appreciated both points.

It was the beginning of Mulroney's second year in office, and he had a problem. His administration was mired in scandal, and it badly needed a new direction. Just over a year before, Mulroney had led the Conservatives to a smashing victory over the demoralized Liberals under Trudeau's successor, John Turner. Turner now led a decimated opposition, unable seriously to oppose whatever Mulroney and the Conservatives might propose. Liberalism was out of fashion, in Canada as in the United States, Great Britain, and even continental Europe. The wisdom of the day held that markets should be free, and across the Western world governments loudly proclaimed that they would draw in their horns and reduced expenditures and taxes.

Everywhere, that is, but Canada. The Canadian government—and Canada's provincial governments too—were running large deficits. The solution was to borrow more and tax more, in the hope of finding a balance at some later date, always postponed. Economics was very much the obsession of the Mulroney government, although it had some subsidiary concerns as well. The contention and antagonism of the Trudeau era had contributed heavily to the Liberals' defeat in 1984. Mulroney promised to do better, but could he keep

139

his promise? It was high time to bring Quebec separatists—the people Trudeau had defeated in the 1980 Quebec referendum—back into the Canadian political mainstream. They found a ready welcome in the Conservative party. Naturally they got jobs, some in the cabinet, but they also got influence and, with influence, the chance to implement their point of view.

There was a price, however, for the Quebeckers' support. Rather than accepting Canada on its terms, especially as those terms had been defined by Trudeau, they wanted to get Canada to take them on theirs—conditions that would involve a substantial devolution of authority away from the central government and toward the provinces. In return, in 1984 the Conservatives swept Quebec. For the first time in many years, Quebec nationalism's viewpoint would be expressed inside the federal cabinet. A reduction in federal power was therefore indicated.

That accorded well with Mulroney's second conciliatory thrust—dismantling Trudeau's complex of government enterprise and regulation, for example over oil and gas, which had been so obnoxious to the governments of Canada's three westernmost provinces, British Columbia, Saskatchewan, and especially, Alberta.

There was a third leg to Mulroney's policy tripod: He wanted to conciliate the United States. Relations with the Americans had suffered under Trudeau, as anyone could see; as Mulroney put it, the Liberals had treated Americans "like enemies, barraged them with insults, never gave them the benefit of the doubt, and then wondered why we never got along." Mulroney's election was greeted in Washington with ill-disguised pleasure. "We are on the way to recreating the 'special relationship,' " according to the assistant secretary in charge of European and Canadian affairs in the State Department.[1] That was important to Mulroney and his cabinet that day in September 1985. His next initiative in relations with the United States would, he hoped, tie all his programs together, crowning and guaranteeing his government's political success in time for the next Canadian election in 1988 or 1989. That was the issue that had now brought them all together in Meech Lake, and they would not leave without resolving it. For Mulroney had on his agenda nothing less than a reversal of Canada's basic economic policy, the protectionist wall around the Canadian economy that dated from 1879. He wanted to negotiate free trade with the United States.

This should have come as no surprise. "Good relations, super relations with the United States will be the cornerstone of our policy," Mulroney had proclaimed, and he set out to make it so. He had met Reagan as leader of the opposition in June 1984 and again immediately after taking office in September. Mulroney made a highly positive impression, "young, dynamic, good looking, dramatic," according to one observer. "The sky was the limit to what he could do for the economy. He could also work out the problems with the provinces, he could provide an integrated political Canada."[2] In September, the prime minister and the president agreed to meet at least once a year

Canadian nationalists considered Brian Mulroney slavishly pro-American. Cartoon by Aislin from the *Montreal Gazette*. *Reprinted by permission of the Toronto Star Syndicate.*

in future, with the next get-together set for Quebec City in March 1985. Speaking to the Economics Club in New York, the same body to which Lévesque had delivered his bomb in 1977, the prime minister stated that both FIRA and the NEP were on the way out.[3] As indeed they were. FIRA was replaced by Investment Canada, whose job it was to encourage foreign investment, while the NEP was gone—lock, stock, and taxes—by the end of 1985.

In defense policy, a major American concern and complaint, Mulroney promised to spend more. That was harder to do than it seemed, because the Canadian budgetary deficit had reached alarming proportions. Under Trudeau, Canada refused to participate in Reagan's Strategic Defense Initiative, better known as Star Wars; under Mulroney, ministers contradicted one another freely as to whether Canada had reconsidered. Joe Clark, Mulroney's minister for external affairs, worried that Star Wars might become a litmus test by which the Canadian people would judge the Conservatives' foreign policy. If Mulroney went too far in accommodating the Americans, would he not be accused of subservience?[4]

The prime minister worked out a deft compromise. His government would not participate in Star Wars, but if private Canadian firms wanted to, he would not stand in their way. It was a mild distancing from Washington's, and Reagan's, enthusiasms, which had the merit that it did not appear to disturb Reagan in any way. Mulroney needed the credit because he was simultaneously dealing with another transarctic expedition along the Northwest Passage, this time by a U.S. Coast Guard icebreaker, the *Polar Sea.*

The *Polar Sea's* Arctic voyage naturally conformed to the American doctrine that Arctic waters were international and not subject to regulation by Canada. On the official level, it was agreed that the voyage would not prejudice either country's claims about the passage in international law, and Canadian officials went along for the ride. Nevertheless, the Mulroney government's complaisance irritated Canadian observers. "We have come out of this looking like a bunch of clowns," one said. "I think the way this has been handled has been a farce, a fiasco." The new American ambassador to Canada, Thomas Niles, admitted that the affair could have been better handled on both sides.[5] He may have done so because there was by then something much more important on the Canadian-American agenda.

FREEING TRADE

That something was trade and trade relations. It was not an area in which Canada or the United States felt especially secure by the mid-1980s. The 1981–82 recession, which had reduced Canada's gross national product, had also diminished Canadians' propensity to import, resulting in a large trade surplus with the United States (C$11 billion in 1982, and C$13.7 billion in 1983, up from C$0.6 bilion in 1979[6]). Canada's trade surplus was a part, admittedly only a part, of the United States' trade deficit of US$67.1 billion in 1983.

Reaction to the trade deficit inside the United States was gloomy, if contradictory. Americans loved to buy Japanese products, yet they hated their growing deficit in trade with Japan. According to pollster Lou Harris, almost 60 percent of Americans wished to restrict Japanese products, unless of course they were made in the United States by American labor.[7] Although polls showed that Americans preferred open trade, on a reciprocal basis, congressmen had no difficulty in perceiving a cautionary note. If a local industry was being gored, protection was called for.

Protection was anathema to the Reagan administration, as it had been to its predecessors since 1945. "The consistent goal of the president was free trade," economist James Niskanen wrote, "both in the United States and abroad." The best way to reach that goal, however, was to survive, and the best way to survive politically was to make concessions to Congress on trade restrictions, "a strategic retreat," as Niskanen put it.[8] Others put it less kindly: Muddle, not management, was the Reagan style with Congress.

As the United States' largest trading partner, Canada was vulnerable whenever the administration decided to take backward steps in defense of free trade. American television broadcast the bad news north: plant closings, money-losing businesses, desperate towns in the "rust belt" just south of the U.S.-Canadian border. There was an uncomfortable awareness that with a common geography came similar natural products: wood, for example, or wheat. Manufacturing was another potentially contentious area. Although the Autopact insulated automobile trade to some extent, its bases were eroding with every percentage point of increased sales of Japanese cars. Canadian autoworkers, under nationalist leadership, took themselves out of the "international" United Autoworkers. Although union cooperation had not functioned too well before, there was no reason that it would be any better after the split.

Other unions faced similar problems, though with not quite the same solution. The United Steelworkers actually chose a Canadian as its "international" president. His credentials, however, had been largely earned in the United States, and he had to mount a vigorous campaign to persuade his members that he would not sell out their interests. It was a sign, although less decisive than with the Autoworkers, that Canadian-American trading relations could easily fall prey to competing nationalisms.

The sense of apprehension was combined with a sense of limitations. The Trudeau government had tried and failed with its "third option." For lack of an external trade strategy, it made do with an internal nationalism, attempting to imbue all parts of the country with a belief in a common purpose and destiny sufficient to override regional and provincial concerns. To that end Trudeau had appointed a royal commission "on the economic union and development prospects for Canada" in 1982, with a former Liberal finance minister, Donald Macdonald, at its helm. As the commission's title suggests, Trudeau expected the commission to concentrate on "union," but it soon veered toward "development prospects" instead.

Macdonald was expected to be orthodox. His background as a Trudeauvian Liberal and his nationalist past (he had been a disciple of Walter Gordon) suggested the direction his thought might take. But Macdonald had a knack for learning from experience and varying his opinions as he learned. One thing he had experienced, as finance minister, was the Third Option's failure to impress either the Europeans or the Japanese. A "contractual link" laboriously negotiated between Canada and Europe had gone nowhere. Canadian monetary policy already mimicked that of the United States; some foreigners observed that it was the U.S. Federal Reserve Board, not the Bank of Canada, that really controlled Canadian interest rates. Not officially, of course: but as the governor of the Bank of Canada was prone to observe, when the United States caught cold, Canada sneezed. It followed that Canada took a bit more interest-rate medicine than the United States, to keep investors happy and dollars flowing north, and when the United States changed its prescription, Canada did likewise.

It was time to try something new and fresh. Everything else had been tried and had failed. Multilateral talks were bogged down and in any case had a doubtful longer-term future; why not free trade with the United States? It was supported by a considerable body of respectable opinion in Canada, including most professional economists. One prediction, commonly held, was that free trade with the United States might increase Canada's gross national product by as much as 10 percent. Though this opinion dwindled over time, the margin for free trade was nevertheless considered positive. Some free-trading academic economists, plus a few from the civil service, were serving on Macdonald's commission.

In November 1984, Macdonald took the plunge. At an ostensibly closed conference in Harriman, New York, he explained to his largely American audience that Canadians had been fearful of "putting in jeopardy" their "rather fragile structure of national sovereignty." Macdonald respected those fears, but it was time to put them aside. "If we get down to the point where it's going to be a leap of faith, then I think at some point some Canadians are going to have to be bold and say, yes, we will do that."[9]

Macdonald spoke for many Canadians. The Canadian Manufacturers' Association had once been viligant against the possibility of free trade with the United States, but by 1984 it was viligant no longer. In 1980, its members had divided evenly on the idea—one-third for, one-third against, and one-third undecided. By the winter of 1984–85, more than three-quarters were for. U.S. investment was rising in popularity, too, or more precisely, opposition to it was falling, down to 50 percent from 67 percent in 1981. One of Trudeau's most nationalist former colleagues sold his company to an American firm, while another, an architect of the NEP, could be found advising Chevron, the American oil company.[10] In public opinion surveys on free trade with the United States, Canadians expressed the opinion that they would be better off in such a circumstance, and a 1983 poll showed large margins everywhere but Ontario and the prairie provinces.

The downward trend of the Canadian tariff also affected the attitudes of formerly protected industries. According to the head of Canadian DuPont, "the tariffs in Canada are no longer high enough to offset the higher costs of producing solely for the Canadian market. On the other hand, even modest tariffs into the U.S. can make it difficult, if not impossible, to set up production in Canada to export into that market." American nontariff barriers— "contingent protection" such as countervailing duties on subsidized imports— added uncertainty and by that token decreased investment prospects in Canada: "Secure access to the American market is mandatory."[11]

Prime Minister Mulroney was not, by conviction or instinct, a free trader. He had even pronouced against it in the past. Yet he liked American business and the jobs that it brought—his father's among them, back in his home town of Baie Comeau, Quebec. There was much to think about. When Mulroney and Reagan met in Quebec City on 17–18 March 1985, the time was ripe for closer relations. Publicly, the two men posed for photographers and attended, with their wives, a cultural evening at a theater. Television viewers long remembered an enthusiastic Mulroney pulling a somewhat embarrassed Reagan onstage for a St. Patrick's Day chorus of "When Irish Eyes Are Smiling." Many concluded from the display that nothing serious could have happened during the meeting, but that was not the case.

Mulroney and Reagan had agreed to examine the possibility of bilateral trade negotiations. Mulroney knew the idea was attractive to Canadian businessmen. He used the spring and summer to ventilate it across the country via a parliamentary committee. The cabinet considered the matter on 6 September 1985. Mulroney proposed that Canada approach the United States to negotiate free trade: Were ministers for or against? Joe Clark, minister of external affairs, suggested that this was a matter requiring some thought and some discussion. Perhaps some special meetings could be scheduled? Mulroney thought not. The cabinet had to decide on a strict up-or-down basis, and it decided up. On 26 September, Mulroney told Parliament that he had that same day phoned Reagan to ask that negotiations begin.

American trade law allowed the president to use a "fast track" to conclude trade agreements. The fast track procedure placed a series of time limits on trade negotiations: sixty days to get approval from Congress for the procedure to be used; then the clock started ticking to spure negotiators toward an inexorable deadline. In return, there was a limit to what Congress could do to a treaty negotiated under the procedure.

There was a momentary pause. Reagan was a very popular president, but he seemed unable to translate his popularity into an effective partnership with Congress. He was, moreover, a lame-duck president, and Republicans in the House and Senate were well aware of the limits of Reagan's power. Canada was hardly in the forefront of Washington's attention, but there were plenty of politicians who were searching for an opportunity to embarrass the president, as well as a few who had specific grievances against Canada or Canadian exports. As one experienced onlooker put it, "When Canada started on this course, it did not realize what it was getting into, how people might want to bite back. . . . They got a consensus at home but did not stop to ask, what about south of the border?"[12] There were interests in the United States, mostly in the natural resources sector, hostile to expanding Canadian trade, and there were irritants that might at any point explode. The United States' vast trade deficit was not improving, contrary to expectations—another point of administration weakness and a spur to protectionists. That, plus Reagan's relaxed attitude toward congressional infighting, made Canada vulnerable. It had taken years for Canadian-American relations to exorcise the ghost of the failed 1911 trade agreement; if the 1985 process failed, it would take years more.

The two countries appointed chief negotiators: the Americans Peter Murphy, a youngish trade official, and the Canadians Simon Reisman, an abrasive veteran of forty years of trade negotiations. "The Americans appointed somebody who couldn't talk, and the Canadian somebody who wouldn't listen," a bystander quipped. They also appointed very different sized teams. Canada's was large and varied; it immediately took over lavish office space in a downtown Ottawa office tower. The United States' was much smaller, though in a pinch it could draw in extra help.

The negotiations attracted very considerable attention in Canada—and very little in the United States. Nobody was particularly surprised that the talks proved lengthy and complicated, stretching on into the spring, then summer of 1987. Outsiders, especially in Canada, would have been very surprised to learn that the talks were going nowhere.

The reason was not hard to find. Canada was the *demandeur*, in diplomatic jargon—the beggar at the feast. To the American side, that suggested a fairly hard line, in expectation of eventual Canadian concessions. Public opinion in the United States was not engaged by the issue, and even in Washington a Canadian trade deal was appealing mostly because it set a good example for other nations to follow and demonstrated American good intentions for all to see. These considerations were laudable, but not strong.

The Canadian side expected some initial opposition; eventually, however, it expected that its mastery of detail would surely tell in Canada's favor. There were limits to what could be conceded. While the negotiations were proceeding, several spectacular battles over varieties of Canadian wood exports to the United States were resolved to Canada's disadvantage by an administration under pressure to help western Republican senators and congressmen. Restricting Canadian imports would do little good to the United States, but it would help the administration beat back worse demands in trade legislation that was then pending. "It was shoving raw meat at Congress," according to an interested bystander. [13]

The surface issue was subsidies and what qualified as a subsidy; a subsidiary concern was the complexity and expense of defending, again and again, Canadian exports in an American trade court where Congress made and remade the rules and the administration imposed couuntervailing duties against purported (and sometimes actual) subsidies. All this put pressure on the Canadian negotiators and the Mulroney government. Reagan sent Vice President George Bush north to explain matters, and Bush did his best. But on the main issue, relief from trade complaints, there was little he or the president could do.

The Canadian trade negotiators still expected progress in the talks, but that did not happen. Talks dragged along through the winter and spring of 1987, then through a painful summer. The Canadians raised issues, and the Americans evaded them. Time was the Americans' ally and delay their instrument. Minor agreements were reached, but divergences between the Canadian and

Many Canadians feared that free trade would miss the mark. Cartoon by Aislin from the *Montreal Gazette*. *Reprinted by permission of the Toronto Star Syndicate.*

American negotiators became more evident. The Canadians wanted a comprehensive agreement, a true agreement in principle, that would provide a disputes-settlement mechanism for the future and avoid repeating the trade embarrassments of the past; the Americans wanted to patch up existing grievances. There was no reconciling the two, and that fact gave the negotiations an unusual character. Instead of becoming engaged in a joint enterprise working toward a commonly understood goal, the two delegations were usually at cross-purposes. The Americans apparently believed that when the final crunch came, the Canadians would see things their way. The Canadians decided that an agreement on American terms would be worse than no agreement at all.

The deadline under the "fast track" was 3 October, but neither side was able to budge. In September 1987 negotiations reached an impasse. The Canadian team staged a televised walkout (televised only in Canada, of course). Relations between Reisman and Murphy could by then charitably be described as bad; bad as they were, they masked the fact that neither negotiator had the authority to make the concessions that the other side deemed crucial. The problem was booted up to the ministerial level. Mulroney put his chief of staff in effective (though not nominal) charge of the Canadian case, and the case was made to Reagan's chief of staff and the secretary of the treasury.

What emerged on 3 October, shortly before midnight, was the shell of an agreement. There would be free trade, phased in over ten years. Existing trade laws, including the controversial countervail process penalizing imports deemed to be subsidized, would continue to apply, but they would be subject to review by a binational panel to determine whether the law was being fairly applied. The two countries gave themselves seven years to negotiate the definition of a subsidy and a solution to the countervail problem it spawned. Future American trade laws would not apply to Canada unless Canada was specifically mentioned in the legislation—a specific against the rampant imagination and creativity of protectionist legislators. How effective this remedy would be, only time would tell. Finally, the two countries adopted what might be called an anti-NEP clause, which provided that the effects of future energy cuts would be prorated according to enduring export patterns. In other words, Canada would not in the future be able to restrict Canadian gas, oil, or electricity to Canada alone if a market already existed in the United States.

Opinions were not lacking. Opponents claimed that the effects of the Free Trade Agreement (immediately baptized the FTA) would be far-reaching and negative. The most perceptive pointed out that the agreement was a time bomb and that the Canadian government had traded the abolition of tariffs for a promise to negotiate, in the future, the true meaning of subsidies and therefore the applicability of countervail. While the tariff barriers were gone, the nontariff barriers were very much present and continuing. Almost 120 years of Canadian protection were being dismantled, and it was hard not to imagine that there would be dislocations as a result. Supporters conceded the point but argued that job formation would far outweight job destruction, even if some Canadian industries—furniture, for example—were likely headed for the scrap heap. American subsidiaries in Canada, established to get around the tariff, would close.

The crucial question of defining subsidies was left open. What if a subsidy were defined to include social benefits, such as Canadian universal health insurance? To that point, the American ambassador replied that Canada was as much a model to the United States as the United States was to Canada. What if Americans were to see the light and adopt Canadian-style health insurance? But there was worry nevertheless. Americans, many Canadians believed, had a tendency to assume that the American way was the only proper one and that deviations were unwholesome, if not illegal. The free trade negotiators vigorously denied that the deal meant any such thing.

Prime Minister Mulroney was, needless to say, pleased. All told, 1987 was a good year. He had free trade and improved relations with the United States. He also, in June, had made an agreement with the new Liberal government of Quebec (under a retreaded premier Bourassa) and all the other provinces to settle immediately outstanding issues in Canadian federalism by devolving further powers to all the provinces, thereby avoiding "special status" for Quebec.

Free trade was obviously less important for President Reagan. To be sure, Canada was not unimportant in his scheme of things. Mulroney reminded him that Canada was a nonthreatening neighbor in more ways than one—stable, peaceful, and prosperous—and his actions showed that his government was remarkably pro-American. Canada was like Reagan's home state of California—it had about the same population and the same gross domestic product. These factors helped in explaining Canada to the president, who could grapple with familiar magnitudes. Because the president was a free trader by conviction, free trade with Canada was no problem, either for him or his administration. "It fit in ideally with what we [were] trying to do internationally," a treasury official enthused. And at home, free trade with Canada kept protectionist forces at bay and off balance.[14]

Free trade was predicted to have a rough ride in the U.S. Congress. The votes were sometimes close and difficult, but in the end free trade was accepted. The main debate was expected to be within Canada, and it was.

Mulroney introduced the FTA to the House of Commons on May 30, 1988. He had the business community on his side, he knew. Less publicly, he had most of the senior civil service and most newspapers on his side as well. Regionally, Quebec's Premier Bourassa and all the western premiers strongly advocated free trade.

That put Bourassa, a Liberal, at variance with the national Liberal party and its leader, John Turner. Turner announced his position in October 1987: "We did not negotiate the deal, we are not bound by the deal, and if the deal and the final contract reflects the principles and general terms of the agreement we have seen, we are going to tear the deal up."[15] Free trade was a sellout of Canadian interests and a threat to Canada's political integrity, he argued. Under Mulroney's agreement the Ottawa government would forever play second fiddle in an American band. When economic sovereignty went, Turner told the country, political sovereignty would soon follow. Some Liberals darkly suspected that that was what Premier Bourassa had in mind: the next stage in the dissolution of Canada by emasculating Ottawa of another of its powers. Mulroney found it hard to take Turner seriously. Free trade was apparently popular, supported by 50 percent of Canadians, and he expected it would become more popular still. "This guy is gone. He's finished. He can't win an election," the prime minister told his deskmate in the House of Commons.[16]

Free trade easily passed the House of Commons on 22 June and moved on to the Senate, an appointed body dominated by holdovers from the Trudeau years. The Senate proceeded deliberately—very deliberately. Its proceedings dragged through the summer, and as time passed, public opinion shifted toward an even balance on free trade.

Mulroney still had certain advantages. The timing of an election was his to choose. His party was united and very well financed. Though pollsters detected some problems with the prime minister's image, things were worse with opposition leader Turner. Turner's Liberal party was divided over Mulroney's constitutional settlement, and quarrelsome. The anti–free trade vote would be split between the Liberals and the NDP, and in the Canadian political system the winner in a constituency does not need a majority—merely to be first past the post.

The election was announced on 1 October and set for 21 November. At first it proceeded as if Mulroney had scripted the entire show, including the opposition. Turner made eloquent speeches, and no one listened. The Conservatives cruised while the Liberals stumbled, and the NDP slogged along, hoping to pick up enough votes replace the Liberals as the principal opposition party. No leader was really liked or trusted, polls showed, but Turner and his party ranked so low in voter confidence that the outcome seemed inevitable.

A televised debate was expected to make things worse for the Liberals. For three hours a night on successive nights, the three party leaders—Conservative, Liberal, and NDP—would debate the issues of the campaign. For the Liberals it was the last chance. As Mulroney spluttered ineffectively in the background, Turner told him (and millions of television viewers), "I happen to believe you sold us out as a country. . . . The political ability of this country to sustain the political influence of the United States, to remain as an independent nation—that is lost forever and that is the issue of this election." Mulroney's response—that his father had worked hard with his hands and that in consequence he, Mulroney, was a true Canadian—did not impress either Turner or, as polls showed, those watching the debate. They abandoned the Conservatives at the rate of one percent per day.[17] The Liberals took over first place in the polls.

The Canadian business community panicked. Sensing a need, they rushed to fill it with brochures, public interest advertising, speeches, and warnings of all kinds. The Canadian dollar trembled: if Mulroney were defeated, it would collapse to the level of the peso. Office workers and factory hands were assembled to listen to dire predictions. Meanwhile on television the Conservatives ran a series of person-on-the-street interviews telling voters that Turner was a desperate liar.

The polls reversed themselves—and just in time, from Mulroney's point of view. In the last week of the campaign the Liberals dropped a percentage point a day. The final percentages (with the comparable 1984 results in parentheses) were: Conservatives, 43 (50); Liberals 32 (28); and NDP 20 (19).

It had been an election about issues. Like 1911 and 1963, it was to some degree a referendum on Canadian-American relations. If the Conservatives won, there would be free trade; if the opposition won or held the Conservatives to a minority, there would be no free trade. It is not surprising that 82 percent of the electorate judged free trade the most important issue. High-income Canadians were more likely to vote Conservative than not; women were less likely to do so than men.[18] Artists and writers, to judge by their published work, were almost unanimously anti-American. Canadian literature was increased, if not enriched, by their outpourings.[19]

The election yielded a majority to Mulroney, and he used it to pass free trade through Parliament in December. On New Year's Day 1989, Mulroney and Reagan in separate ceremonies proclaimed the advent of free trade. As they signed, the first percentage points tumbled off the two countries' tariff schedules. In Canada and the United States, business sighed with relief.

Dropping tariffs and setting up the binational panels called for in the agreement were almost the only things Reagan and Mulroney were authorized to do. The really difficult questions, those dealing with subsidies, had been postponed till later, and until they were resolved, the menace of American countervail and Canadian antidumping legislation would linger. For the moment, it seemed that things were getting slightly better, and the odds were that they would not get worse. As Reagan transferred power to George Bush, he left Canadian-American relations in improved shape.

The longer-term effects of free trade have been difficult to seize or to judge. Even the enthusiasts of free trade thought that some Canadian industries would suffer. They suffered more rather than less in 1989 and 1990. The Canadian dollar appreciated against its American counterpart, losing exports with every cent it gained. The Canadian government kept it high with interest rates a few percentage points above the American. Taken together, these policies were enough to drive the Canadian economy into a spate of plant closures and recession, by the end of 1990. How much worse, or better,

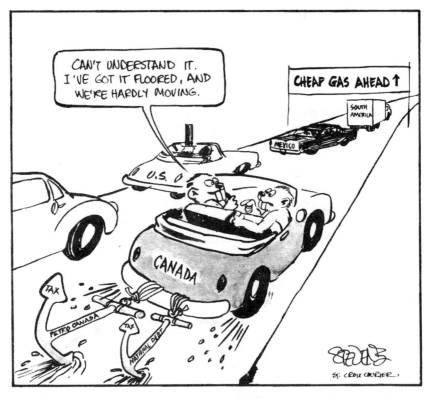

The Canadian economy heading into the 1990s. Cartoon by Dave Stevens from the *St. Croix Courier. Courtesy Dave Stevens.*

things were because of free trade was a matter of lively dispute, in which the protagonists adopted entirely predictable positions.

On the American side, gains and losses were equally difficult to measure. Buffalo anticipated that it would have an influx of Canadian businesses, and certainly in the first few years a number chose to move. Some American subsidiaries decided they could usefully consolidate, in some cases as far away as Mexico, which was looming as the latest zone of enterprise in the North American economy. That came as no surprise to American states south of the Great Lakes. There the only surprise in some areas was that Canada, especially Ontario, still had some plants to close. One effect of free trade may eventually be to reunite some of the regions of North America to confront common problems: New England with the Maritimes, the Great Lakes states, including New York, with Ontario, British Columbia with the Pacific North-West, and the prairie provinces with the plains states.

American-Mexican free trade was next on the American trade list, and to nobody's great surprise Canada asked for, and got, admission to the talks. At this writing, a conclusion to the issue is some time away.

REGIONAL RUMBLINGS

Free trade was, of course, concluded between two countries, Canada and the United States, whose boundaries had been stable since the 1840s. The boundaries helped define and protect two distinct political systems that in the twentieth century kept getting more different as Canada and the United States separately indulged their talents for government and legislation.

That did not eliminate their cultural differences or prevent economic contacts. Any Canadian government foolish enough to try to hive off the Canadian economy would not have endured past the next election. Trudeau's Liberal government went farther than most, and the Liberals paid the price in Canada's 1984 election. The 1988 election confirmed the trend toward greater integration. Mulroney told an amazed television audience that the Canadian-American Free Trade Agreement was a treaty like any other, to be canceled on six months' notice. Many, and possibly most, Canadians did not believe him. To Canada, the Free Trade Agreement has the air of an irrevocable choice.

The realities that may emerge in the aftermath of free trade—bilateral or trilateral, including Mexico—are unknowable. Ambassador Enders warned in 1977, and the State Department echoed the warning, that Canada's internal problems had implications for Americans. As long as Canada was a stable, self-confident national entity, Canadians would keep their problems at home. An unstable Canada might export them, might indeed unwittingly beckon intervention.

Canada in the years after free trade was not stable. In the short view, that was because Prime Minister Mulroney's internal agenda came unstuck in 1990, with the defeat of his package of constitutional compromises that traveled under the name of the Meech Lake Accord, another 1987 achievement at the government retreat house. A longer view argued that differences between French and English Canadians had finally frayed their mutual tolerance. The search by successive Quebec governments for more autonomy continually pressed the federal government to concede more power. Trudeau for the most part refused and was strong enough inside Quebec to make his judgment stick. Trudeau's vision of Canada was of a nation of individual citizens enjoying a number of individual rights, including the right to the *reasonable* use of either French or English. To that end, Trudeau put into place a Charter of Rights, resembling though more limited than its American cousin, and in doing so he struck a chord that continued to reverberate after he was gone.

Universal rights for all citizens were incompatible with the beliefs of Quebec nationalists who wished to restrict the linguistic rights of the English-speaking minority in Quebec. Without such restrictions, the Quebec nationalists argued, French culture and French language would perish in North America. French had made notable strides, especially inside Quebec, under the existing constitution, but the nationalists craved the symbolic affirmation of actual sovereignty: independence, in fact, with enough controls so as to guarantee the perpetuation of French in Quebec and, as far as was decently possible, the simultaneous disappearance of English. Except for clergymen, professors and a few other such creatures, job qualifications by 1991 required French.

For the first time since the eighteenth century, the basic political shape of northern North America came under scrutiny. The fact that Canada's trading relationships with the United States seemed to have been secured encouraged separatists in Quebec to dream of a free trade future for an independent French-speaking republic on the banks of the St. Lawrence, a fact that was noticed and resented by English-speaking Canadian nationalists. The resentment exacerbated relations between English-speaking and French-speaking Canadians and encouraged one American observer to speculate that "the other provinces may well secede first, leaving Quebec to fend for itself." Shortly thereafter, Marvin Cetron prophesied, four more states would be added to the American union as politics ratified what economics—the Free Trade Agreement—had created: "Quebec at last would receive its wish and become an independent nation, if in name only." He did not add that it would recreate, within somewhat different boundaries, the strategic situation of 1759. Cetron's vision created a minor stir in Canada when it first appeared in 1989: the rush of events since then has not discredited it. Canada's national feelings became increasingly strained as separatism gained ground in Quebec and Canadians pondered what the future might hold without Quebec. Whether Canada's nationalist defenses can withstand any number of shocks is an open question.

Ultimately Quebec's restrictions on the use of English—and the provincial government's use of legislation to bypass inconvenient court decisions—diminished the tolerance with which Quebec was regarded in the rest of the country. Bigots, English- and French-speaking, naturally rejoiced, but the increasing rejection of Quebec by English Canada, and of English Canada by Quebec, was a movement that was not confined to nationalist fanatics. The continual depletion of Ottawa's authority by concessions to the provinces suggested to Canadian nationalists that Quebec's demands for more elbow room put the whole country at risk. Their sympathy for Quebec swiftly drained away. By the end of 1991, the possibility of Quebec's secession from Canada posed the dilemma for the United States of dealing with two nations on the northern border where there had been only one before. And what if Quebec proved to be the key thread in the Canadian tapestry, without which the fabric would unravel? And would that thread be cut off at the U.S. border?

A SPECULATION IN THE GUISE OF A CONCLUSION

In 1979 a *Washington Post* reporter named Joel Garreau published an article that argued that instead of three or four nations (counting Cuba) in North America, there were really nine. Six of these spanned the Canadian-American border; of all the existing jurisdictions only Quebec maintained its frontiers in Garreau's New World. Garreau's vision was not free of American ethnocentrism: His nine new nations, with the exception of Quebec, all had American capitals. Kansas City would rule as far as the Quebec border, and Denver would project to the North Pole.[20] For those Canadians who bought the book and read it, it confirmed how little even cosmopolitan Americans knew about Canada. Such knowledge was hardly necessary since, as Garreau pointed out, "in western Ontario, cultural boundaries become a little thin, since there are too few people to make cultural distinctions about."[21]

It was an elaboration of Thomas Enders's 1977 nightmare that Canadian disunion could affect the American union. Despite its minor absurdities, Garreau's argument had a point. If Canada resembled the United States, Canada's regions resembled their American neighbors. The people of North Dakota and Manitoba at least sometimes grumbled about the same things and identified the same enemies. That could be true on a grand scale, as when Canadians and Americans blamed gasoline prices on large multinational oil companies, or in countless lesser delusions and convictions.[22]

Will such thinking lead to a weakening of federalism in both countries, or even to its disappearance? The idea seems far-fetched. The inertia of institutions, traditions, and precedents is not something that can easily be dismissed. Two hundred years of separation have left a clear political imprint. Much of the American political experience (and American nationalism) is necessarily foreign if not entirely unfamiliar to Canadians; the contrary proposition, it need hardly be said, is also true. The negative barriers between Canada and the United States, the lack of certain shared experiences, are powerful. For Canadians, it was the positive factors that were in danger of breaking down in 1991.

The 1990s appear destined to be a time of shocks. The end of the cold war, the collapse of the Soviet system, and the emergence of a new pattern of international relations are profound events that may well transform the nature of politics in these two countries of North America. (The advent of free trade with Mexico, under negotiation in 1991–92, may affect it even more.) Governments and voters oriented to resist communism through alliance and heavy military expenditure now have to reformulate their relations. Canada, which partially—but only partially—checked out of the cold war in the late 1960s, found a coincident rise in regionalism and rivalries between the central power and that of its provincial governments. It is not entirely far-fetched to suggest that the same thing might happen in the United States.

Sociologists have correctly emphasized the divisions between Canadian and American societies; at the same time, as Seymour Martin Lipset concedes, "the two [countries] resemble each other more than either resembles any other nation," in their liberal values, in their settler backgrounds, and in their estrangement from Europe, with differences as measured by public opinion samples "often in the range of 5 to 10 percent."[23]

Canada and the United States were once united in a continent that divided along linguistic or cultural grounds. The resemblances persist. Both countries have been constrained by the burden of history, Canada more obviously than the United States. Immigrant countries endowed with vast natural resources, both sought and created mass-production and mass-consumption societies. For most of the time, people moved freely across the border, Canadians more than Americans, finding no very large personal differences in crossing the border.[24]

That was guaranteed by the phenomenon of television, reinforced by the universality of pop music. As Canada's connection to the British Empire dwindled during the twentieth century, Canadians reformulated their sense of self and country into their own particular nationalism. Oddly enough, this was accomplished by legislating a liberal agenda that in 1945 had considerable resonance in the United States as well as in Canada. Because it took a fuller, more developed form in Canada, the Canadian social welfare system became a significant point of national difference between the two countries and a reference point in debates over Canadian-American relations in the 1980s and 1990s.

Canadian governments thus shaped Canadians' concept of themselves, using tools that were not uniquely Canadian in origin—or execution, a point frequently lost on Canadians and ignored by Americans. The perpetuation of the division between the two countries thus is more likely than not, but not certain. But certainty, even in such a long-lasting relationship as that between Canadians and Americans, is most notable by its absence. That this should be so is perhaps the most striking constant in Canadian-American relations, suggesting that in the twenty-first century Canadians and Americans will continue to experience the shock of recognition across a defined border.

CHRONOLOGY

1940   17–18 August
               Ogdensburg Conference between Canadian prime minister Mac-
               kenzie King and president Franklin D. Roosevelt establishes the
               Permanent Joint Board on Defense (PJBD) to coordinate Cana-
               dian and American defense efforts.

1941   20 April
               Hyde Park agreement between King and Roosevelt for pooling of
               defense production efforts.

1945   12 April
               Death of Franklin Roosevelt; Harry Truman becomes president

               11 June
               Liberal party under Mackenzie King narrowly returned in Cana-
               dian general election

               September
               Ignor Gouzenko defects from Soviet embassy in Ottawa, reveal-
               ing atomic spy scandal.

               29–30 September
               Mackenzie King sees president Harry Truman on the subject of
               the spy scandal.

               10–15 November
               Washington conference between Mackenzie King, Truman and
               British prime minister Clement Attlee on the international con-
               trol of atomic energy.

1946   16–17 December
        Ottawa conference between Canadian and American officials
        postpones implementation of a common air defense system.

1947   13 January
        Canadian external affairs minister Louis St. Laurent, in a speech
        in Toronto, defines Canadian foreign policy as involving coopera-
        tion with the United States, and a community of interest be-
        tween North America and Europe.

        29 October
        Canadian government approaches the US government to explore
        a bilateral trade agreement.

        17 November
        Successful conclusion of GATT in Geneva; simultaneous an-
        nouncement of Canadian controls on imports to stave off foreign
        exchange crisis.

1948   February
        Political crisis and communist coup in Czechoslovakia

        11 March
        British government proposes American-British-Canadian discus-
        sions on western security

        22 March–1 April
        Tripartite discussions in Washington lead to a decision to seek to
        negotiate a wider North Atlantic security arrangement.

        1 April
        Mackenzie King derails negotiations for a Canadian-American
        customs union.

        6 July
        Washington exploratory talks begin between United States, Can-
        ada, and western European powers

        November
        Harry Truman wins US presidential election

        15 November
        Mackenzie King retires as Canadian prime minister; Louis St.
        Laurent succeeds as prime minister.

1949   4 April
        NATO treaty signed in Washington by United States, Canada
        and western European countries.

        27 June
        Liberal party returned to power in Canadian general election

1950   25 June
        Outbreak of Korean War

1951	**10 April** External affairs minister Lester Pearson makes speech claiming that "easy and automatic relations" with the United States were over.
	11 April Dismissal of Douglas MacArthur as commander of United Nations forces in Korea.
	October–November Canadian troops sent to Europe as part of NATO
1953	**20 January** Dwight D. Eisenhower becomes president
	10 August Liberal party wins Canadian general election.
1956	**May–June** "Pipeline debate" in Canadian parliament stirs anti-American sentiment
1957	**4 April** Suicide of Canadian ambassador in Egypt, Herbert Norman, in the wake of American congressional charges that he was a Soviet agent.
	10 June In Canadian general election Conservative party under John Diefenbaker defeats the Liberals under prime minister Louis St. Laurent
	22 June Diefenbaker becomes prime minister at the head of a minority government
	1 August North American Air Defense agreement announced, creating the joint North American Air Defense Command at Colorado Springs.
1958	**31 March** Diefenbaker wins snap Canadian general election, securing a majority government and defeating the new Liberal party leader, Lester Pearson.
1961	**17 January** Columbia River treaty signed in Washington
	20 January John F. Kennedy becomes president
	16–18 May President John F. Kennedy visits Ottawa

1962	**18 June** In Canadian general election, prime minister Diefenbaker narrowly avoids defeat, and loses his parliamentary majority.
1963	**30 January** US State Department press release condemns Diefenbaker's statements on nuclear defense policy
	5 February Diefenbaker government defeated in vote of confidence in parliament; election called
	8 April In Canadian general election Liberals under Pearson oust Diefenbaker and the Conservatives, but miss securing a parliamentary majority.
	22 April Lester Pearson becomes prime minister.
	10–11 May Pearson visits Kennedy at Hyannis Port
	9 October Canadian-American agreement on nuclear weapons at Canadian military bases.
	22 November Assassination of John F. Kennedy; Lyndon B. Johnson president
1965	**16 January** Canada-United States automotive agreement (Autopact) signed
	2 April Pearson speech on Vietnam at Temple University in Philadelphia
1967	**26 July** French president Charles de Gaulle makes "Vive le Quebec libre" speech in Montreal
1968	**21 April** Pierre Elliott Trudeau becomes Canadian prime minister.
1969	**March** Canadian cabinet decides to cut Canada's German-based NATO contingent.
1971	**6–7 December** Trudeau-Nixon meetings in Washington realign Canadian-American relationship.
1972	**13–15 April** Nixon visits Ottawa
	30 October Trudeau almost defeated in Canadian general election; obliged to function with a minority government

1973 **24 January**
Canadian participation in Vietnam peacekeeping force as a result of the Paris Accords announced.

29 May
Canada announces withdrawal from Vietnam peacekeeping.

26 November
Bill creating a Foreign Investment Review Agency passes Canadian parliament

1974 **8 July**
Liberals under Trudeau win majority government in Canadian general election

1976 **15 November**
Separatist Parti Quebecois wins Quebec election.

1977 **20 January**
Jimmy Carter becomes US president

22 February
Trudeau addresses US Congress

8 September
Trudeau and Jimmy Carter agree on natural gas pipeline from Alaska across northern Canada.

1979 **22 May**
Conservatives under Joe Clark defeat prime minister Trudeau in Canadian general election, but secure only a minority government.

14 December
Joe Clark government defeated in parliament; general election called.

1980 **18 February**
Liberals under Trudeau win majority government in Canadian general election.

28 October
Canadian government announces National Energy Program designed to enhance Canadian control over oil and gas industry.

1981 **20 January**
Ronald Reagan becomes American president

10–11 March
Reagan visits Ottawa

13 October
Ministerial meeting between Canadian and American governments in Ottawa fails to resolve dispute over Canadian oil and gas policy.

1983   31 August
Canadian (Liberal) government committed to seek sectoral free trade with United States

1984   30 June
Trudeau resigns as prime minister and is succeeded by John Turner.

4 September
Liberal government of John Turner trounced in Canadian general election; Conservatives under Brian Mulroney secure overwhelming parliamentary majority.

19 November
Donald Macdonald, chairman of Canadian Royal Commission on Economic Union, calls for a "leap of faith"—free trade between the United States and Canada.

1985   17 March
"Shamrock Summit" in Quebec City between Reagan and Mulroney; commitment to explore free trade

26 September
Prime minister Mulroney announces that Canada had asked the United States to negotiate a free trade agreement.

10 December
Reagan notifies Congress of his intention to seek free trade with Canada.

1986   21 May
Free trade negotiations began in Ottawa.

1987   23 September
Free trade negotiations suspended

3 October
Agreement in principle reached on free trade

10 December
Free trade negotiations finally concluded

1988   21 November
Canadian general election on issue of free trade won by Conservatives under Mulroney.

1989   1 January
Free Trade Agreement takes effect

NOTES AND REFERENCES

List of Abbreviations

DEA	Department of External Affairs, Ottawa
FDR Library	Franklin D. Roosevelt Library, Hyde Park, N.Y.
FRUS	Foreign Relations of the United States (periodical)
JFK Library	John F. Kennedy Library, Boston, Mass.
NAC	National Archives of Canada, Ottawa, Ontario
USNA	United States National Archive, Washington, D.C.

Chapter 1: Distant Neighbors, 1763–1945

1. FDR Library, F. D. Roosevelt Papers, PSF 35 Canada, 1944–45, Joseph Grew, memorandum for the president, 8 March 1945: "He is seeking to rebuild his prestige and thus may want to meet the press here and capitalize discreetly on his friendship with you."

2. David Brinkley, *Washington Goes to War: The Extraordinary Story of the Transformation of a City and a Nation* (New York, Knopf: 1988), 268; J. W. Pickersgill and D. F. Forster, eds., *The Mackenzie King Record*, vol. 2 (Toronto: University of Toronto Press, 1968), 329.

3. Ibid., 331.

4. Ibid., 365.

5. Quoted in William T.R. Fox, *A Continent Apart: The United States and Canada in World Politics* (Toronto: University of Toronto Press, 1985), 38.

6. David Hackett Fisher, in his *Albion's Seed: Four British Folkways in America* (New York: Oxford University Press, 1989), 8–9, proposes twenty-four categories ranging

from "Speech ways" and "Building ways" to "Power ways" and "Freedom ways" by which cultural patterns can be compared. In most of his categories except the last two, adjacent Canadian and American regions would be very close if not identical; and even their attitudes to freedom and power are not entirely dissimilar. See Alan Gowans, *Building Canada: An Architectural History of Canadian Life* (Toronto: University of Toronto Press, 1966), 46–54, 66–71.

7. Gerard J. Brault, *The French-Canadian Heritage in New England* (Hanover, N.H., and Montreal: New England University Press, 1986), 55, 193.

8. Franklin D. Roosevelt to Mackenzie King, 18 May 1942, reproduced in Jean-François Lisée, *Dans l'oeil de l'aigle: Washington face au Québec* (Montréal, 1990), 454–55.

9. See, for example, Wallace Stegner, *Wolf Willow* (New York: Viking, 1962) and Edward Hoagland's more recent *Seven Rivers West* (New York: Penguin, 1989).

10. U.S. figures are from the Bureau of the Census, *Historical Statistics of the United States*, bicentennial edition (Washington, 1975), series F1-5; Canadian figures are from estimates by O. J. Firestone, in M. C. Urquhart and K.A.H. Buckley, eds., *Historical Statistics of Canada*, 1st ed. (Toronto: Cambridge University Press and Macmillan of Canada, 1965), E214–244.

11. Dalhousie Law School, in Halifax, was the first maritime law school. Other provinces simply resisted the idea that law required academic training.

12. This point, first developed by Richard Risk of the University of Toronto, is a fruitful area for scholars.

13. In 1868, 52.3 percent of Canadian exports went to the United States, while 36.9 percent went to Great Britain; but only 33.8 percent of Canadian imports derived from the United States, and 56.1 percent from Britain.

14. NAC, Brooke Claxton Papers, vol. 62, Pearson to Claxton, 16 October 1943. Pearson added that Congress had "a level of intelligence somewhat below that of the Upper House in Haiti!" Pearson's comment is a classic example of Canadian anti-Americanism, intended for domestic and private consumption only.

15. Defense Secretary James Forrestal was one, but his comments have to be taken as quite unrepresentative. Walter Millis, ed., *The Forrestal Diaries* (New York: Viking 1951), 474–45: diary for 18 August 1948.

16. Michael Bliss, *Northern Enterprise* (Toronto: McClelland & Stewart, 1987), 303–4.

17. H. B. Gates, *The Dominion of Canada: Its Interests, Prospects and Policy* (Montreal, n.p., 1872). This conception was later dubbed the "linchpin" theory, meaning that Canada was a "linchpin" between Great Britain and the United States.

18. The major sore point was a dispute over the boundary of the Alaska Panhandle, which Canada lost in an arbitration in London in 1903.

19. Chandler P. Anderson, reporting on Root, quoted in C. P. Stacey, *Canada and the Age of Conflict*, vol. 1 (Toronto: Macmillan, 1977), 111.

20. Queen's University (Kingston, Ont.), John S. Foster Papers, Foster to Charles Pepper, 15 March 1911.

21. See David Potter, "Canadian Views of the United States as a Reflex of Canadian Values: A Commentary," in S. F. Wise and R. C. Brown, *Canada Views the United States: Nineteenth Century Political Attitudes*, Seattle: University of Washington press, 1967). For a more recent example, see John Irving, *A Prayer for Owen Meany*, New York: Morrow, 1989), in which a Canadian character describes *strong opinions* as "American."

22. Yale University Library, House Papers, diary, 6 February 1919.

23. The classic definition of a Canadian mine of the period is "a hole in the ground with a liar on top."

24. Quoted in John Herd Thompson and Allan Seager, *Canada 1922–1939: Decades of Discord* (Toronto: McClelland & Stewart, 1985), 146.

25. Ibid., 187–89.

26. A point emphasized by the media historian Paul Rutherford in his very sensible discussion of Canadian television, *When Television Was Young: Prime Time Canada, 1952–1967* (Toronto: University of Toronto Press, 1990), 143–44.

27. Arthur Irwin, "Can We Stem the Exodus?" *Maclean's* 11, 15 May, 1927, 3, 34.

28. NAC, Lester B. Pearson Papers, vol. 3, Hume Wrong to Pearson, 15 July 1936.

29. See Robert Bothwell and John Kirton, "A Sweet Little Country: American Attitudes toward Canada 1925 to 1963," *Queen's Quarterly* 90 (Winter 1983), 1079.

30. Charles P. Kindleberger, *The World in Depression, 1929–1939* (Berkeley and Los Angeles: University of California P. 1973), 191–92.

31. Quoted in Robert A. Pollard, *Economic Security and the Origins of the Cold War, 1945–50* (New York: Columbia University Press 1985), 12.

32. Dean Acheson, *Grapes from Thorns* (New York: Norton, 1971), 231–32.

33. FDR Library, Harry Hopkins Papers, vol. 312, Author unknown, "Canadian labor and the war," 9 September 1942. I am obliged to differ with some of the assertions of Seymour Martin Lipset, *Continental Divide: The Values and Institutions of the United States and Canada* (New York: Routledge 1990), 164–71. It seems clear that in the 1930s the United States was more oriented than Canada toward class consciousness and socialism, values that he believes are over time more characteristic of Canada.

34. *Foreign Relations of the United States: Diplomatic Papers, 1935*, vol. 2 (Washington: Department of State, 1952), 27–30.

35. C. P. Stacey, *Mackenzie King and the Atlantic Triangle* (Toronto: Macmillan, 1976), 49–50.

36. Raymond Moley, quoted in Robert Dallek, *Franklin D. Roosevelt and American Foreign Policy, 1932–1945* (New York: Oxford University Press 1979), 109.

37. This paragraph is based on discussions with Jack Hickerson and Theodore Achilles in Washington in 1980.

38. Public Record Office (Kew), FO 371/20670/A2082, Sir R. Lindsay to Sir R. Vansittart, 8 March 1937, with comment by Vansittart, 31 March 1937.

39. See "F.D.R.'s Adviser on Canada," *Financial Post* (Toronto), 29 May 1943.

40. Stacey, *Mackenzie King and the Atlantic Triangle*, 50.

41. C. P. Stacey, *Arms, Men and Governments: The War Policies of Canada, 1939–1945* Ottawa: Queen's Printer 1970), 329–32.

42. Quoted in ibid., 340.

43. Robert Bothwell and William Kilbourn, *C. D. Howe: A Biography* (Toronto: McClelland & Stewart, 1979), 139.

44. FDR Library, Adolf Berle Papers, Berle Diary file, 26 June 1941.

45. USNA, State Department Records, 842.20 Defense/245, Lewis Clark to Graham Parsons, 22 July 1943.

46. John English, "Canada's Road to 1945," *Journal of Canadian Studies* 16 (Fall–Winter 1981), 100–9

47. Alan S. Milward, *War, Economy and Society, 1939–1945* (Berkeley: University of California Press, 1977), 331, 351–53.

48. NAC, J. W. Dafoe Papers, vol. 12, Chester Bloom to Dafoe, 20 October 1941.

49. NAC, Mackenzie King Papers, King Diary, 22 March 1943 50; King Diary, 11 August 1943. American officials nevertheless misread the situation. "Canada can be counted on to back Great Britain on any major international issue," one analysis reported in November 1943. "She is strongly tied to her by tradition, trade and overall interest." (USNA, RG 165, G2, regional file Canada A-C, box 425, file Canada and Newfoundland, Current Situation, "Interview with Miss K. Norton, North American Branch, November 1943 by M. H. Williams, British Isles Branch.")

51. Typical of Pearson's point of view is a letter from Pearson to Wrong, 18 March 1943 in *Documents on Canadian External Relations*, vol. 9 (Ottawa: Department of External Affairs, 1986), pp. 1138–42.

52. Lipset, *Continental Divide*, chapter 10, takes the fashionable view that Canada is more "mosaic" than "melting pot." Nevertheless, some of his evidence (pp. 182–84) indicates that Canadian policy in the interwar period was skewed toward creating a "Protestant, Anglo-Saxon" society within the *British* Empire. I would argue that the expectation that immigrants would and should assimilate continues to this day, as a recent poll, which Lipset considers an aberration, suggests. (The poll, which appeared in *Maclean's* magazine in July 1989, suggests that more Canadians than Americans believe that immigrants should assimilate toward a cultural norm.)

Chapter 2: Postwar Convergences, 1945–1950

1. J. W. Pickersgill interview by author, 4 April 1990.

2. Harry Truman, "Isolationism: Our First Foreign Policy," in Margaret Truman, ed., *Where the Buck Stops: The Personal and Private Writings of Harry S. Truman* (New York: Warner, 1989), 191. Truman repeated the same sentiment in an essay on James K. Polk, in ibid., 320.

3. See John English, "Canada's Road to 1945," *Journal of Canadian Studies* 16 (Fall–Winter 1981), 100–9.

4. Such, at least, was the result of a poll conducted in Kitchener, Ontario, and Vancouver, British Columbia, by the Canadian Chamber of Commerce in 1944. See

R. Bothwell, I. Drummond, and J. English, *Canada since 1945*, revised ed. (Toronto: University of Toronto Press, 1989), 477.

5. Alonzo K. Hamby, *Beyond the New Deal: Harry S. Truman and American Liberalism* (New York: Columbia University Press, 1973), 66–67.

6. Georgetown University Library, Foreign Affairs Oral History Collection, Willis Armstrong interview.

7. In 1946, Americans spent $214 million in Canada, and Canadians, $131 million in the United States. See *Canada Year Book, 1947* (Ottawa: King's Printer, 1947), 914.

8. Article 7 of the lend-lease agreements prescribed trade talks and looked to the abolition of trade barriers such as imperial preference.

9. R. Bothwell and J. English, "Canadian Trade Policy in the Age of American Dominance and British Decline," *Canadian Review of American Studies* 8 (Spring 1977), 54–65.

10. Ibid.

11. Lewis Clark to Graham Parsons, 28 December 1945, State Department Records, 842.00/12-2845.

12. On this point, see Bothwell and English, "Canadian Trade Policy," 64.

13. During 1946, Canada furnished $750 million in credits to Britain and Europe; in 1947, it was $563 million. After the exchange crisis of 1947–48 these totals were drastically reduced to C$105 million in 1948. See *Canada Year Book, 1950* (Ottawa: King's Printer, 1950), 901.

14. See Arthur Donner, "Inter-provincial Economic Links Getting Weaker," *Toronto Star*, 18 February 1991, C1–2.

15. See Bothwell, Drummond, and English, *Canada since 1945*, 21.

16. This point was made to the Canadian minister of trade and commerce, C. D. Howe, by his senior economist in August 1947. NAC, Howe Papers, vol. 87, file S48-10, Alexander Skelton to Howe, 18 August 1947.

17. Ray Atherton, ambassador in Ottawa, to secretary of state, 22 August 1947, in *FRUS, 1947*, vol. 3 (Washington, 1972), 116–7.

18. USNA, State Department Records, 842.51/9-2447, memorandum of conversation, 24 September 1947. Participants were Ty Wood, Paul Nitze, Wayne Jackson, Andrew Foster, and Alexander Romanson.

19. *FRUS, 1947*, vol. 3, 123, Atherton to secretary of state, 11 September 1947.

20. Ibid., 127–28, Atherton to secretary of state, 29 October 1947.

21. DEA Records, file 265(S), Hume Wrong to secretary of state for external affairs, 1 November 1947.

22. NAC, Howe Papers, vol. 87, file S48-10-6, Hume Wrong to L. B. Pearson, 25 November 1947.

23. DEA, "Soward manuscript," 15, quoting the views of Norman Robertson, then Canadian high commissioner (ambassador) to Great Britain.

24. Hickerson interview, November 1978.

25. DEA Records, file 265(S), H. R. Kemp to Max Mackenzie, 27 December 1947.

26. State Department Records, 611.422/10-2649, memorandum by E. C. Moline, 29 October 1947. Moline saw opposition from wheat and cattle interests in the West, from Wisconsin dairy farmers, the Maine potato industry, the New England fisheries, and West Coast lumber companies.

27. See R. Bothwell and W. Kilbourn, C. D. Howe: A Biography (Toronto: McClelland & Stewart, 1979), 219–20. Howe's American birth was held against him by the more rabid of Canadian nationalists, who took it as proof positive of treasonable intent.

28. See note 19.

29. Queen's University Library, Grant Dexter Papers, box 4, file 31, Max Freedman to Dexter, 20 September 1947, reporting the views of John Deutsch.

30. "The Nation's Business," Financial Post, 29 November 1947.

31. Woodbury Willoughby to Willard Thorp, n.d., enclosed in Willard Thorp to Robert Lovett, 8 March 1948, FRUS, 1948, vol. 9 (Washington: Department of State, 1972), 409.

32. Bothwell and Kilbourn, Howe, 219–20.

33. Statistics Canada, Review of Foreign Trade, 1966–72 (Ottawa: Information Canada, 1974), 123, table A.

34. DEA, "Soward manuscript," chapter 7, 40ff.

35. R. D. Cuff and J. L. Granatstein, American Dollars, Canadian Prosperity (Toronto: McClelland & Stewart, 1978), chapter 4.

36. See Martin and Susan Tolchin, Buying into America: How Foreign Money Is Changing the Face of Our Nation, paperback ed. (New York: Times Books, 1989).

37. Figures for the Canadian economy are based on gross domestic product and are derived from the various Canada Year Books, the Historical Statistics of Canada, 2nd ed., and the 1987 historical supplement to the Canadian Economic Observer.

38. J. L. Gaddis, The United States and the Origins of the Cold War, 1941–1947 (New York: Columbia University Press, 1972), 252–53.

39. His most famous essay, at least to Canadians, is entitled "Stern Daughter of the Voice of God."

40. W. A. Mackintosh, quoted in Bothwell, Drummond, and English, Canada Since 1945, 86.

41. A point made in J. J. Jockel, No Boundaries Upstairs: Canada, the United States and the Origins of North American Air Defense, 1945–1958 (Vancouver: University of British Columbia Press, 1987), 14–25.

42. Ibid., 16–29.

43. This is a point also made by Denis Smith, Politics of Fear: Canada and the Cold War, 1941–1948 (Toronto: University of Toronto Press, 1988), 230.

44. Quoted in ibid., 28.

45. Ibid., 29.

46. Canadians did read and appreciate American journalists. For example, Anne O'Hare McCormick's comments on "Soviet Political War" were approvingly drawn to the attention of the prime minister and the minister of external affairs after the Czech coup. NAC, King Papers, J4, vol. 344, file 3713, Escott Reid to Mackenzie King, 25 March 1948.

47. Assessments of Canada's security requirements may be found in the memorandum and enclosures from the Joint Chiefs of Staff to the State-War-Navy-Coordinating Committee, 12 May 1947, in FRUS, 1947 vol. 1 (Washington: Department of State, 1973), 734–50.

48. Quoted in John English, Shadow of Heaven: The Life of Lester Pearson, vol. 1 (Toronto: Lester & Orpen Dennys, 1989), 328.

49. On King's state of mind in this period, see C. P. Stacey, A Very Double Life: The Private World of Mackenzie King (Toronto: Macmillan, 1976), 209–12. Stacey is careful to note that King used his spirits to confirm rather than originate policy, and that Roosevelt in any case never warned him specifically about Korea, merely telling him not to forget Asia (seance of 23 October 1948).

50. Hume Wrong to Lester Pearson, "Influences Shaping the Policy of the United States Towards the Soviet Union," 4 December 1947.

51. J. W. Pickersgill interview, 4 April 1990.

52. See Lawrence Kaplan, NATO and the United States: The Enduring Alliance (Boston: Twayne, 1988), 22–23.

53. Kennan to secretary and undersecretary of State, 24 May 1948, FRUS, 1948, vol. 3 (Washington, 1974), 128.

54. Canadian cabinet defence committee minutes, 16 August 1948, NAC, King Papers, J4, file 2384. Forrestal was visiting Ottawa.

55. Minutes of the third meeting of the Washington exploratory talks on security, 7 July 1948, FRUS, 1948, vol. 3, 159, and concluding memorandum, 9 September 1948, ibid., 245.

56. Report of the international working group to the ambassadors' committee, 24 December 1948, ibid., 337.

57. The story was recounted by Hickerson in an interview in Washington in 1980.

Chapter 3: The Cold War: Dependence and Independence, 1950–1957

1. USNA, State Department Records, RG 59, vol. 2773, 611.42/3-1951, "Policy Statement Canada," 19 March 1951.

2. Ibid.

3. DEA Records, file 1415-10, Holmes, "Relations between Canada and the United States in the United Nations," 26 March 1951.

4. Ibid.

5. The history of the Seafarer's International Union, is ably described in William Kaplan, *Everything That Floats* (Toronto: University of Toronto Press, 1988).

6. That does not mean that security issues were absent. Security screening was in place, and some Canadian civil servants came under suspicion because of their previous associations back in the 1930s. See James Barros, *No Sense of Evil* (Toronto: Deneau, 1986).

7. This paragraph relies very heavily on an M.A. paper by Robert Prince, "The Limits of Constraint: Canadian-American Relations and the Korean War, 1950–51," to be published in the *Journal of Canadian Studies.*

8. The official was obviously anonymous. See Blair Fraser, "Backstage at Ottawa," *Maclean's,* 1 September 1950.

9. Quoted in R. Bothwell and W. Kilbourn, *C. D. Howe: A Biography* (Toronto: McClelland & Stewart, 1979), 254.

10. Canada had been part of the wartime atomic triad and remained a contractor to the American atomic energy enterprise through the sale of uranium and the rental of test facilities in Canada's own atomic project. At the United Nations, Canada was a member of the UN Atomic Energy Commission, and in the face of discouraging circumstances the Canadians were still, in 1950, urging the Americans to resume discussions on nuclear controls with the USSR.

11. Cited in Prince, "Limits of Constraint," 21.

12. DEA Records, file 1415-10, A.F.W. Plumptre, "Relations with the United States," 31 March 1951.

13. Acheson was ready to give up and had to be ordered by Truman to persist. Truman Library (Independence, Mo.), Acheson Papers, memorandum, 22 November 1952; NAC, DEA Records, file 1415-40, vol. 2, "St. Lawrence Deep Waterway and Power Project," 29 March 1951.

14. DEA Records, file 1415-40, vol. 3, R. L. Rogers to Escott Reid, "The Effect of the Far Eastern Crisis on Relations between Canada and the United States," 30 March 1951.

15. Ibid.

16. State Department Records,

17. DEA Records, Statements and Speeches, 51/14: "Canadian Foreign Policy in a Two-Power World."

18. DEA Records,

19. H. F. Wood, *Strange Background: Official History of the Canadian Army in Korea* (Ottawa: Queen's Printer 1980), 257–58.

20. NAC, Brooke Claxton Papers, vol. 31, Claxton to George Ferguson, 27 May 1953.

21. Dean Acheson, *Present at the Creation: My Years in the State Department* (New York: Norton 1969), 703–704; Pearson in his memoirs, *Mike,* vol. 2 (Toronto: University of Toronto Press 1973), called Acheson's account "a travesty of the facts."

22. A disappointment Hickerson expressed when I interviewed him in Washington in 1980.

23. J.J. Jockel, *No Boundaries Upstairs: Canada, the United States and the Origins of North American Air Defense, 1945–1958* (Vancouver: University of British Columbia Press, 1987), 47.

24. NAC, Louis St. Laurent Papers, box 175, file External Affairs, Defence, Pickersgill to Claxton, "Facilities in Canada for Joint Canada–US Defence Operations," 23 April 1951.

25. Jockel, *No Boundaries Upstairs*, 47.

26. Canadian diplomats once again, as in 1950 over Korea, misinterpreted American policy. Canada at first believed that Eisenhower would press Chiang to give up the islands; later, when it became apparent that the Americans would risk war on Chiang's behalf, the Canadians were simply incredulous. I am grateful to Philip Charrier, a graduate student at Cambridge University, for this information.

27. These figures are derived from indexes of real domestic product, *Historical Statistics of Canada*, 2nd ed. (Ottawa: Statistics Canada, 1983), series F225–240.

28. Quoted in Joseph Barber, *Good Fences Make Good Neighbors: Why the United States Provokes Canadians* (Toronto: McClelland and Stewart, 1958), 115.

29. "C. D. Howe of Canada," *Fortune*, August 1952.

30. See, for example, the U.S. embassy annual economic reports for 1950 and 1951, State Department Records, 842.00/1-2551 and 842.00/2 452.

31. Alfred E. Eckes, *The United States and the Global Struggle for Minerals* (Austin: University of Texas Press 1979), 110–11.

32. Barber, *Good Fences*, 114–15. See also Hugh Aiken, *American Capital and Canadian Resources* (Cambridge, Mass.: Harvard University Press, 1961). C. D. Howe and his friends demonstrated their invincible optimism at their country's mineral and industrial prospects in a volume entitled *Canada: Nation on the March* (Toronto: Clarke, Irwin, 1953).

33. R. Bothwell and W. Kilbourn, *C. D. Howe: A Biography* (Toronto: McClelland & Stewart 1979), 277.

34. See Robert Bothwell, *Eldorado: Canada's National Uranium Company* (Toronto: University of Toronto Press, 1984).

35. Barber, *Good Fences*, 117.

36. Barber, *Good Fences*, 62, tells the story of a dinner party he attended at which most of his dining companions turned out to be Americans, like himself.

37. Ibid., 51. By 1958 there were an estimated one million Canadian expatriates in the United States, of whom 750,000 were naturalized citizens.

38. A large majority of Canadians—69 percent—said yes when asked if it was "good for Canada" that development was U.S.-financed. See poll dated 18 July 1956, cited in Mildred Schwartz, *Public Opinion and Canadian Identity* (Berkeley: University of California Press, and Scarborough, Ont.: Fitzhenry & Whiteside), 68.

39. The story of the pipeline is told in great detail in Bothwell and Kilbourn, *Howe,* chapters 17 and 18.

40. Schwartz, *Public Opinion,* 70–71: polls from 1955 and 1956.

41. Burt Marshall, quoted in Leonard Mosley, *Dulles: A Biography of Eleanor, Allen and John Foster Dulles and their Family Network* (New York: Dell, 1979), 358.

42. USNA, State Department Records, RG 59, vol. 3552, 742.13/5-1353, John Morgan to Dept. of State, 13 May 1953; Donald Barry, "Eisenhower, St. Laurent and Free Trade," *International Perspectives* (March–April 1987), 8–10.

43. Truman Library (Independence, Mo.), Dean Acheson Papers, memorandum of conversation with the president, 3 November 1952; *FRUS 1952–1954,* vol. 6 (Washington, 1986), 2074ff. The National Security Council formally recommended the seaway on 23 April 1953: ibid., 2077–2078.

44. See Bothwell and Kirton, "A Sweet Little Country," *Queen's Quarterly* 90 (Winter 1983), 1078–1102.

45. John Holmes, *The Shaping of Peace: Canada and the Search for World Order,* vol. 2 (Toronto: University of Toronto Press, 1982), 281–82.

46. Coarse grains were a problem because of surpluses encouraged by U.S. farm subsidies. See T. H. Peterson, *Agricultural Exports, Farm Income, and the Eisenhower Administration* (Lincoln, Neb.: University of Nebraska Press 1980), 28.

47. Quoted in Dan Morgan, *Merchants of Grain* (New York: Viking 1979), 101.

48. The most extraordinary surplus disposal was in 1956—to France! See Peterson, *Agricultural Exports,* 79.

49. *Historical Statistics of Canada,* 2nd ed., series H161–175.

50. NAC, DEA Records, file 1415-40, part 4, "Summary Record of the United States-Canadian Committee on Trade and Economic Affairs held in Ottawa on September 26, 1955."

51. NAC, Arnold Heeney Papers, vol. 2, file memoirs 1955, diary, 26 and 27 September 1955.

52. The Norman affair still generates controversy in Canada. Since 1985 there have been two books and a government report on the subject. The *Globe and Mail* is quoted in James Eayrs, *Canada in World Affairs, October 1955 to June 1957* (Toronto: Oxford University Press, 1959), 158.

53. Ibid., 159–60.

54. DEA Records file 1415–40, Maurice Pope to Pearson, 20 April 1951.

Chapter 4: The Time of Troubles, 1957–1968

1. Basil Robinson, *Diefenbaker's World: A Populist in Foreign Affairs* (Toronto: Univeristy of Toronto Press, 1989), 103.

2. K. J. Holsti and T. A. Levy, "Bilateral Institutions and Transgovernmental Relations Between Canada and the United States," in A. B. Fox, A. O. Hero, and J. Nye, eds., *Canada and the United States: Transnational and Transgovernmental Relations* (New

York: Columbia University Press, 1976), 290–91. The agreement exempted Canada from the Buy America Act of 1933. An alert Congress immediately modified the agreement to exclude shipbuilding.

3. J. J. Kirton, "The Consequences of Integration: The Case of the Defence Production Sharing Agreements," in A. Axline, J. Hyndman, P. V. Lyon, and M. A. Molot, eds., *Continental Community? Independence and Integration in North America* (Toronto: McClelland & Stewart, 1974), 116–35.

4. "Northern European Chiefs of Mission Conference, London, September 19–21, 1957, Summary of Proceedings," *FRUS, 1955–1957*, vol. 4 (Washington, 1986), 617–18.

5. See Alistair Horne, *Macmillan*, vol. 2 (New York: Viking, 1989). Macmillan considered Diefenbaker "something of a mountebank," 355, 356.

6. Diefenbaker on 20 February 1959, quoted in Jon B. McLin, *Canada's Changing Defense Policy: The Problems of a Middle Power in Alliance* (Baltimore: Johns Hopkins University Press, 1967), 87–88.

7. Canadian Institute of Public Opinion poll, quoted in Peyton Lyon, *Canada in World Affairs, 1961–1963* (Toronto: Oxford University Press, 1968), 539.

8. John Paul and Jerome Laulicht, *In Your Opinion*, vol. 1 (Clarkson, Ont.: Peace Research Institute, 1963), 84. The most reliable sample is the "national" one of one thousand persons; the other samples are much smaller. The poll was conducted for the Canadian Peace Research Institute in November 1962, just after the Cuban missile crisis.

9. On Robertson's beliefs, see J. L. Granatstein, *Man of Influence: Norman Robertson and Canadian Statecraft* (Ottawa: Deneau, 1981), chapter 11.

10. NAC, Arnold Heeney Papers, vol. 1, file United States—ambassador to Washington, 1960, "Memorandum of conversation with the Prime Minister in Ottawa, Tuesday August 30, 1960 and Wednesday, August 31, 1960."

11. A poll taken in September 1961 revealed that 60.7 percent of Canadians had heard that Canada had undertaken to acquire nuclear weapons, and that of those 61.5 percent believed Canada should honor its commitment. See Peyton Lyon, *Canada in World Affairs, 1961–1963* (Toronto: Oxford University Press 1968), 537–38.

12. Diefenbaker's conversation with Heeney, quoted above, note 10, specifically credited Eisenhower and his administration with great knowledge about Canada.

13. JFK Library, Kennedy Papers, POF, box 113, file Canada Trip, National Intelligence Estimate no. 4, 99-61. "Trends in Canadian Foreign Policy," 2 May 1961.

14. Willis C. Armstrong to author, 29 October 1990.

15. JFK Library, POF, box 113, file Canada Trip, National Intelligence Estimate no. 4, 99-61, "Trends in Canadian Policy," 2 May 1961.

16. Keith Davey, quoted in Knowlton Nash, *Kennedy and Diefenbaker: Fear and Loathing across the Undefended Border* (Toronto: McClelland & Stewart, 1990), 302, and diary entry for 18 January 1961, in Robinson, *Diefenbaker's World*, 168.

17. Ibid., 90–100, citing Robert Kennedy and Arthur Schlesinger, Jr.

18. Ibid., 104, quoting a dispatch from Heeney.

19. DEA Records, file 1415-40, vol. 3, John Holmes, "Relations between Canada and the United States at the United Nations," 26 March 1951.

20. "Many of us familiar with both Canada and the U.S. thought this the dumbest idea of the year. We had enough troubles with both the OAS and Canada and didn't need to compound them." Willis C. Armstrong to author, 29 October 1990.

21. Nash, *Kennedy and Diefenbaker*, 121–23, 128.

22. Ibid., 159–62. See also Benjamin C. Bradlee, *Conversations with Kennedy* (New York: Norton, 1975), 181–85, especially 183, where Kennedy is quoted as saying: "I didn't think Diefenbaker was a son of a bitch. . . . I thought he was a prick."

23. Lyon, *Canada in World Affairs*, 335–37.

24. Quoted in Nash, *Kennedy and Diefenbaker*, 196.

25. Ibid., 189–90.

26. Canadian Peace Research Foundation poll and R. A. Bell, quoted in ibid., 204–5.

27. *Canadian Annual Review for 1963* (Toronto: University of Toronto Press, 1964), 284.

28. Nash, *Kennedy and Diefenbaker*, 166–7.

29. Poll cited in Lyon, *Canada in World Affairs, 1961–1963*, 540.

30. Butterworth was Kennedy's second choice for the post; his first was Erwin Griswold, dean of law at Harvard. See JFK Library, POF, countries, box 113, Griswold to Kennedy, 1 August 1962. On Butterworth, Joe Scott interview with author, Washington, 1978.

31. Quoted in Nash, *Kennedy and Diefenbaker*, 239.

32. Quoted in ibid., 246.

33. Armstrong to author, 29 October 1990.

34. Quoted in Peter Stursberg, ed., *Lester Pearson and the American Dilemma* (Toronto: Doubleday, 1980), 188; see also Charles Ritchie, *Storm Signals: More Undiplomatic Diaries, 1962–1971* (Toronto: Macmillan 1983), 48–49, entry for 10 May 1963.

35. JFK Library, National Security Files, meetings and memoranda, box 340, NSAM 234, Canada Government, Bundy to secretaries of state, defense, treasury, commerce, and interior, attorney general, director of the CIA, chairman of the AEC, and the special representative for trade negotiations, 18 April 1963.

36. Ritchie, *Storm Signals*, 49.

37. See Paul Rutherford, *When Television Was Young: Prime Time Canada, 1952–1967* (Toronto: University of Toronto Press, 1990), 138, 142–143.

38. JFK Library, T. Roncalio oral history, 20 December 1965.

39. Seymour Martin Lipset, *Continental Divide: The Values and Institutions of the United States and Canada* (New York: Routledge 1990), 138–42, sees the distinctiveness of Canadian and American welfare and medical institutions as a major difference between the two countries. While today that may be so, it is a relatively recent phenomenon, and a historian would be chary of labeling it fundamental.

40. The figures for 1962–63 and 1967–68 are derived from *Historical Statistics of Canada*, 2nd ed., tables H148 and H161, and for 1970–71 from *Canada Year Book, 1973* (Ottawa: Information Canada, 1973), 818.

41. Quoted in J. L. Granatstein, "When Push Came to Shove: Canada and the United States," in Thomas G. Paterson, ed., *Kennedy's Quest for Victory: American Foreign Policy, 1961–1963* (New York: Oxford University Press, 1989), 103.

42. JFK Library, National Security Files, countries, box 19-20, Butterworth to secretary of state, 29 July 1963. See also Peter C. Newman, *Distemper of Our Times: Canadian Politics in Transition, 1963–1968* (Toronto: McClelland & Stewart, 1968), 418–19. James Rockefeller's discussion with Gordon later became a bone of contention.

43. Ibid., 422–23.

44. JFK Library, National Securities Files, countries, box 19-20, Canada-General 9/5/63–9/10/63, Raymond Vernon to undersecretary, 10 September 1963.

45. Armstrong to author, 29 October 1990.

46. Arnold Heeney, *The Things That Are Caesar's: The Memoirs of a Canadian Public Servant* (Toronto: University of Toronto Press, 1972), 193–94.

47. Pearson's version of the Autopact is in L.B. Pearson, *Mike: The Memoirs of the Rt. Hon. Lester B. Pearson*, vol. 3 (Toronto: University of Toronto Press, 1975), 127–28.

48. Lawrence Martin, *The Presidents and the Prime Ministers* (Toronto: Doubleday, 1982), 224.

49. Douglas Ross, *In the Interests of Peace: Canada and Vietnam, 1954–73* (Toronto: University of Toronto Press, 1984), 202–21.

50. Pearson, *Mike*, vol. 3, 137.

51. A restrained account of the interview is in Ritchie, *Storm Signals*, 81–84.

52. Charles Ritchie interview, Ottawa, May 1990.

Chapter 5: Odd Couplings 1968–1974

1. Larry Martin, quoted in Kim Willenson et al., *The Bad War: An Oral History of the Vietnam War* (New York: NAL, 1987), 259.

2. Senator Allan MacEachen interview in a television program, *America: Love it or Leave it* (Canadian Broadcasting Corporation, 1990).

3. *Manual for Draft-Age Immigrants to Canada*, 5th ed. (Toronto, Summer 1970), revised and edited by Byron Wall, 24. Sixty-five thousand copies were sold by 1970; see Myrna Kostash, *Long Way from Home: The Story of the Sixties Generation in Canada* (Toronto: Lorimer, 1980), 61. On Canadian immigration experiences, see Joyce Carol Oates, "Customs," in *Crossing the Border: Fifteen Tales* (New York: Vanguard, 1976), 106–117.

4. Quoted in K. F. Emerick, *War Resisters Canada: The World of the American Political-Military Refugees* (Knox, Pa.: Knox, Pennsylvania Free Press, 1972), 112.

5. The 125,000 estimate is derived from a careful and detailed CBC documentary, broadcast in 1990, on the draft dodgers, *America: Love it or Leave it.*

6. Statistics Canada, *Perspectives Canada III* (Ottawa, 1980), 297, 304–305, and tables 15.21, 15.22 and 15.23.

7. Ibid., 115.

8. A point made by Oates in "Customs," 114.

9. Canadian Institute of Public Opinion, *The Gallup Report,* 27 November 1968. Fifty-one percent of Canadians disapproved of draft dodgers.

10. Kostash, *Long Way from Home,* 65–67.

11. Trinity College archives, George Ignatieff Papers, box 2, memorandum of conversation between P. E. Trudeau and U. Thant, 2 November 1968.

12. Privy Council Office, Ottawa, cabinet minutes 27, 29, 30 March 1969.

13. Quoted in J. L. Granatstein asnd Robert Bothwell, *Pirouette: Pierre Trudeau and Canadian Foreign Policy* (Toronto: University of Toronto Press, 1990), 51.

14. USNA, Nixon Papers, WHSF, SMOF Haldeman, memorandum from Nixon to Haldeman, Ehrlichman, and Kissinger, 2 March 1970.

15. Uranium was an area where, Nixon was told, "our domestic political requirements with the mountain state senators" precluded any action, even though Canada had "a legitimate concern." USNA, Nixon Papers, WHCF, C028, Peter Flanagan to Alexander Haig, 3 December 1971.

16. Quoted in Seyom Brown, *The Faces of Power: Constancy and Change in United States Foreign Policy from Truman to Reagan* (New York: Columbia University Press, 1983), 418.

17. NAC, Arnold Heeney Papers, vol. 15, file Permanent Joint Board on Defence, Heeney memorandum of 10 July 1970.

18. Jean-François Lisee, *Dans l'oeil de l'aigle: Washington face au Quebec* (Montreal, 1990), 130–35

19. See the sensationally titled article by Milton Viorst, "An Analysis of American Intervention in the Matter of Quebec," *Maclean's,* November 1972, 22–23, 72, 74. Viorst reached the tame conclusion that there had been *no* American intervention.

20. USNA, Nixon Papers, WHCF, C028, Flanagan to Haig, 3 December 1971.

21. The latter poll, dated 14 October 1970, showed little divergence between labor and management, or between Ontario, Quebec, and the prairie provinces. Only the Atlantic provinces, economically underdeveloped, diverged somewhat from the pattern. See Canadian Institute of Public Opinion, *Gallup Report,* 14 October 1970.

22. Ibid., polls of 28 November 1970 and 23 January 1971.

23. The Gray Report was leaked to the media and published in the left-wing journal of opinion *Canadian Forum* in December 1971.

24. These statistics are found in *Canada Year Book, 1975,* 824–25; the definition of statistics is in M. J. Moroney, *Facts from Figures,* 2nd ed. (London: Penguin, 1971), 1.

25. Figures derived from Statistics Canada, *Review of Foreign Trade, 1966–1972* (Ottawa: Statistics Canada 1974), 44–46. The United States in 1972 took 69.4 percent of Canada's exports and supplied 69 percent of Canada's imports. On U.S. policy, see USNA, Nixon Presidential Materials, Committee on International Economic Policy, 71-33880, "U.S. Trade Policy Towards Canada," October 18 1971.

26. Steven Globerman, *U.S. Ownership of Firms in Canada* (Montreal and Washington: C.D. Howe Research Institute, 1979), 29–33.

27. The classic case was the location of a Michelin tire factory in Nova Scotia, where the intention was obviously to supply the American market. See the annoyed comments of a State Department analyst, quoted in Walter Stewart, *As They See Us* (Toronto: McClelland & Stewart, 1977), 132–33: "You were trying to solve your problem at our expense."

28. USNA, Nixon Papers, WHSF, staff member files, H. R. Haldeman, chronological files, box 197, Haldeman to Ray Price and William Safire, 30 August 1971.

29. Gerald Ford Library, Arthur Burns Papers, box K31, Safire file, "Notes on Camp David Weekend—8/13–8/15/71."

30. That this was the intention is confirmed by a memorandum from Peter Flanigan to Nixon, "Trade Negotiations with Canada," 10 February 1972 (USNA, Nixon Presidential Materials, WHCF, C028), in which he refers to the cancellation of the Autopact and the Defense Production Sharing Agreement as strong possibilities in the event of a breakdown in negotiations. With Kissinger's and Rogers's support, he urged that this not occur.

31. See Granatstein and Bothwell, *Pirouette*, 161.

32. NAC, Don Jamieson Papers, vol. 329, DEA "Canadian Identity and Independence," 5 April 1972.

33. Emerson Brown interview with author, Washington, 11 January 1988.

34. The official term for the phenomenon was "the shit list." See Granatstein and Bothwell, *Pirouette*, 53–54.

35. USNA, Nixon Presidential Materials, White House Tapes, US *v.* John N. Mitchell, 22 March 1973.

36. Willis Armstrong interview with author, 15 April 1990.

Chapter 6: Keeping Warm, 1974–1984

1. John Davis, *Canadian Energy Prospects* (Ottawa, Queen's Printer, 1957), 382, table 17. The ratio of Canadian costs per kilowatt hour for electricity compared with American costs was 38:88 in 1945, and 29:53 in 1955 (measured in constant cents per kilowatt hour).

2. Quoted in Joseph Barber, *Good Fences Make Good Neighbors* (Toronto: McClelland & Stewart, 1958), 64.

3. USNA, Nixon Presidential Materials, WHCF, C028, G. A. Lincoln to Peter Flanigan, 17 November 1972, "Notes on Canadian Oil in relationship to the MOIP."

4. USNA, Nixon Presidential Materials, WHCF, C028, Peter Peterson to Bill Eberle, Jules Katz, John Petty, Hal Scott, 14 December 1971.

5. The offer was made by Donald Macdonald, the new minister of energy, mines, and resources in Trudeau's government. See J. L. Granatstein and Robert Bothwell, *Pirouette: Pierre Trudeau and Canadian Foreign Policy* (Toronto: University of Toronto Press, 1990), 84.

6. See note 3.

7. Canadian and American polls reveal this.

8. USNA, Nixon Presidential Materials, WHCF, C028, [W.C. Armstrong], "Consultations with Canada on Oil," 9 October 1973.

9. Ibid., Flanigan to Deane Hinton, 5 November 1973.

10. Granatstein and Bothwell, *Pirouette*, 86–87.

11. Ibid., 102–104.

12. *Canada Year Book, 1976–77* (Ottawa, 1977), 684, table 13.1. Canada's favorable balance on electricity exports was $2.6 million in 1965, and $92.5 million in 1975.

13. Jean-François Lisee, *Dans l'oeil de l'aigle: Washington face au Quebec* (Montreal, 1990), 195–96.

14. Thomas Enders interview with author, 13 May 1988.

15. Lisee, *Dans l'oeil de l'aigle*, 209–10.

16. Ibid., 243. Some American investors seem to have decided that Quebec separation was not likely and that they might as well go on as usual.

17. Gaddis Smith, *Mortality, Reason and Power: American Diplomacy in the Carter Years* (New York: Hill & Wang, 1986), 246–47, notes Carter's appreciation for foreign leaders who flattered him.

18. Robert Hunter interview with author, 15 November 1988

19. "The Quebec Situation: Outlook and Implications," August 1977, reproduced in Lisee, *Dans l'oeil de l'aigle*, 462–80.

20. NAC, Don Jamieson Papers, vol. 377, Tokyo Summit 1979 file, "Proposed Scenario of Discussion with President Carter, n.d.

21. Charles Doran, "Canada and the Reagan Administration: Left Hand, Right Hand," *International Journal* 36:1 (Winter 1980–81), 238.

22. See Viv Nelles, "The Unfriendly Giant," *Saturday Night* (February 1982), 28–34.

23. Granatstein and Bothwell, *Pirouette*, 318–19.

24. On these subjects, see Granatstein and Bothwell, *Pirouette*, 319–29.

25. Lisee, *Dans l'oeil de l'aigle*, 410–12.

26. Sidney Weintraub, "Fear of Free Trade," *Policy Options* (July–August 1981), 9.

27. On this point see Steven Globerman, *U.S. Ownership of Firms in Canada* (Montreal and Washington, 1979), 74–85.

28. Economic Council of Canada, *Twentieth Annual Review* (Ottawa, 1983), 33.

29. *Maclean's*, 11 July 1977, cited in C.L. Barnhart et al., *The Second Barnhart Dictionary of New English* (Bronxville, N.Y.: Barnhart/Harper & Row, 1980), 6.

30. Peter Dobell, *Canada in World Affairs, 1971–1973* (Toronto CIIA, 1985), 101–103.

Chapter 7: Free Trade and Its Discontents

1. Quoted in Stephen Clarkson, *Canada and the Reagan Challenge: Crisis and Adjustment, 1981–1985,* 2d ed. (Toronto: Lorimer 1985), 359–60.

2. Confidential interview by author.

3. Quoted in ibid., 358. He had already said as much in a preelection visit to Washington.

4. David Bercuson, J.L. Granatstein, and W.R. Young, *Sacred Trust? Brian Mulroney and the Conservative Party in Power* (Toronto: Doubleday, 1986), 248–49.

5. Quoted in ibid., 254, 256.

6. *Canada Year Book, 1985* (Ottawa: Statistics Canada, 1985), 679. Trade statistics as between Canada and the United States sometimes differ considerably owing to different concepts used by the two countries in collecting and reporting data.

7. Louis Harris, *Inside America* (New York: Random House, 1987), 377–78.

8. James Niskanen, *Reaganomics: An Insider's Account of the Policies and the People* (New York: Oxford University Press, 1988), 137.

9. Quoted in *Canadian Annual Review of Politics and Public Affairs, 1984* (Toronto: University of Toronto Press, 1987), 81–82.

10. Richard Gwyn, *The 49th Paradox: Canada in North America* (Toronto: McClelland & Stewart, 1985), 150.

11. Speech to the Conference Board of Canada, 24 February 1985. I am indebted to Michael Hart for this reference, and for much besides. His unpublished study of the achievement of the FTA, "Expletives Deleted," written with Bill Dymond and Colin Robertson, is the best and most complete available account of the free trade negotiations.

12. Willis Armstrong interview by author, 25 June 1986.

13. Confidential interview by author.

14. Ibid.

15. Quoted in Graham Fraser, *Playing for Keeps: The Making of the Prime Minister, 1988* (Toronto: McClelland & Stewart, 1989), 94.

16. Ibid.

17. Robert Mason Lee, *One Hundred Monkeys: The Triumph of Popular Wisdom in Canadian Politics* (Toronto: MacFarlane, Walter & Ross, 1989), 206–207.

18. Poll results in Alan Frizzell, Jon Pammett, and Anthony Westell, *The Canadian General Election of 1988* (Ottawa: Carleton, 1989), chapter 7.

19. See William Johnson, ""People of the Word," in A. R. Riggs and Tom Velk, *Canadian-American Free Trade (The Sequel)* (Halifax: The Institute for Research on Public Policy, 1988), 43–47.

20. Joel Garreau, *The Nine Nations of North America* (Boston: Houghton Mifflin 1981). Garreau's enthusiasm for his concept outran his proofreading: Ontario is consistently referred to as "Ottawa," doubtless a measure of his research in the area.

21. Ibid., 73.

22. One set of opinions on corporate concentration is quoted in Seymour Martin Lipset, *Continental Divide: The Values and Institutions of the United States and Canada* (New York: Routledge, 1990) 131. Lipset notes that Canadian frustration with corporate concentration is less than American; to this observer, what is striking is that the Canadian level of frustration is nevertheless at 68 percent.

23. Lipset, *Continental Divide*, 212

24. See the collection of short stories, *Crossing the Border: Fifteen Tales* (New York: Vanguard, 1976) by Joyce Carol Oates.

BIBLIOGRAPHIC ESSAY

It is usually Canadians who write about Canadian-American relations. So important is the United States to Canada, that even books on domestic Canadian topics often have an American dimension: politics, literature, even national identity are defined in an American (or non-American, or anti-American) context. No essay can hope to cover the consequent literary output. The reader will, however, notice that little of the material that follows is American in origin. Speaking a common language, Americans interested in Canada can easily obtain Canadian materials written in English— and English-language studies predominate, even in Canada.

The most obvious point of departure is the standard Canadian foreign relations series, *Canada in World Affairs,* sponsored by the Canadian Institute of International Affairs and covering the period between 1935 and 1965, and from 1971 to 1973. The United States figures prominently in each individually–authored volume. The history of Pierre Trudeau's foreign policy, by Jack Granatstein and Robert Bothwell, covering 1968 to 1984, *Pirouette* (Toronto: University of Toronto Press, 1990) counts as the last volume of the series. The period since 1984 is covered in *Canada Among Nations,* an annual publication from Carleton University in Ottawa. Its coverage is, however, rather idiosyncratic, depending on a variety of authors with disparate interests. It also lacks an index, which further limits its utility for researchers unfamiliar with the field.

In documentary collections, the American documents outclass the Canadian. The *Foreign Relations of the United States* (Washington: Department of State) documents series is extremely useful to students of Canadian-American relations in a variety of areas (for example, Canadian policy towards Cuba under Castro). The comparable Canadian series, *Documents on Canadian External Relations* (Ottawa; Department of External Affairs), covers only 1945, 1946, 1952, and 1953 in the post–World War II period, although a few other volumes, covering the late 1940s and early 1950s, are due for publication. Some Canadian records dealing with Canadian–American relations are open to historians at the National Archives of Canada or at the Department of External Affairs in Ottawa, even down to the 1970s, but scholars are inhibited by a cumbersome and restrictive "Access to Information" process. Ironically, information is more open while still in the custody of the department than at the archives. American materials on Canada abound, both in the records of the Department of State and in the several presidential collections, including Jimmy Carter's in Atlanta and Gerald Ford's in Ann Arbor, Michigan.

Canadian-American economic relations were extensively studied by several government commissions, including the Royal Commission on Canada's Economic Prospects (Ottawa: Queens Printer, 1957–8) and the Royal Commission on the Economic Union and Economic Prospects for Canada (Toronto: University of Toronto Press, 1985–6). The latter's main report is in three volumes; its special studies are seventy-one in number and include several specifically on Canadian-American relations. The C.D. Howe Research Institute in Toronto periodically publishes surveys of aspects of Canadian-American economic relations.

The autobiographies and biographies of some of Canada's prime ministers and ministers of external affairs are of considerable interest. Prime Minister Mackenzie King's diary affords a unique insight into his relations with Franklin D. Roosevelt and Harry Truman. Excerpts have been published in four volumes as *The Mackenzie King Record*, edited by J.W. Pickersgill (Toronto: University of Toronto Press, 1960–1970). The original is available on microfiche. Lester B. Pearson, Canadian ambassador to the United States and subsequently minister of external affairs and prime minister, wrote three volumes of memoirs, *Mike* (Toronto: University of Toronto Press, 1972–5). These have been superseded for the period down to 1948 by the first volume of John English's *Shadow of Heaven: The Life of Lester Pearson* (Toronto: Lester & Orpen Dennys, 1989). John Diefenbaker, his rival for the prime ministership and J.F. Kennedy's bête noire, left behind another three-volume work, *One Canada* (Toronto: Macmillan of Canada, 1975–7). They are not well regarded by scholars because of their exaggerations and misstatements. More useful is an oral history collection edited by Peter Stursberg, *Diefenbaker: Leadership Gained, 1956–1962* (Toronto: University of Toronto Press, 1975) and *Diefenbaker: Leadership Lost, 1962–1967* (Toronto: University of Toronto Press, 1976). Less well edited is his comparable collection of interviews about Lester Pearson, *Lester Pearson and the American Dilemma* (Toronto and Garden City, NY: Doubleday, 1980). There is considerable material on Canadian-American economic relations in Robert Bothwell and William Kilbourn, *C.D. Howe* (Toronto: McClelland & Stewart, 1979). Few American politicians mention Canada in their memoirs, and their biographers have followed their example.

On defense relations, American scholars predominate. J.T. Jockel, *No Boundaries Upstairs: Canada, the United States and the Origins of North American Air Defence, 1945–1958* (Vancouver: University of British Columbia Press, 1987) and Jon T. McLin, *Canada's Changing Defense Policy, 1957–1963* (Baltimore: Johns Hopkins University Press, 1967) are well researched and well regarded. Political relations over the years are dealt with in J.L. Granatstein and Robert Cuff, *American Dollars, Canadian Prosperity* (Toronto and Sarasota: Samuel-Stevens, 1978). J.L. Granatstein, *A Man of Influence* (Ottawa: Deneau, 1981), and in Granatstein's essay, "When Push Came to Shove: Canada and the United States," in Thomas G. Paterson, ed., *Kennedy's Quest for Victory* (New York: Oxford University Press, 1989). A variant interpretation of the same period is Jocelyn Ghent's article, "Did He Fall or Was He Pushed?" in the *International History Review*, I (April 1979), 246–70. Basil Robinson, who worked in

Diefenbaker's office, has produced *Diefenbaker's World* (Toronto: University of Toronto Press, 1989). Also useful is Knowlton Nash, *Kennedy and Diefenbaker* (Toronto: Mc-Clelland & Stewart, 1990).

Canada and the Vietnam war are covered in Douglas Ross's authoritative *In the Interests of Peace* (Toronto: University of Toronto Press, 1984) and, from a very left-wing point of view, in Victor Levant, *Quiet Complicity: Canadian Involvement in the Vietnam War* (Toronto: Between the Lines, 1986).

Pierre Trudeau's relations with the United States are covered by Granatstein and Bothwell, *Pirouette*, mentioned above, and by Steven Clarkson's very useful book, *Canada and the Reagan Challenge*, 2d edition (Toronto: James Lorimer, 1985). A collection of papers by political scientists and economists, Annette Baker Fox, A.O. Hero, and Joseph Nye, eds., *Canada and the United States: Transnational and Transgovernmental relations* (New York: Columbia University Press, 1976) still repays scrutiny.

Richard Gwyn, *The 49th Paradox: Canada in North America* (Toronto: McClelland & Stewart, 1985) is the reflections of a thoughtful journalist; and Seymour Martin Lipset's *Continental Divide: The Values and Institutions of the United States and Canada* (New York: Routledge, 1990) is a stimulating if not always convincing analysis.

Quebec's relations with the United States are covered in a memoir by a separatist academic-politician, Claude Morin, *L'art de l'impossible* (Montréal: Boréal, 1987) and in a fascinating history by a Montreal journalist, Jean-François Lisée, *Dans l'oeil de l'aigle* (Montréal. 1990).

Trade relations and investment account for a vast literature. Of particular interest are Richard Caves, *Diversification, Foreign Investment and Scale in North American Manufacturing Industries* (Ottawa. Information Canada, 1975) and John Dales, *The Protective Tariff in Canada's Economic Development* (Toronto: University of Toronto Press, 1966), as well as the background studies for the Canadian Royal Commission on the Economic Union, such as John Whalley and Roderick Hill, eds., *Canada-United States Free Trade* (Toronto: University of Toronto Press, 1985). More recently the Free Trade Agreement of 1987 has attracted considerable interest. G. Bruce Doern and Brian Tomlin, *Faith and Fear: The Free Trade Story* (Toronto: Stoddart, 1991) is an especially useful study, the more so because it breaks with traditional political science forms in favor of a narrative history.

INDEX

THE AUTHOR

Robert Bothwell is professor of history at the University of Toronto. A specialist in international relations and Canadian history, he has written numerous books in the field, including *The World of Lester Pearson* (1977), *C.D. Howe* (1979), *Eldorado: Canada's National Uranium Company* (1984), and *Nucleus* (1988). He is co-author of two standard Canadian histories, *Canada 1900–1945* (1987) and *Canada since 1945* (1981 and 1989).